ULSTER FOLK OF FIELD AND FIRESIDE

Michael J. Murphy

ULSTER FOLK
OF
FIELD AND FIRESIDE

by
MICHAEL J. MURPHY

Printed and Published by
Dundalgan Press, Dundalk, Ireland
1983

DEDICATION

*For Patrick, Michael, Peter, and The Glens Girl, Winifred,
who, with their mother, shared the rigours—and some of
the delights of the collector's quest for folklore by the
fields and firesides of Ulster.*

© Dundalgan Press
ISBN 0-85221-107-4

CONTENTS

page

Mountainy Folk 1
Drama on a Fireside Hob 13
I Follow the Fairies 15
The Residenter 19
Drinkers in a Gale 21
Spring on Slieve Gullion 23
Moon and Cloud over Carlingford Lough . . 25
The Tinker in Glen Dhu 27
The Pig Smugglers 29
Stalemate on a Border Road 32
One Brave Droll Fella 35
His Last Leprechaun 38
The Story-teller of Donaghmoyne 41
A Deal in Calves and Women 44
A Breath of Summer 47
Watching the Mare at Foaling 50
Thinning the Turnips 52
A Coat of Whitewash 54
Did Ghosts Really Walk in the Summer Evening? . . 56
The Mourne Man Remembered 59
Return of the Yank 62
Rendezvous with a Tyrone Match-maker . . 65
When Oweny Cut His Harvest with a Scythe . . 67
Wet Harvest Interlude 73
Magic in the Harvest Moon 76
In an Antrim Glen 78
The Glens Fairy Woman Talked 81
The Hare on the Hearth 85
A Man with a Charm 88
The Ould Lammas Fair 91
A Bad Run on the Shores 93
On a Rathlin Rock 96
The Holly and the Hazel and the Flailing of the Hay 99
Potatoes for Hallow Eve 102
I Followed the Threshing Mill 105
The Ageless One 107
Sentimental Journey in the Snow 111

Contents—*continued*

	page
Turkeys in the Straw	113
A Quiet Ramble round the Roads	116
The Ghost Train of South Armagh	119
The Two Hawthorns	121
Slieve Gullion, Mystery Mountain of the North	126
South Armagh's Outlaw Poet	130
The Last Score in Dromintee	133
Who Banished the Banshee?	136
Old Lord Erin's Son	139
Poteen in the Thatch	148
Paddy the Prophet	150
History from the Mournes and Ravensdale	153
Long Night in the Spike	157
The Widow's Son	161
Charlie Gets His Own Back	163
Katchy the "Box" Player	165
Loan of a Scythe	169
I Would Not Wear That Mexican Sombrero	173
A Village by Carlingford Lough	175
Bus Along the Border	177
Banter in the Bar	180
A Walk Near the Mournes	182
Making Hay in Shane's Ground	185
The Tinkers That Nearly Tied Hay	188
Spring Comes to the Glens of Antrim	191
Television in a Glen of Antrim	194
One Fair Day in Cushendall	196
Wild Strawberries in Glenariffe	198
The Mower and the Carters	200
Rathlin Islander Swore Me to Secrecy	202
The Raghery Mermaid	204
Scholars in a Barn	205
The Cobbler Was a Rebel	207
Old Cows Sold Well in Newtown	210
Evening Interlude in a South Armagh Pub	211
A Cavan Welcome for the Man from The Fews	217
Hunting Ghosts on Christmas Eve	221

LIST OF ILLUSTRATIONS

Michael J. Murphy . . . . . *frontispiece*

facing page

The " Granny Rock ", Quay Yard, Ballycastle . . 22

Lammas Fair in Ballycastle 23

Pier Wall at Ballycastle 23

" Boating " it to Ballycastle 38

Hauling out Cattle from Rathlin at Ballycastle . 38

Forge Scene at Hilltown, 1944 39

The late Anne Savage, Story-teller, near Hilltown . 39

Thrah-hook or Rope-twister 86

Twisting a Grass Rope, Clontifleece . . . 86

The late James Loughran with a " pannel " he made 87

Harvest Scene 102

Stacks of Oats at Clonallon, County Down . . 102

William Carleton's Cottage 103

Blaeberry Baskets made from Rushes . . . 150

Griddle, Pot Oven and Three-legged Pot . . 150

James McLeigh with Flail 151

The Fallen Fairy Bush 151

Horse Harness which includes
Bridle, Collar, Back-band and Traces . . . 166

Ox Collar from Julianstown 166

Back Sugan 167

Rush Saddle from Curraghinalt 167

ACKNOWLEDGEMENTS

I acknowledge, with grateful thanks, assistance with the proofs by colleague Séamas Ó Catháin, Archivist of the Department of Folklore, University College, Dublin. And my grateful thanks also to the Head of the Department of Irish Folklore, Professor Bo Almqvist, for permission to use folk-tales.

As well as some original material the following articles have appeared in *The Irish Press, Irish Independent, Irish News and Irish Weekly, Belfast Telegraph, Belfast News-Letter, The Manchester Guardian, Times Pictorial, Irish Digest, Literary Miscellanea (Ulster Tatler)*, BBC, *Evening Press, Ulster Folklife, Ulster Social Studies.*

My sincere thanks to the National Museum of Ireland for permission to reproduce the jacket illustration and the plates facing pages 166 and 167.

INTRODUCTION

I WAS working late at a threshing mill in Padgey O'Hare's in Dromintee in 1941 when news was brought that I was urgently wanted at home. Of course I feared the worst: my mother knew one was expected to stay at a threshing until the job was finished, even if it ran on past midnight.

At home I got the surprise of my life to learn why my mother had been unable to restrain sharing her sheer delight as she held up a copy of *At Slieve Gullion's Foot*, her voice silent, her eyes brimming. I knew that the late Harry Tempest of Dundalgan Press in Dundalk had accepted the book, a compilation mainly of printed articles similar to this one, but because of the war-time scarcity of printing paper publication would have to wait until normality had returned with the end of the war in Europe.

Next morning's post brought a letter from a Dr. Séamus Delargy, Hon. Director of the Irish Folklore Commission at University College in Dublin, inviting me to join the collecting staff of the Folklore Commission. At that time I had neither heard of Professor Delargy—as he was to become later—nor the Irish Folklore Commission. Harry Tempest himself was equally pleased with this outcome following publication of the book.

To Harry Tempest of Dundalgan Press and to Professor Delargy—a man of cultural vision if ever there was one—I express a debt of gratitude which introduced me to a way of life that was to become both challenge and vocation for over forty years. Indebted, too, must be the social historians and students of folk life studies for the hundreds of volumes I have contributed to the archives of the Department of Irish Folklore in UCD: because I know I have written one of the greatest—if not *the* greatest—stories to have come out of Ulster. I can make that claim unblushingly. Apart from my journals they represent the story of a people told by the people themselves for the first—and no doubt—the last time.

All that began with *At Slieve Gullion's Foot* in 1941. Now in 1983 Dundalgan Press has again accepted a current book arising from that quest. I could not wish for a more fitting and gratifying close to a career and destiny for which it would now seem nature and my upbringing in field and at fireside at the foot of Slieve Gullion had been unobtrusively and patiently preparing me all along.

MICHAEL J. MURPHY

Dromintee
South Armagh
April 1983

MOUNTAIN FOLK

THE MOUNTAINY MAN

SIXTY years ago I was a boy of ten living in the mountains of South Armagh. Since then I've lived and worked, not only as a labourer in South Armagh, but as a folklore collector in the Mournes in County Down, the Sperrin Mountains in Tyrone and Derry, in the Glens of Antrim and Rathlin Island, and in the mountains around Carlingford Lough, through Monaghan, Cavan and the Fermanagh lake country. Now, with the Old Ulster folk quest safely behind me in the archives in Dublin in tape and transcription I am back again like the hare in the chase to my den at the foot of Slieve Gullion in South Armagh. So by upbringing, sentiment and everything except birth I'm a Mountainy Man myself.

Thirty-six years ago, if I had said " I'm a Mountainy Man ", someone in the mountain valley where I was reared would have given me a back-handed rebuke for classing them, by implication, as " Mountainees ". And the people we then looked on as " Mountainees " would, in an even firmer way, have let me know I was no Mountainy Man at all; they would have suspected me of being satirical. Outside the hills, however, we were all " Mountainees ", all on the defensive.

The Mountainy Man seems to have shed much of this self-consciousness. I remember it now as a kind of odd inferiority complex, a touchiness sustained by an independence and a pride that could be aggressive: many a man at a dance or fair went home with a buzz in his ear for making uncalled-for remarks about the Mountainy Man—the man who, they said, took his spade to bed, who let the heather grow out of his ear.

This pride was partly traditional and had its roots in the conquest of little fields won from the heath and moor and heather. That's why the Mountainy Man, more than any other country-man, was instinctively conservative, resisting change of any kind. That's why you could live in the mountains without ever really becoming a Mountainy Man—you wouldn't be truly accepted.

I

In the Glens of Antrim you were a " runner " till you'd had two or three centuries of mountain living behind you: you'll hear these things quoted to-day with the same half-apologetic laugh which excuses talk of other traditions, like belief in fairies, witch-craft and so on. In other parts you'll be told that " comers have no errand here "—that is, newcomers who, in this sense, could be from a distant part of the same parish. I've lived in places where I was referred to as being from " outside ". Even around Warrenpoint and Omeath on Carlingford Lough you were " in-blown wrack " if you had no roots in these areas.

I doubt if any countryman's mind really changes much, but the frame of mind behind these sayings has certainly lost the old force. I knew of mountain townlands where you were apt to be rough-handled if you walked there at night, certainly if you went to court one of their girls. I knew of townlands where no " outsider " could buy a farm—a " place " as they phrased it: the Mountainy Men by agreement helped one of themselves to out-bid the stranger. The same applied to marriage; boy and girl had to be from the immediate area.

All that had changed greatly, though some inner strains of it may hang on. You could blame much of it on instincts inherited from the old clan system; you could blame it, too, on the physical and mental complexities of mountain living; because more than anyone else the Mountainy Man's fields, and his neighbours' fields, were part of his own living personality; he knew every inch of them as intimately as the lines and callouses on the palm of his hand or the corns on his feet.

Individual as they were, the sense of community was strong. If a man required some implement he took it without asking. And everyone must have heard of the system of co-operative ploughing teams known as " Joining " and " Neighbouring " and " Morrowing " in which a man joined with his neighbour's horse to form a ploughing team.

That has changed, too, and you can't blame the Mountainy Man. The ties of his community spirit have begun to come apart and he is more self-centred to-day. There are several reasons. The Mountainy Man is better off, his standard of life is higher. Tractors are as common in the mountains as elsewhere—on

Rathlin Island they outnumbered the horses when I was there. Farms have expanded as neighbours died or sold out.

The Mountainy Man to-day is the man who was bred and who works within the hills, or at least lives there; he's no longer the man who actually lives *on* a mountain itself or within its immediate shadow. That may sound like the townsman's notion of the Mountainy Man. What the townsman apparently doesn't know is that you get social groupings in the mountains just as you get them everywhere else.

I lived for some years on a hillside of farmed land over the sea outside Cushendall in County Antrim; to many Cushendall folk I was a puzzle because I " lived on the mountains " as they said. Along Carlingford Lough shore people still talk of the " mountainees " who live less than a mile away. " Is there much snow out in the mountains? " a Gortin shopkeeper in the mountains of Tyrone asked a man from a few miles outside. In Waterfoot in Glenariffe and elsewhere I've had similar instances of this old notion of mountainy social groupings.

The Mountainy Man takes town talk with defensive banter or a dead-pan expression—and laughs his head off about the poor townsmen when he gets back to his own mountain. The mountain has been coming to the town, so to speak, and the townsman should be aware of this: after all, scratch a Mountainy Man they say, and you're apt to get a druid; but scratch our townsman and you get the clay, possibly the moor and rock of the mountainy fields as well, all just a few generations down.

The Mountainy Man is no longer physically remote or in isolation from the events of the modern day unless he wants to impose these strictures on himself. Radio, and now TV, the daily newspaper, the motor car, the truck and the bus have changed that. Yet he is a less satisfied, a more lonely man culturally than he was when I first met up with him.

There's an adage which says: " The want of the people is a poor want ", and that's partly what is wrong—fewer people in the mountains. And now fine roads made under forestry schemes run through rock and heather—and over abandoned fields. His old conservative, self-sufficient world has been slit and he wears it in a tighter re-stitch like a hand-me-down jacket: the pockets, so to speak, no longer bulk with the makings of his own social entertainment and culture, which was mainly folk.

His culture and pastimes were traditional and shaped by the standards of the tough hills around him. He had games that exhibited physical hardiness and a wiry skill, like the roadside game of " bowls " (or " Long Bullets " as we called it), played with a stone ball. But his pastimes were few. He played cards and he talked of the people and the world around him, or he walked among his neighbours or his land, or to a fair, a wedding, a wake, a christening: the Mountainy Woman was usually with him, for it was the custom, and his social and cultural life was intimately bound up with hers.

When I think of the Mountainy Man's pastimes I'm reminded of the story of the man who worked for a Mountainy Woman. She said to him: " You can rest yourself after your dinner, digging the garden for me ". Work of some sort was his true pastime.

THE MOUNTAINY WOMAN

AT a North of Ireland fair a man was sympathizing with a friend over the death of his wife. The friend sounded the virtues of the dead woman and the bereaved husband echoed every word. . . . " Aye then in sowl an' he'd lost one good woman. He'd miss her, indeed, miss her sorely. . . . Feth, then, she worked hard all her life. . . . Aye' they'd been a brave span together surely, the most of sixty years. . . ."

Then, as if compelled to keep intact his manhood and independence by speaking out, the husband had to say, " But do you know what? I never really liked thon woman of mine ".

I told that story to a young mountainy woman who'd recently come home after a spell in factories in England. She said she could believe it. No man could really like a woman and ask her to live as the mountainy woman lived and worked thirty-five years ago. She didn't say " love a woman " mind you: in rural Ireland " love " is a word you must jib and jibe at. " What's love? " runs the saying, and the answer tells you: " It's an itchy feeling in at your heart and you can't get in to scratch it ". This County Down woman's opinion of mountain living was that it was a " great way for getting old fast ".

Our young mountainy woman was speaking in her own house, and her " boy friend ", as they say these days, was present as well as her parents. They " make dates " to-day. Years ago it was " a set " or " a scud of a coort ", " your hoult " and so on. If that boy had as much as shown himself at the gate, let alone come into the house, he was better than half-married already.

The mountainy woman, as I saw her, was, and in fact still is, the backbone and brains of the mountainy man, the architect of his work, his fortune or his failure: a valiant, devoted woman who could be something of a tyrant at times.

She might have had too much of a rather fatalistic courage, but there was no doubt about her tremendous endurance—even sometimes with her mountainy man in his vanities and tantrums. She knew what she was letting herself in for when she married him, and accepted life as she found it—until ambition, thrust upon her rather than shared, showed her how to lead towards a change.

She always had to work hard; you'll never convince a city woman of the amount and variety of work her country sister has to get through in a day. But she doesn't have to work as she did thirty-five years ago, thank heaven. Don't mix sentiment with your sociology in this; you mustn't forget the tradition behind the mountainy woman even today.

For instance, you couldn't commend a woman or girl better than to say she was " a powerful worker—in or out of the house ": that meant outside in the fields; even hired servant girls were expected to work in the fields those days. There was a counter-balance to flattery of course, and you had satirical cracks about the over-praised, like " she could make a meal's meat out of a dish-cloth ".

Other instances of this tradition come to mind—the bride in her new home, for instance: you just couldn't have kept many of the " new women " out of the fields; they *had* to show their paces, their own family reputation and prestige and future were at stake. Old labourers used to advise us: " Never work for a woman; she doesn't know what's in a day's work ". Quite true; she was in the habit herself of putting two or three days' work into one and thought little of it.

This tradition sprang from the pattern of life of the migrant labourer. The mountainy woman's husband usually had to be such a labourer until around the beginning of this century. The men, helped by the women, did the ploughing or digging. The oats were sown and the potato ground prepared; if in rigs the men shaped the outline of the ridges out of lea or grassland. Then they left for seasonal work in Scotland and England.

The remainder of the work was done by the women: manuring, planting potatoes, digging them in, weeding and all the rest of the endless attention the crop needs throughout the year. Cattle, pigs and poultry had to be looked after, and a family, if any, as well as the aged. The men returned again in late harvest.

That was the original pattern; but only the tail-end of it remained when I came among the mountainy folk in 1922. Neighbour still helped neighbour of course—often by a request that could be, in effect, an order: " Maybe you could give us a hand the morra to drop a lock of seed spuds ", or " Tie a few sheaves of hay " (or oats and so on).

I remember my mother, hardly a month back in the country after twenty years, answering this kind of request and coming home at dark just as tired as other women who worked beside her in the fields for wages. There was recompense, of course: you got butter and milk or potatoes. In fact no one those days without milk would be allowed pay for it, or for buttermilk, which always had a small print of butter floating on top. That spirit is still there: everywhere we've lived in the mountains of the North people of all creeds brought us gifts: "A wee share of my kitchen".

The familiar changes in social life have had much the same meaning for the mountainy woman as for her husband; the bus and the motor car and radio enable her to share pleasures and benefits that used to be enjoyed solely by townsfolk. Housing is better. But interchange between friend and neighbour isn't as free. You must knock more often on a closed door, where before you were half in the house once you opened the now vanishing half-door.

Old-time market-making in a stiff farm cart in all sorts of weather was a ritual. I remember women carrying baskets of butter ten miles to town because the horses were needed in the fields. They didn't grumble, but isn't it wonderful that all that hardship has gone. Anyhow, the talk is usually there: get into a country bus on a market day going out of a town to the mountains and it can be like a céilí-house on wheels.

Two other things have changed the outlook of the mountainy woman—the labourers' cottages and the local dance-hall. Thirty-five years ago the meanest mountain dwelling was held to be superior to the best council cottage ever built. In a cottage you were only a half-step above the cottier or " cotter-house " tenant who lived on sufferance according to the will and whim of the farmer who owned the house.

The dance hall helped to restore some of the healthy inter-mixing any society needs: it restored in another way the shrinking social orbit of the hills which was making a stranger of a man from the far end of the parish. The family céilí in the neighbour's house had had its day and was crying to be transferred to a community setting, even before local halls were needed.

A mountainy woman's daughter could now marry a labourer, a tradesman, a shop-boy without scaling down: the peasant complex—which puts prestige, house, lands, cattle and everything else above people—began to disappear. Boys and girls went by bus to work in town—factory work was no longer the disgrace they used think it was, even if you had only a few acres. No longer has the mountainy woman that single outing in the year to look forward to: the 13th or 14th July if you dug with one foot, the 15th of August if you dug with the other; she may even go on a week's holiday! This isn't so much a change as a return to an older order of things.

I've said our mountainy woman could be a bit of a tyrant. I'm taking a well-known instance, our low rural marriage rate.

It's said that the low rural marriage rate is largely due to the possessive mother who won't let the sons marry. She may wish her own daughters readily enough on to some other fellow's mother, but no one else's daughter must come in as her own son's wife.

B

Until the Land Acts became law just before the beginning of this century, tenants hadn't owned their land, not even in the days of the clans. People did marry young till then: why not?... What did it matter? But when suddenly they found they really owned the land, marriage of a son, particularly the eldest son, *did* matter, and in a purely material way.

The mountainy woman instinctively wanted to consolidate, to strengthen the grip. So when a son married and left home, his act was like a traitorous pulling away of a stake of support. How often have I heard them use phrases like " He goes an' marries, just when we were gettin' our heads above water an' risin' in the world ".

The change here isn't as rapid as it might be. But we can't blame this valiant woman without first understanding the whys and the wherefores. Responsibility was thrust upon her rather than shared.

I heard of a mountainy man who'd made money in England declare in boastful enthusiasm: " I've hundreds for land, hundreds for law an' hundreds to work on. I can never be broke—for I started with nothin' ". Except thon mountainy woman of his.

THE MOUNTAINY CHILD

THIRTY-FIVE years ago most mountainy folk liked to say, or better still, have it said, that their children were great workers. It meant more than being " a great scholar ", though "learning was no load to carry".

By " work " they meant manual labour in the fields or around the farmhouse. Work was the recurring decimal in the child's life; it mixed with play, before and after school, and with recreation.

Children still help around the farms, of course: reasonable tasks will do them good. But how many times have men, and some women, bragged of the size of rocks their sons in early teens could handle, or the weight of a sack they could carry? Fathers could be as possessive about work as mothers about marriage: if a boy lifted his head from a task he was apt to hear, in a gulther of a yell: "Is it countin' the crows y'are?"

Boys, incidentally, were praised more often than girls. In parts of Ulster no one shakes your hand over a birth unless a son is born. You hear the birth of a girl commented on with jocular though sardonic phrases like: " Another priddy-washer ".

An old relative of mine in South Armagh, a wonderful mountainy woman who died in the 1930s aged about eighty-five, was one of the last of the native Gaelic speakers. And she often pointed out a long, steep lane up which she used carry a three hundredweight sack of oats. Only now do I realize why she used make that boast—she was no mere "priddy-washer", anyway!

There were traditional reasons behind much of that, and other reasons. So many people had to live from hand to mouth, one ha'penny chasing another. A man trying to rear a family in the 1920's on a few acres of mountainy land couldn't afford to let his bone go with any dog. Prices were poor; I remember potatoes sold for sixpence and ninepence a hundredweight. A labourer was lucky to get constant work " at two shillings a day an' your meat "—three meals. When I left the land in the 1940's wages were still around a half-crown a day.

There was another reason behind this recurring decimal of work in the child's life. Many people in the hills—in most of rural Ireland as well—seemed to have an idea about talent that was oddly at variance with Christian ethic; saying, in effect, that brains and talent would benefit you nothing.

Educational ideas, which meant that children should go to schools in the towns, seem to have thrust that aside. You find people who deplore this change; who look on youngsters " gallivantin' ", rather than travelling in buses and trains to schools in the town. One man recently phrased it for me as " nothin' short of expeditions to courtin' dens ".

I must add one further remark on another tradition behind the work of the mountain child. Thirty-five years ago—indeed much later—the gantry of the hiring fair loomed ahead of most like a social gallows. They didn't see it like that at the time, nor until they'd grown up, and had left the land or emigrated. Then back came those letters: " For heaven's sake get rid of the ass, the thatched cabin, the barefooted boys and girls, and the hiring fair ".

Here lies a real cause behind much of the rural discontent that disturbs us to this day. Imagine a town or city parent taking a boy or girl of fourteen to a public street and bargaining their labour for six-month terms as they would bargain for cattle, hand-slapping and all the rest. The Hiring Fair, thank heaven, has gone, and I like to think I had a part in abolishing it. Although thirty years ago I could find them in towns like Strabane and Newry and Derry City and elsewhere.

There was a tradition behind it. Most of the parents had themselves been " hired " at ages as low as ten, and usually bare-footed. Some " boys ", need I say, came back when man-big to beat up a bad master on the Hiring Ground. Yet I knew of " houses " where children followed elder brothers and sisters, even parents, into hired service and were as well looked after as if at home.

But behind it all, good, bad and indifferent, was something else which could be positively tragic, although it was maintained by parent and servant alike. Work-prowess was a fetish; the ability to stick out a job, no matter how tough, was something you just were supposed to do. Well, if a boy or girl " left their place " before the term of employment was up, they were held in contempt by everyone at home and in the district.

" Aw sure you done *Kacka-a-sherrivish* " (left your excrement in the nest) I once heard it said to a lad at a cross-roads gather-ing. He was barely fourteen and he'd been expected to do a man's work in a " place " or farm about fifty miles from his home. He'd refused and walked back; there were no buses then in the late 1920's and, anyhow, where would he get the fare?

Despite such trying things life wasn't dull for the child. Among hiring anecdotes, for instance, I'd like to tell just one:

A boy asked his master to let him home to see an uncle who, he said, was dying. The master thought this an excuse to run away; he asked what the boy hoped to gain. " Me uncle ", says

the boy, " might lave me thon field a-back of the house ".
" Which ", said the master, " would be a bit of a garden in your
country ". " It's a quare bit of a garden ", says the boy; " there's
six hundred acres in it ". He meant the mountain itself, which
his uncle didn't own anyway.

Now, if that retort sounds over-adult to-day it was manly and
humorous and showed intelligence. The mountainy child had to
grow up fast; responsibilities came early. For youngsters shared
in much of the full, adult run of the social life of older people:
there was thus a greater respect for age and ability; if a child got
over-smart or impudent—" old fashioned " as they said—it was
certainly put in its place without mincing words.

At night there was storytelling and talk and, I admit,
hereditary spleens and prejudices and prides and—politics, all
handed down. You were what your father and grandfather were
no matter what you said later in life. But you learned at least
that few rows—however flaming—last for ever.

Children were allowed to go to dances, to attend weddings
and wakes, and in some parts got clay pipes full of strong tobacco:
" Lord-a-mercy pipes " at wakes. Radio, the cinema and the bus
had yet to come (although folklore had prophecies which told
you all about them—on Rathlin Island didn't one even foretell
TV. . . .!). But there were compensations in the fireside talk or
or in a céilí-house.

Mountainy men were usually travelled men: you heard
colourful tales of fairs and of work in England or abroad. In the
Glens of Antrim, as well as folklore, the tales were of local seamen
and skippers who sailed the wind-jammers. In the Mournes
there'd be talk of mining in Butte, Montana, of Salt Lake City.
In South Armagh we could hear talk from seamen, from dealers
and Yukon gold miners and pedlars or pahvees who'd traded with
peoples as far apart as the Eskimo in the Arctic and the Maori in
New Zealand: a fine way to learn geography and the facts of the
outside world and of strange peoples. (You always went " among
the stranger " once you left the hills.)

Radio and the cinema in town or the local hall, and now
TV have long since replaced most of that.

Little time was allowed for games, except perhaps on the
longest of summer evenings or on Sundays. Games were inter-
mixed with work. The child herded fowl, for instance, from a
neighbour's oats as " sport ". But if hens strayed and were seen,
the complaint came as a call to the owner's dog that everyone
understood: " Soup, Carlo, boy—soup, soup thonder Carlo ".
Or it came in a half-domesticated clan-cry once used in battle
and still known as " A Mountain Gowl ". With this bellowing
yell some men could startle crows half a mile away. Girls played
a game with small stones called Jacks; it seems to have gone,
along with others. I'll mention one famous boys' game which
has also gone: Ducks and Drake. Modern parents would be
horrified to know how dangerous it seemed—flinging cobs of
stones more than a pound weight while some boy dodged in to
retrieve his " duck " or tig another boy and get a chance to " fire
at a duck on the drake ", a large stone or embedded boulder.

Between about May and September few boys or girls wore
boots to school, church, or anywhere else. Schoolmasters encouraged youngsters to get rid of their boots for the summer; the same
master who, unless you kept your hair cut short, was likely to
grab it in one hand and use the other in punishment. All this
went along with slates and slate-pencils.

Children nowadays cry if they don't get to school. This is
surely a change. Some old mountainy folk would note this
change, too, and explain it by quoting a phrase: " Every genera-
tion gets weaker and wiser "—weaker in bodily strength, they
mean, wiser in their ideas and attitude to life.

THE PHYSICAL ASPECT

All mountainy folk respected the work-tradition: some even
took a grim delight in a physical strength which was a half-
instinctive legacy from an ancient Gaelic idea. In Gaelic myth
and legend, as well as in historic fact, no king or chieftain with a
physical blemish could reign.

Why, in a marriage-match the parents of the girl took note
even of a man's baldness; the boy's parents took note of the
build, looks and shape of the girl, right down to her ankles.

DRAMA ON A FIRESIDE HOB

SOMEONE'S Christmas dinner died on the Old Lassie's hob and the Oul Fella and I thought it a timely end. You feel as lonesome as the thud of a single flail when everyone has turkeys to sell and you have none. The misery of yesterday makes happy reminiscence for today, even when the inspiration of such common human phenomena is the countrywoman's worry and pride—her turkeys.

Again, if this last turkey of the flock had lived, it mightn't make a Christmas dinner this year at all—not until it had parented next year's flock, when a fresh bird would be retained, letting all bad luck go with the old one—after we had camouflaged the scales on her legs to look like a young hen, a manipulatory cult on par with the artist in your ritzy beauty parlours.

All of which, if you're a countryman or woman, will tell plainly that the Old Lassie herself was deadly ill when her turkeys took the same turn, in late infancy. If the turkeys of an old countrywoman must die at all—bar they're blitzed by rat, dog or weasel or Red Rogue Reynard—they die on the hob at the fire. Sometimes you see chickens die in an old tin on the hob, too; but when it comes to a case of turkey versus chicken, the " birds " can die where they please. Even in death the turkey must be an aristocrat.

The Old Lassie herself got the chill out in the wet following the same turkeys, for they mustn't get a drop, and they're so gawky or snobbish they don't even know to go in out of the rain like other beings in feathers. So the doctor put the Old Lassie to bed, and she went, moaning about her turkeys, while the Oul Fella and I promised to care for them as lightly as you promise to meet a man who is looking a loan.

And, as the Oul Fella said, we started the dinner with soup. That very evening we had casualty Number One when the Oul Fella caught one of their heads in the half-door. That started the devastation; for they don't even know, as chickens do, to get out of the way of flat feet wearing boots the size of sleighs. Two more died mysteriously in the night.

And we damned our souls in answering the Old Lassie's calls from the room about the welfare of her turkeys. If the merest sign of rain blurted on the window she shouted to take them in. By that time, unfortunately, the Oul Fella could easily carry the survivors in both hands.

And so on, until she heard that last one making its final cheep in a wheezy falsetto from the tin box on the hob, and the calamity could be hidden no longer.

" Aw, I may rise outa this, or there won't be a livin' thing about the place—is the birds with the moggy hen at self all in it ? "

The Oul Fella stamped through the floor, saying desperate, unprintable things about turkeys, old women, and fowl generally.

" Put him in a tin box on the hob, an' put that bit of flannel out of the drawer around him ", she beseeched.

" Sure, isn't he smothered in flannel as it is, woman! "

" Keep the lid I blow the fire with on top, an' a boot or a brush or somethin' on it, so's the cat can't get at him ".

To convince her the Oul Fella rattled the tin the way the delph-sellers used to rattle plates in Newry market.

She didn't know, of course, that it was the last of the flock. But every other minute the Oul Fella lifted that lid and peeped in, and as if afraid of a gruesome sight, or another swan song, always plopped it back. Then he'd look apprehensively at the room door. " The draught through that door's no good for you, me girl. I'll shut it for a while anyway ".

" You'll shut none of it! I'm fryin' as it is ".

After that he peeped into the tin again, and in sudden frenzy carefully took the turkey out and stood it on its feet beside the blaze, bending around the pot towards the hob. The turkey's head plopped dismally like a slain flower. He turned it round the other way, but it was trying to die, miserably, of course, but on its feet, like the aristocrat it was. He held it, making grimaces.

" Wouldn't they drive any ordinary man up the wall, the same turkeys ", he croaked. " One wee gurry of a pig that'd ate he's fill and sleep after is worth a countryside of them—Woops a daisy! . . . Blast the same turkeys anyway! "

" Aw. What's up now? " she wailed from the room.
" He's feet up, an' the divil much loss! "
" The last? . . . The last o' me darlin' turkeys. . . ."
He took a deep breath and said to me: " Take him the hell outa me sight an' bury him a mile deep in the dung-hill ". And as I went: " An' take this oul' tin, too! "
And he flung it down the floor.

I FOLLOW THE FAIRIES

IN a week's growth of beard, and wearing duds which might embarrass a modern tramp (but excellent nevertheless for clabbering through wet priddy-stalks) I was riding on the back of a cart through Newry, past the bus shelters.

Two Mourne women, laden with market-making, looked hard at me: it was one of the last of the horse-drawn carts and I thought that was why till I heard one say:

" Isn't he the dead livin' spit of thon fella was after the fairies down our way last year or so . . .? "

" Ach, he couldn't ", says her companion. " Sure I heerd that fella on the wireless about all that after. . . ."

It was meself all right: even though to their dear minds a man who gave a talk or two on the radio was then reckoned to have landed it rich for ever. That had been my first venture into the Mournes and the mellowness of collecting there rose in a wistful glamour in my mind from the very sound of their voices.

It was even enough to blot out the din of the town about me: the cart itself rattling on the granite setts, the stink of buses roaring by, a curly-headed boy yelling the name of a local paper. Mourne . . . poetic and mysterious, the name murmuring of strange silhouettes and hidden valleys, like Attical above Kilkeel, The Waste Land and Clontifleece, where I would yet live with a family. And the people too: " Kindly Mourne: ask for tea and they fry you bacon; ask for the time and they give you the clock ".

I had been a puzzle at first to the people of the heights and vales around Hilltown. I was " following the fairies ": a pictur-esque interpretation of the job of the folklore collector, and as I was used in South Armagh vernacular to refer to them as " Wee People " the Mourne talk of " The Good Neighbours " puzzled me at first: I thought they were actually referring to their mortal selves. Even so, people looked on my quest as something ideal for the legitimate vagabond, no matter how often I might explain that we needed more than folk and fairy tales: we needed the details of the lives of the people as well, old standards of living, habitation, social customs and taboos and practices in wide association.

But because I could use the vernacular, though bamboozled by some idioms, people found it hard to accept me for what I said I was. I kept quoting a paraphrase of the words of the old ballad:

> " I buttered my brogues
> And shook hands with my spade,
> And went following fairies
> Instead for a trade ".

Because I was embarrassed: I had never been out of the Slieve Gullion country before in my life. Hilltown I had heard of: the hired boys and girls all seemed to disappear into Hilltown, famous as Eight-Mile-Bridge where South Armagh's rapparee, Redmond O'Hanlon, had met with a treacherous end—although later I found that local tradition refuted the historically accepted version of the tale.

Spring was tussling with winter when the bus dropped me in Hilltown. Bare hedges shuddered in the wintry blasts tearing across country from the north where Rathfriland sat on its hill. Sleet added tails to the shower as I sought out a man I knew, going from house to house as directed. Then it started to snow as dusk fell. I found a lodge. When the snow ceased the frost set in and moonlight shone.

The Mournes piled like stacks behind Hilltown were magnifi-cent in a regal and aloof beaten silver of the light. In the square of Hilltown itself the trees—each twig with its mane of frozen snow—might have become old ladies in a secret pantomime quietly awaiting their cue.

There was a different kind of silence in Spelga Pass next day. The boulders, dark with old moss, were part of a strange, watching stillness chaste under the snow. Against it the Bann looked quite black, while the staring sheep startled me when they moved, so indistinguishable from the boulders. A thousand souls might have been holding their peace at the intrusion of the stranger.

A man slithered down the hillside to the road. He was looking for sheep. I was unable to help, but when he found out (my accent told him I was a stranger) what I was after he began to fling phrases in Gaelic at me. He said his name was Rooney, and took me to a nearby house where an old woman of over ninety years sat at the fireside of turf working her spinning-wheel. I had never seen one in use before and her skill fascinated me . . . as it continued to fascinate on the nights I later spent at her fireside writing down her tales and traditions. Her name was Anne Savage.

They suggested the names of people who should be of use to me. But I should make myself known: I might be taken to be a pension officer in disguise, a secret policeman, an official from the Government department which deals with subsidies for this and that. I knew all this, and knew why country people are curious first and cautious afterwards with any stranger, however hospitably they may greet them: I had to remember the townlands where I had been reared to realize what was happening in their minds.

In the end most of them accepted me, tried to play pranks on me (like directing me at night to the house where a man was said to be jealous of his wife), while to others the caution remained, the curiosity still unsatisfied. One day a man called after me on a road in those Mourne hills:

" Hoigh! Hold on. I won't take a slate off you and I don't suppose you'll take a slate off me ". He had been pointed out to me as a man with folklore, but he either avoided me or made some hurried excuse for failing to let his talk expand to the reaches of Mourne hospitality. He came up to me and we walked along the road near Goward. We talked of sheep and weather and crops and then he asked:

" How long are you going to be here? " I told him. Then he says: " You must have money behind you to do this kind of thing ". I told him I was being paid by the Folklore Commission. And then he went on: " You're sure you're not a clerk? "—who had robbed a till and fled?—" or a brucken-down schoolmaster? "

Men who walked an area, unless hired farm labourers or tradesmen, were always wandering scholars and schoolmasters to the folk mind. I assured him I was neither. And then says he: " Well, I've been over a fair share of the world in my time. I've been to Butte, Montana, to the silver mines (many Mourne emigrants went to Montana), I've been on the Pacific coast and where have I not been. An' I've seen all sorts of quare jobs. But damme if I ever met a man before who made his livin' out of the fairies ". I wonder now why he hadn't said " Good Neighbours ". Perhaps he'd been away too long.

Yet outside Hilltown I spent nights with an old man who just loved to meet someone like me. He had a phenomenal store of folk knowledge of all kinds, and his name was McCumiskey. He came to be associated in my mind with a mystical experience in those early days in the Mournes.

I had walked to the foot of Crottlie Mountain after spending an afternoon and evening with him. In a field nearby a young man was burning scutch-grass on a fire of whins. A girl with folded arms watched silently. She stood sideways to the blaze, and as if oblivious to the man piling on the dried grass. And the glare of the blaze from the fire in the thickening dusk speared past her, making rays about a transparent rain-cap on her head.

For those few moments the young man and the girl became beings from the mythological age I had been dwelling in all that afternoon: they might have been performing an early Druidic rite in steel and fire to the first movement of a Mourne spring, humouring the new growth by burning the rags of last year's raiment. Into the darkening sky—deep, cool, calm and soon star-studded, the smoke from their fire curled up in bracken-staff spirals of obeisance to the mountain of Crottlie.

THE RESIDENTER

HALF-WAY up Newry Hill going south, between the road and the railway, a yellow-painted bulldozer was levelling off a building site. Beyond the site was a housing estate erected several years ago; and the man beside me in the bus had something to say about both.

" Nothin' but buildin' goin' on ", he observed. " An' they'll get takers for them all. There's houses beyont thonder at fifty bob a week an' they get takers for them. How it's done bates me. I idle no time, an' I'm neither out on the door nor lickin' the stones, but hell to me skin if I can see how some of them manage it. Labourin' men I mean ".

His voice was soft and slow and it matched a smile pleasantly wry and imperturbably philosophic.

Search

" No one these days ", he went on after the conductor had collected our fares and punched tickets, " wants to live in a country house any more. Not that I blame them ", he added quickly, and gave that wry, almost introspective smile out of grey eyes. " But the thing that bates me is this: There's not all that scarcity of land around here. What's the sense in buildin' town houses in a country place? "

I was reminded of the South Armagh flax-pullers making a festival of their search for work one time around the Bann. They met a man taking his constitutional stroll and asked him what was the name of the town ahead. He told them Banbridge.

" Isn't it a helluva fine town ", says one, " to be built out in a country place ".

My companion in the bus had heard the tale and gave that slow smile once more. Then he went on to explain what he had meant by " town houses " in a country place.

" Take the labourers' cottages built long ago. There was a good garden, half an acre, between every one. Now that was useful. Look't the houses they build now out in the country: everyone's stuck in everyone else's teeth.

" An' every door's closed—not a half-door in sight. You daren't make a noise or shout hard. You can't take a bite to ate bar some neighbour's child is lookin' in at you through the window. An' you daren't rise your voice to it—or that's another fault an' another row. They're never out of variance ".

" Mind you ", he went on, after the bus swung under the railway bridge and for a while ran parallel with a train, " I'm not sayin' the old people in their day hadn't many a barney; but it amounted to nothin': they weren't at it all the time over wee footherdy things ".

Before us, on the hills of South Armagh, in Clontigora beyond Killeen, the mountain face exposed an intricate plan of fields and scattered houses. Here and there I could trace the remains of the low earth fences of the rundale divisions running diagonally across the hillside of fields.

I wondered if my companion knew any tradition of those days, when land was held almost communally, and the houses were in small clusters known here as " Bahwins ", a word which means " bawn " or cattle enclosure. Before I could ask he observed:

Peace

" When all's said an' done, any man or woman's two ends of a fool that has a country house that's half like the thing to leave it to live in a cottage. But they're leavin' them just the same, good slated houses.

" 'Course, they're beside the bus, an' they have light an' water an' a dry foot. An' the TV. It's all right—an' it's not all right, if you know what I mean.

" But ", he said as he got up to leave the bus, " I think a bit o' peace is like the water in the well: you think nothin' of it till it's not there ".

I looked over the white houses of Killeen, and up the rise to Clontigora and Edentubber, where the mountainside had been carved into fields by the forebears of the man who valued a particular kind of peace and quiet—with independence, whatever about tradition.

DRINKERS IN A GALE

BLASTS of the gale in Newry made flying grabs at hat-brims and skelped a few signs hanging along the street. I turned back towards the pub, the swing doors of which didn't open when I pushed. A bright little man, who might have spun out of a whirl of the gale, opened the door and I followed him in.

" No heat ", he said to the barman who, in a steel-grey smock, was talking to a group behind one of the bar partitions. " Either that or the blood's far back in me ".

Inside the pub the wind sounded worse than ever—as if someone with heavy rubber boots was kicking a tattoo on the door. It clung like invisible swallows to crevices around the windows and shrieked like infant banshees throwing fits of spite.

Beside my boot a bit of tinfoil, no larger than an elfin silver birch leaf, rocked and shuddered along the floor.

" It'll tell a tale ", the barman said to the little man as he set up his drink.

" It won't ", said the other, " for it's told it already ".

The barman drew me a pint with expert ritual, returned my change with quiet courtesy, and went back behind the partition.

" But anyway, this day the Head come in to me in the bar . . .". He was a born narrator, pace and pause instinctively measured as he told about a retired Head Constable of the town. Winds rushed against the door and thudded around the whole house.

There were two snugs under the windows. Behind me, along the wall, was a form, where two men, heads close together, collogued on their own. There was no glamour or glitter; the sort of bar that makes its reputation on the quality of the drink.

". . . . When he was Head here, now wasn't he clergyman, counsellor and everything else? Sure, whenever a man got into a bit of bother, what was the cry of the women? ' Run for the Head—get the Head '."

They all agreed; and each began to tell of incidents in which this policeman, evidently an expert at his job, knew the way to

wink at the exigencies of human nature in order to counter-
balance the open-eyed demands of the Act.

When I filled my pipe and lit it a man told me he liked the
smell of my plug tobacco and asked what it was. The little man
then said he knew—from the " brogue " I had—that I must have
come from around " Dhrementee ". Did I know this man and
that? The name of The Jock Traynor (God rest the man!) came
up. Did he know him?

". . . I mind one time the Head talked to old Paddy . . .".

That was the moment another barman turned on the radio at
full strength. The voice of a news announcer thundered raucously
and indistinctly like infiltrating demons of the wind.

The barman toned down the volume and we learned from the
announcer of a threat of a delayed, insidious death; Russia had
exploded an outsize Hell-bomb in the Arctic. No one yet knew
if it was *the* Bomb, but he went on to detail precautions against
fall-out.

The moment of pause among the talkers in the bar was sudden
and long. And the winds seemed to howl in malicious jubilation,
as if aware of the predicament in which we found ourselves.

Man, with his ages of vanities, tied to the ever-turning wheel
of folklore, you up to-day, me tomorrow, never really getting
anywhere; the infantile jealousies and jostlings for the delusions
of snobbery and advantage and power. All, like ourselves, waiting
for a Godot and afraid he might turn up. The winds seemed to
know we had created a machine which was past controlling.

The first words in the bar came with almost ludicrous sanity
from one of the men on the form behind me: ". . . an' when your
bluddy feet's wrong, you're all wrong . . .".

Topics were picked up where they'd been suspended, and the
talk resumed. But our words seemed to refute every idea and
image of that moment of pause. I wondered if indeed the perfect
tragedy, as someone has said, has to be written in terms of a
comical farce.

Outside again, the winds seemed to cavort and jeer and bellow
in traffic-sound with a terrible irony.

Original caption: "Lammas Fair MCMXX"
The "Granny Rock" now enclosed in the Quay Yard, Ballycastle.

Lammas Fair in Ballycastle

" A run on the shores . . .! "

Breakers and swells going over pier wall at Ballycastle

SPRING ON SLIEVE GULLION

IT was, I think, that spring before I left Slieve Gullion: but it was so vivid I re-live it.

The radio had given out fog; and fog it was next morning—fog choking the spring gems as completely as cotton wool in the jewel case of the hills. Not a breath of air. No sign of sunrays, eager as a jeweller's morning fingers to lift and tease it and arrange the sparkle underneath. No birds sang. Only for an optimistic robin it could have been eerie. Somewhere voices were talking. Next came the roar of a bus. It was the Newry bus, but still hidden in the fog. Sometimes one saw it as a forerunner from a fable, seeking news of the excitement of our mountain spring, hurtling back to startle the town. But that morning it was a dim and fugitive hulk fleeing through rifts in the fog past the church.

Even the church was sombre, like a thing of the night trapped by dawn greys. The lyrical background of knuckled rock in Tievecrum had gone to leave it in hazy solitude, the cross on the front gable and the spires of the belfry outlined nakedly against the fog.

The voices from the road were complaining. I heard stones being built in a gap and knew the speaker had come to turn his cows out to graze: but I could see neither. Now the voices complained of the weather; of the work; complaining of the tangle of buds on the potatoes they had picked from the pits the day before. It was queer to listen to spring talk in such episodes without the great theme in the sight of earth to present the thrill as a single impression.

A hare came loping out of the outlet of the fog and sat on its haunches, startling a blackbird which scattered a throatful of alarm notes as a sower might scatter grain. Now the crows were on the wing, but their cawings came leadenly in twos and threes.

The Gentle Thorn

I walked to the road; and walked on towards The Gentle Thorn. There are dozens of these lone Fairy Thorns in the Slieve Gullion country but this one is a dramatic sight. It went down in a gale some years ago and, while one branch rots in the grass, the other, like an arm, flings a fistful of dainty blossoms skywards every year in a bribe for prolonged life. I remember looking closely and seeing that the hawthorn buds were bursting on that high branch: no more than a fistful, pale yet, and as tremulous as the drops gathered by the fog under the bars of the gate entering the field.

Beside the Gentle Thorn there is an old gable sporting a busby of ivy, like a sentry dourly watching. By then the fog had begun to thin. More birds took heart. A cart was on the road somewhere. There was some movement from the fields, and a ploughman was making a litany of the names of his horses, urging them to breast the cold collars and tighten the traces hooked to the plough. Then a tractor roared from a field beyond the church. I remember seeing a horse and slipe coming through a gap out of the fog like a ghost of a dim age, the driver riding as the primitive thing skidded along. A few evenings before I had been ironically stirred to see a crowd of homing schoolboys ignore a new tractor and beg for a ride in a slipe after it had delivered its load of manure through the treacherous passes.

Spring Magic

Just then, it seemed, the fog lifted. Spring spirits had used it as a magician uses his cloth. Up went a fistful of larks towards the light, boring through fog: one could imagine them as drills shredding angelic music behind. And down came the rays of light like brisk fingers to whisk away the cloth of fog.

All was changed: Spring magic was everywhere. The old gable had no busby now, but a head-dress of diamonds. The Gentle Thorn was bowed in curtsey. Carts blocked the field gaps with shafts riding high, sporting a regalia of harness with brasses like belated stars. There was so much sudden movement it seemed that men had been working all the time, the fog (true to tradition) a mere fairy sleep on the eyes of the watcher. An eight-bull harrow combed the scutchy head of a field on Garriba ridge, chuckling and lilting among the stones as it trailed and jogged along the earth. Across the bog, in the hollow, a lone potato-picker knelt at his pit like a worshipper of an old rite caught unawares at his conical shrine of earth and bud. And, impishly enough, on the ditch beside me, a half-burnt heap of mouldy scutch, with black and grey and brown ash pitted inside the smouldering cowl of weeks, was a monkey's face impaled ridiculously on a blossoming Irish whin.

By now the fog had ascended to the heights and was on the move, but tails clung like sheeps' wool to the barbs of heather. Where a compact scroll remained it was wonderfully shot with light. But it didn't remain long. The sunrays came like a shepherd's staff and gently herded them to the far north-east among the peaks of Mourne; while spring merriment laughed till it wet the eyes of the little green mountain fields on Slieve Gullion, laughing through the tears of fog.

MOON AND CLOUD OVER CARLINGFORD

FOR two nights running, high over Carlingford Lough, moon and cloud might have been staging a spectacle in light and shade.

I saw it quite by chance when my youngest son, on his way to bed, called excitedly from an upstairs window to come and see the moon. We are not long enough in the hills above Warrenpoint in County Down to have seen it like that before, and I stayed on when he and the rest of the family had been hooshed off to bed.

I watched until the movement of light and shadow became almost like an expressive gesture, till it seemed I was watching a mime of Man in relation to the poetic fulfilment of fields and landscape.

On the second night the mood was altogether different. It all became more of an allegory of Man, at once giddy and apprehensive, beneath achievements which were noble and frightening at the same time.

There was a field of oats in view near our townland of Clontifleece, and the mystic excitement in the imagery of bursting grain may have touched off impressions of both mime and allegory.

On that first night when I reached the window I found it wasn't exactly the moon I had been called to see. I was told to look at how the moon was lighting up the Lough.

From this window can be seen the swing and dip of the Omeath and Carlingford Mountains till the range rises up and over the craggy heights of Slieve Foy. Tall trees in our valley hide all sight of the Lough except at one point. The angle of the Lough glowed like the tail of a fabulous fish airing itself in the moonlight somewhere along the beach.

The moon that night was brilliant in a clear sky. Out of view around Rostrevor were some of the peaks of the Mournes, their timbered slopes clinging like moss on the roof of a steeple. They would be in shadow just as the hill to the east of our valley was also in shade.

But light in full glory showed up hedge and house on the hillside to the west. Here was a field of shooting oats like a packed tray of dull green pearl in a jeweller's window tilted to catch the slant of ingenious lighting.

That was when the mime began. The children were laughing over images which came to them when the moon seemed to be hanging in a tree on the ditch. There were " ahs " when a wisp of cloud folded about the moon and light in the cornfield vanished. Then the light was back and gone again. One of the youngsters said the tree was like a hand or claw round the moon.

I hooshed them off to bed, but watched on till the fingers of that hand took the coin of light from its purse of cloud and squandered brilliance once more below.

That night and most of next day it rained, but there was no wind. Towards dusk the rain ceased and mist filled in. It lifted once to let a finger of sunlight trace vivid colours on the hills of Omeath.

The moon came up that night above packed cloud which might have been upholstery haphazardly finished, all veined and tucked with shadow. Just enough light seeped through to make a dull glitter on that fish-tail angle of the Lough in view. I watched until the light slowly unfolded the massive outline of a cloud sprawled like piled fleeces on top of Slieve Foy.

No real light seemed to touch anything except that fantastic cloud lit up at the edges, while underneath on the mountain and its skirting of fields shadow deepened into a curious gloom. A single house light shone through and there wasn't a sound.

All the time the cloud mass seemed to mount, to get top-heavy and threaten to topple and engulf both Lough and town, mountain and field and every living thing.

I waited for a stray touch of light to awaken the cornfield. None came. There was only a stillness and that beautiful cloud on the mountain, soaring higher and higher above Carlingford Lough.

THE TINKER IN GLEN DHU

IN lovely Glen Dhu where, as you walk up the hill, the road sinks at each step between shoulder-pips of rock to bring up Slieve Gullion in ever fresh magic, the April shower caught up with me. It caught up with the young tinker as well; and together we lay close under the brow of a high ditch with only the briars and the grasses for shelter. Our feet were planted against the brow of a *sheugh* where tiny puddles shimmered. Around our ears the dead grasses of last year trembled with a sound like tinsel.

Three miles back in Louth I had seen the shower coming over Monaghan, and then emptying its gauze of rain on the famous Crossmaglen country. I reckoned that with stout pushing I should, however, make home before it caught me. But I had misjudged a spritely wind; the telling and abrupt silence of the birds, and the strange mood of spring shadow which falls before a shower.

There is always a breeze in Glen Dhu on the calmest of days: a cool breeze which, as we say, would " sometimes starve you ". Now the wind of the shower seemed to be cutting through Forkhill and curling back down the mountain valley. There was no hope, anyway, of riding the hill into the Glen. The first frolic of the shower, indeed, was upon it: a cloud-shadow furleyed along by a ray of sunlight as a boy furleys his hoop with a rod. In among the rocks on the Boill-Breaga of Tiffcrum the soil of little fields went as brown as turf; the green blush went from the heather as if it had been a light switched off. In that mood there was a terrible pathos in the sight of slain timber lying around a Big House now bare and incongruous somehow, its garrison atmosphere naked to the world. I dreamed for a moment of days when I rambled its grove with a ropeful of dead sticks on my back.

Sound sank under the shadow also. There wasn't even the cackling of a laying hen from any of the houses where the land, ascending from the plain, breaks into quick hillocks and clumps of bushes and fairy forts. Two old folk crouched at one end of a priddy-pit seemed to be oblivious to everything—to Spring, its lilt, to the coming shower. A moody task this, with fruitful quiets and your fingers gloved in naked earth.

An April shower is no more than the laughter-tears of Spring; but, like the famous Scotch mist, it can wet an Irishman to the skin for all that. I cycled down the hill into the Glen and had reached the high ditch when the rain came like quivering silver rods. Then the tinker joined me. He might have passed on had I not been there. But he stopped, his head bent to the shower, and then he came over, slipping a bandolier of shining pint-tins off his shoulder as he came.

He also carried two cans on the crook of his arm.

" That's a wicked one, sir ", he began, digging his heels into the channel of the sheuch to thrust his shoulders further into the briars like me. " An' the shelter could be better ".

He was a young man, and I wondered had I seen him before. Young and freshly-shaven, his hair blue-black, and his eyes like two coals as they begin to light. Was this the man who came to us one spring day asking " all sorts of prices " off herself while we took our " 10 o'clock tay " and while she wanted a basin " for half nothin' " ? I mightn't ask him. He would say " Yes " or " No " just as he thought the reply might suit him. What can you do with a brazen tongue that, in these austere days of uncertain rations, blandly asks you for a share of your tea and sugar ?

" Would you ere have the lend of a match, sir ? "

I asked him was he the tinker I had in mind, and he said he might—and, again, he might not. By now the *sheugh* at our feet was beginning to run brown and a dampness settled on our shins.

I remember that young tinker, wandering the floor with a tin of buttermilk in his fist, while he exposed for us the wiles and waywardness of Irish cities; the wonder and bewildering silliness of it all; the people peering through bay-windows as he approached and then sending a servant to say there was no one in. God forgive us, we kept him going, lying repeatedly that neither of us had ever seen a city.

" There's some coarse Christians in the world, too ", said this tinker from the ditch beside me; and his voice caught the dream-chord of my thoughts in living tongue and an old rhythm of sentiment became alive again. " Further down the road ", he went on, " I thought to sell a can to a woman at the head of her field. Her man, God help him, was turnin' the plough at the bottom. Well before I had crossed breath with her, sir, he started to shout—shout, God help us?—he called me anythin' but a gentleman, sir. . .".

My laughter stopped him. I knew the man; I knew his stony field, and I knew his old horse. I knew that once that old mare sees a can she decides it is dinner-time and, regardless of stones or bawls to " Go easy " makes for the head-rig as fast as she can.

I was still chuckling when the shower passed, while raindrops twinkled on the tinker's tins as he went his way, and while the light of spring laughter glistened in Glen Dhu.

THE PIG SMUGGLERS

THE pigs were being moved north from Louth into South Armagh in broad daylight in a pony and van and the neighbours merely called on me to " give them a hand to scout ". A regular man was not available.

" You'll stand at Frank's ", I was told.

Frank's, a carpenter shop, was a small place without a gate. Stripes of stony fields beyond Frank's led to the rise of the

mountain hills. I would take up my position across the road
facing Frank's gable-end.

To my left the road circled the hills and climbed through
South Armagh out of sight at Moyra Castle in the famous Gap of
the North. To my right the road led to Newry town or the village
of Forkhill. If a policeman came cycling from that direction I was
supposed to be able to spot his approach by the glint from the
peak of his cap at a point just under a quarter of a mile away
beyond some trees. At this spot the road dipped: he would be
out of sight for perhaps ten seconds or so. But how was I to signal
his approach?

Handkerchief

" Just wave this ", I was told.

And I was handed a white handkerchief as big, it seemed, as
the bed-sheet from which at the time seed oats used be sowed.
Someone I couldn't see on the hillside would spot the waving
handkerchief. He would instantly wave another handkerchief
to someone further on and up the mountain; in turn the second
man waved to someone else. It all meant that my wave could set
off transmission of a message which said " Stop "—or take
evasive action such as driving van and pigs headlong into a
neighbour's street out of sight of the Moyra Castle Road in the
north. Radio communications such as R.U.C. and Republican
Customs officers now use hadn't even been thought of at that
time.

Escape

Having waved I was to " make myself scarce ". I could either
saunter innocently into Frank's, a noted céilí-house; or scale the
ditch of stones behind me; or, by running hard reach a narrow
road which shot off to the right north of Frank's. In fact I lived
down that old road at the time.

But here I suddenly saw a snag: supposing a policeman came
cycling up that way? How could I wave my big handkerchief
without his seeing and suspecting?

" Let on ", I was instructed, " to blow your nose. But it's
not likely: only the Newry patrol car comes that way sometimes
an' it's not due for an hour ".

I was at my post for twenty minutes before I saw the glint of a glazed peak beyond Johnny Oiney's trees. I watched it disappear into the dip. I waved my handkerchief, pocketed it, strolled into Frank's and up to the door. But he wasn't in. I pretended to examine an old cart awaiting repair, boldly waiting for the man with the glint of his cap to go by.

It was the postman.

To this day I can recall the consequent feeling of utter loneliness, of a warm foolishness, of a cold alarm. I had done as directed; but I felt a renewed warmth when one of the boys came down from Moyra Castle on a bike, his face dark with frustration. My wave had halted the pony and van and pigs less than a mile away. Now the rest of those engaged in this operation would feel like hens on a hot griddle until the cyclist reported back and gave the all-clear. Before I could tell him something about takin' a runnin' jump he had turned like a circus stunt man and was cycling back up the road.

Stayed put

The unuttered code of our communal fealty held me to my post. And it is absolutely true that less than five minutes later I saw a policeman's cap—no need to watch out for glint at that range—moving along the top of a cut hedge along the old road to my right. Blow my nose nothing: I waved like merry hell. To " make myself scarce "—now with urgency—I crossed the road and into Frank's street once more. The old cart was lying on its shafts, the back-shafts or " trams " cocked towards the road.

Why I got into that cart I'll never properly know; but I was there with one eye to a dungy rot-hole in the tail-board when the policeman came into view. He stopped and got off his bicycle; my heart stopped as well. I watched him leave his bicycle along the wall and look at Frank's closed door. He took out a cigarette. Then he crossed towards the cart. My heart stopped again, then began to leap like a salmon.

Paused

He paused to light the cigarette in cupped hands, turned, and, for a moment, rested one elbow on the point of a " tram " of the cart: above me his shoulder in the dark bottle-green uniform

seemed to be as menacing as the back of Slieve Gullion before
a storm. I could even see the creases in his polished belt, valleys
of them; and I remember thinking swiftly of Forkhill Courthouse
and a magistrate chirping with singular indifference, as he seemed
to chirp in most cases dealing with nabbed smugglers: " Fined
a hundred pounds or six months in Crumlin Road ".

Knew him well

But not once did that policeman look over his shoulder.
I knew the man well. Having smoked his cigarette he rode off
towards Moyra Castle. Less than half an hour later the pony
and van and pigs went by like a runaway.

I had saved a neighbour: I was one helluva tight fella—God
spare me me health an' long days till I was better paid: because,
you see, I was merely " giving a hand " according to custom,
green and very young, I could expect no payment and got none
either. It was only half a crown, but that amounted to a day's
wages for me then just the same. Nor was I ever called on another
run on the Border. Maybe they thought I had jinxed them.
Maybe they knew that, edict or not, I just wouldn't go.

STALEMATE ON A BORDER ROAD

TREKKING across the wide and windy spaces of The Square
in Warrenpoint in County Down I met a man from South
Armagh; he was a neighbour I hadn't seen in years. On the
sheltered side of an establishment in the centre of The Square we
sat and admired the magnificent scenery in mountain-girthed
Carlingford Lough; and we talked and reminisced about many
things and many people, including the smugglers.

Among the legends of events on the Border he reminded me
of the one about the sergeant and the mountainy farmer. When
I lived in South Armagh everyone else also swore it was true and
told it around firesides like a folk-story.

It happened, they said, on an old mountain road which crosses
one of the South Armagh hills into Louth. The road, with a

surface like the bed of a dried-up river, is wide enough at each end to allow an ass or horse to zig-zag or " cut the hill ", as we said, but on top it became just wide enough to allow a farm-cart to pass between the boulders of the stone fences in comfort and safety. Faring south at this level the land on the left of the road is in " the State " (as we always said when alluding to the Twenty-six Counties); on the right the land is in the North—" The Wee Six ". The line may be crazy, but the view is splendid.

On the left-hand side one day a farmer was working in his field with a long-tailed shovel. Up the hill came a sergeant of the R.U.C. The legend says he carefully and dutifully leaned his bike on the right-hand fence or " ditch " and then stretched himself beside it and filled a pipe. The farmer, whose name could be Kevin, leaned on his shovel, and the two men got into talk.

There was a third party with Kevin, and he realized the idiomatic drift of the dialogue: knowing both the sergeant and the farmer, I would accept it almost as gospel.

" Now there's a fine laddybuck of an infant ", says Kevin, " that looks like his grub—an' his time to take it ".

" Good meat's wasted on some people ", countered the Sergeant. He was from either rural Fermanagh or County Cavan and could swop traditional repartee with the best of them.

" You don't have to look for your answer anyway, Sergeant ", Kevin says in a traditional line which defines the spirit of wit better than any phrase I know. " Nothin' like being able to give an' take a joke ".

" True . . ." the Sergeant says.

Kevin propped his other shoulder to his shovel and went on: " Get through this world as easy as you can is my motto. We've only one life to live, an', as the ould people used to say, the longest liver has only a short céilí of it on this earth in the long run . . .".

Other verbal overtures were exchanged, and the crack turned to many things, including the view. It was worth noting. North lay Slieve Gullion, mysterious mountain of Ireland, rising to a pure, temple-like dome: a score of myths had been christened in the rock-bound font of the lake on its summit. Between the mountain and the almost mystical circle of hills lay the bogs and

corrugated valleys of tightly packed fields and white houses. To
the south stretched the wide acres of Louth into the haze of
distance.

Out of this reflective quiet would come that spark of nagging
tension the legend mentions: as if the folk-gods of those hills had
begun to sky-write in Ogham out of a haze. Each other's company would become uncomfortable. The Sergeant, they said
broke it.

" Hear the game on Sunday? "

" Sure only I had a bitch of a heifer past her time at the
calvin' I'd a-been at it, man. A draw, too. You weren't at it
yourself by any chance? "

He wasn't: a football game broadcast from Croke Park in
Dublin. Next they discussed hurling, then soccer; after that it
was boxers from Belfast and Derry. Finally, the Sergeant fingered
the breast pocket of his tunic and said:

" The crack's good but . . . I have a summons for you, Kevin ".

" Aw no . . . ? " Incredulously. "⸙ What for . . . ? " A perfectly
timed pause here: and then even more incredulously: " Not thon
few scaldy bags of priddies surely? "

It was the bags of potatoes: bringing to a place for illegal
importation was the legal jargon for this kind of commodity
juggling or, according to direction, exportation if going south.
The Sergeant told Kevin to come across the dtich—and the
Border—on to the road and take the summons. Kevin naturally
told the Sergeant to come across the road and hand the summons
to him over the ditch.

" I can't serve it on you over there and you know I can't ".
The Sergeant in the end got heated, they said.

" You're right; I forgot; it wouldn't be legal ". And holding
his long-tailed shovel by the tip of the shaft, the head extending
across the Border, Kevin says: " Just drop her on that, Sergeant ".

" This has got to be served on you personally—over here in
the North. Hop over the ditch like a wise man and accept it ".

" Man alive, a body would think you were addressin' someone
as supple as a hare. Put it on the shovel, Sergeant, an' get rid of
it, man . . .".

According to the legend phrase and counter-phrase spiked one
another on interruptions which must have sounded like echoes of
the one that had gone before. Since Kevin owned land in the
North as well as the South there was talk of " arrest when he
crossed some day ". There were each-way and up-and-down
appeals for " sense " and a " grain of wit " and " who'll be any
the wiser ". Finally, legend says, there was a laughing reference
for settlement of the impasse by the methods of the boxers they'd
discussed earlier.

That brought them level and together again. The shovel was
withdrawn and talk was tossed once more from boxing to football
and again to boxing. The summons had by then gone back into
the Sergeant's pocket.

The legend never definitely claimed a victor. Some time later
Kevin (as we say to-day) finalized the sale of his mountain farms
and went to live permanently in the South. As in that game
they'd been discussing you might say the interlude ended in a
draw.

ONE BRAVE DROLL FELLA

HE was a bachelor who lived with a bachelor brother and had
spent a lifetime working as a navvy in England; a small,
slight man with bloodshot dark eyes in a pale complexion that
had a sardonic droop.

His voice came slow and soft with a minimum of lip movement.
And he had the drollest sense of humour, not wit, of any man
I'd met.

When he said he had come home to South Armagh to " leave
his bones beneath Slieve Gullion " I thought he was indulging
a perverse turn of that sense of humour and gave him the
traditional counter: " Twenty years good in you yet, John—
without care ".

" Another clean shirt ", he said, " would be a waste of time
an' labour. A good rinse of the two I have should see me home

an' dry ". Admittedly he had a wrecking cough, but then he was a heavy smoker of cheap cigarettes.

Quiet

Less than twelve months later, after a few days in bed, he died quietly. He was decently waked and the neighbours talked of him and his quiet nature and of his " long days beyont in England ".

When we set off to follow the hearse at his funeral the men repeated all that had been said at the wake. These comments are customary; once disposed of the men drift into crack about land, life, work, war and politics.

" One brave decent quiet fella anyhow, Lord rest him ".

" Never hear his wrong word ", another confirmed.

" Could come an' go at Christmas an' take a drink or leave it alone an' away again . . .".

And so on. Later it occurred to me that none of the men had once made any comment on his sense of humour; someone should have remarked that he was also " one brave droll fella " and recall some incident from his life, such as the time he met the beggarman.

He had come home to help his brother with a heavy harvest extended by conacre takings. A night of heavy rain stopped harvest hopes and the brother had gone off to Newry with a cart-load of new potatoes. John had been digging more.

When I called he was changing boots and socks thoroughly soaked and clabbered; he had a dry sack on the floor beside him. Then we heard the beggarman come to the half-door groaning the familiar chanting litany of those days:

" May the Lord an' His Blessed Mother an' all the Saints in their High Heaven have mercy on all the poor souls ever went out this door on their last journey! "

" Come in. . . . Come in ". John had already been calling as he pulled on a wet, heavy navvy boot.

The beggarman came in, a tall man about sixty, fairly full of body under a dust coat. He wore a hat and carried a stout, crooked stick.

Inside the threshold he dropped a butt-sagging sack laden with his prog; he knew—even in those early iconoclastic days of Welfare State attention—to slide the sack off his shoulder outside, for it wasn't considered lucky to carry anything over the shoulder into a dwelling-house.

Accent

" How's times? " John asked, with just a hint of acquired English accent, not sounding at all disgruntled. I should have watched then for the unexpected.

" Poor enough, *avick*. Poor enough ".

" No luck on your travels at all? "

" Many's the time a lot better. The world's hardenin' its heart more an' more every day ".

" I'd well believe you ". John by then was lacing the other boot. He says: " Which way did you come? "

" From the Newry way, *avick*. Up the Dromintee Old Road here ".

" An' headin' for Dundalk now, I suppose? "

" Sure, there's nothin' else for it ".

" Up by Moyra Castle way? "

" I am, bless you an' all belongin' to you ".

And the beggarman's voice drifted off into an incomprehensible muttering of the old chant.

Stick

" Take your time ", says John, head still bent, " till I get this old brogue laced an' I'll keep you company ". Face impassive, voice indifferent. " All I need is the stick; I have the bag ready an' was on me way out for the high road meself.

" Me an' you can take house an' house about an' split the bunce when we get as far as the New Inn near the town . . .".

The beggarman jerked, stiffened, straightened and then stared. John hadn't looked up.

Then the old man let fly a flurry of telescoped oaths, curses and hoary profanities, seemed to find a surprising energy not hitherto surmised, swept up his sack and even more swiftly swept out, slamming the half-door behind him, still cursing.

John went to the back window, leaning across the table, to watch the beggar-man go towards the end of the Old Road. I joined him.

Bobbing

Twice the beggarman whirled to shake his stick back at the house; we could see his head bobbing on a langled emphasis of expression as if an invisible lightweight boxer as small as John were punching the head in a tattoo from behind.

John says in his disgruntled, even lugubrious way: " As the old people used to say, I'd rather have the curses than the blessin's of a laddo like that. He makes a better fist of the cursin' than the blessin' anyway. I delused he would ".

He turned, picked up his sack and, solemn and sardonic, went off to dig more spuds.

HIS LAST LEPRECHAUN

STRICTLY speaking, this is not an orthodox folktale about a leprechaun, or lauchraman as we say in Slieve Gullion fairy nomenclature; but it has an extraordinary feature. It began with the raciest of our Slieve Gullion shanachies, and only last week I attended his funeral. I recalled the interludes I used to have with him over his Belfast lauchraman.

When Walt Disney himself was over here we used the incidence of that visit to open the subject again. He was an earnest talker and a natural word-artist, but though he had moments of doubt—when his awareness brought rebuke in down-to-earth rural colour—he took this matter of the Belfast Lauchraman seriously. As if eager to settle the matter he sometimes broached the topic himself, as when the price of tobacco and cigarettes went up and he remarked about a priest in Newry who was " tryin' to make the young fellas teetotallers on cigarettes ". Naturally, I reminded him of his Belfast lauchraman; and once again his temperament went up like boiling milk.

Preparing to hobble, throw and tie a horse before " boating " it to Ballycastle

Hauling out cattle from Rathlin at Ballycastle.
Cattle usually have to be trussed.

A typical forge scene taken at Hilltown, 1944

The late Anne Savage, story-teller, near Hilltown.
As a young girl Anne ploughed with a team of horses.
Urn cailleach on display over milk strainer.

Because this Lauchraman in Belfast wasn't following the traditional occupation of cobbling boots. Instead, he was running a tobacconist's shop when our shanachie visited that city for the first time not so long ago. And more extraordinary still, our shanachie refuted the idea that this person was a lauchraman at all.

Not that he meant to imply that a fairy in Belfast would be as sensational as a Unionist meeting conducted in Gaelic. For nights and nights he had told tales about their trips to strange places, even overseas, especially to Spain, where they had a rollicking time. From such a source the late Stephen Vincent Benet may have got the idea for his fine yarn, " O'Hara's Luck " in which the family lauchraman (who apparently clung to a family of the old strain in adversity, as the banshee clung to them in death) went into exile with the last man of a family, and went with him through Yankee-land, sometimes visible, sometimes not, until eventually he assisted the emigrant to hold down a job for which he hadn't any capabilities at all except his native flair for wit and adaption.

Once I suggested to our shanachie that this is probably what happened to him in Belfast. Up went that temperament, and rebuke ran out more colourfully than banners. How extraordinary! How often had our shanachie wasted mental energy and a talent for the traditional in trying to convince numbskulls like me that his fairy tales were true tales; that fairies existed; that in fact he had seen one himself. But by all that's high and holy, it was no Belfast lauchraman who served him with that two-ounce plug of an unknown but unbeatable brand of tobacco.

And again invoking the authority of Stephen Vincent Benet, I went so far as to reason that the Belfast fairies, smothered in industrialism, ordered that touch of consideration, because he represented one of the last of a dwindling body of souls who vindicated the entire fairy clans; who became indignant when someone disbelieved; who, amid quotations of evidence from personal and local tradition, looked at you as a cat might at a mouse behind glass.

" I tell yeh ", he would affirm, " he was a rale man. A wee man surely, but a rale wee man. Dammitskin, sure he gimme

D

change outa ten bob, an' sure you can't go past that now ".
And he would go on, unaided by any teasing: " It was a wee
shop, an' what's more, I was in the shop. A wee shop wedged
between these big houses like a duck-craw between a byre an' a
barn. I thought nothin' of it, an' went in an' asked him for two
ounces of plug. ' I have none in now ', sez he, ' but here's stuff
that's no way bad. Same price an' all ', sez he. A wee man
clean shaven an' not a dust of hair on he's head ".

A pity he couldn't give a few details of the street. If he had,
and the discovery was made known I could see the crowds
collect—hard hats an' all!

" Talk about tobacco! Talk about last! " the shanachie
would enthuse. " No name to it. A pipeful would do you half
a day. I wanted to get more of it, an' took me cousin's man,
Tam, with me. For I couldn't find the shop. Nor could he.
I could mind the corner I went round, an' see the same big houses,
but neither hilt nor hair of the wee shop. An' better nor all, Tam
never minded a shop there an' him bred, born an' reared in the
city o' Belfast ".

Here one used to paraphrase a tale of his own telling: of the
man who, in his charity, gave his last pipeful and pipe to a wee
man who said he was dying for a smoke. The wee man smoked
his fill, emptied the pipe and, handing it back told him not to
tell a soul. He didn't, but later, when looking ruefully at the bowl,
found that instead of being empty it was now packed full. Smoke
as he might the pipe never emptied. Then he realized who the
wee man had been. He never told. Not until his wife—as usual—
wondering why he wasn't reminding her of late to get his tobacco
with the weekly groceries and save his own pocket money, worried
the secret from him. No doubt she regretted it too, for from that
the pipe emptied.

But if one introduced that as an explanation for the mysterious
disappearance of the wee shop, the shanachie used to blow up.
Then he would wheel about on his backless chair, thrust his boots
over the hearth, fold his arms and pretend to sulk—till a new
thought sped down his brain to the tip of his tongue.

That was our racy shanachie and his Belfast lauchraman.
It was his last story, too. Last time I met him he was out of

tobacco. We both lit up, but neither of us mentioned the lauchra-man. Age had come to him as swiftly as a cloud-shadow, but it clung, dragging his steps. But I remembered him then as I did the other day when this item of the Disney people appeared. . . . Hot and bothered by the notion of a clean-shaved lauchraman with nost a dust of hair on his head, selling tobacco in the city of Belfast.

THE STORYTELLER OF DONAGHMOYNE

OUTSIDE Inniskeen, in County Monaghan, two women having a gossip threw back their heads and gave a concerted laugh when they heard I was searching for folklore.

" God help you ", said one with some sarcasm. " There's not a word of that here this years " said the other with an indulgent sympathy.

But a man on the road near Donaghmoyne had heard folk stories told, though he " had no head for that sort of thing ".

He directed me to a house and added: " If old Barney's at himself at all, he should mind somethin'. If he can't there's no one left here fit to tell you anythin'.

" Mind the road, though, on that auto-cycle—you could drown a dog in the holes o' water in it in places. I'm sorry I can't be of any service to you ".

Riotous

Around me the countryside rose in hillocks like pieced caps plucked up by the button on the crown, with riotous thickets and hedge-heavy ditches in fresh green.

Somewhere a dog barked, as if awakening from sleep. I thought I heard an old-type " stiff " farm-cart chortle in ruts in a lane or field.

I came to a road that might have been cast with crushed stone recently spread from the back of a moving lorry, and then rode along a pass through a field to the house I believed I had been directed to.

With red sheds and a pebble-dashed dwelling, the setting may have been far from the sentimental idea of the abode of a folk storyteller, but one never knows. No dog charged at me. There was no half-door. I knocked.

Unabashed

A young lassie of about nine appeared, with younger sisters pushing heads past her to view me. She was unabashed as she ate a potato in its jacket; and I soon discovered I was at the wrong house, and that her own parents had gone to Carrick.

To allay the curiosity of her parents upon return, I concocted a remark about fireside cracks, and asked the wee lassie if she had ever heard her father tell stories.

" I never did " she replied with such startling finality that I almost expected her to reprove me.

Instead, she pointed to a house far over the fields and said: " Old Barney, they say, used to be good crack. What time is it? Our clock's stopped ".

Silent

Barney's house was also at the end of a long, lonely lane. Once through the gate a dog made the expected charge, but silently.

A woman appeared to investigate the clamour and " chewed " the dog, as I was doing, and, in relief, I sauntered to the doorway, talking in vernacular, self-consciously using the idioms of the countryside.

I told her what I was after, and a strain of caution on her face softened to something like a mixture of curiosity and disbelief.

He was in bed, not doing the best, and she doubted if he could help anyway. But I was told to come in, though I said not to bother; I could call again. By then she was at the room door and calling out: ". . . An' it's only a man wants to meet the old people. You needn't be upset; he's only a country fella like ourselves . . .".

Medicine

I was taken up to the room and given a seat alongside the old man. Beside him stood a small table with his matches and pipe with its shiny, notched lid, a glass with dark medicine, and his rosary beads.

He was over ninety, but had full red cheeks and a white and tawny moustache with long tails. He had dark eyes still vivid, a strong voice, and a remarkably firm hand-shake.

He thanked me for calling to see him, and again I explained, adding that I was not going to bother him that day.

But he said I was " no bother ", asked where I came from, could I " make a wee livin' out of what I was at . . ." and before I quite knew it was talking of spring work.

' In petticoats '

He remembered the wooden ploughs in use in the area, and because his own father died early had " ploughed with one himself in petticoats ".

He couldn't move, except to sweep a hand slowly over head and face with a final gesture as if giving a twist to the moustache; but when telling some tale or event he would ask me to rise and go to the window.

Did I see a hill with a ditch running across the top. . . . I did? . . . Did I see an ash bush a bit over—in the corner. . . . That was the spot where it had happened.

Several times I had to rise and go to the window and identify sites on the ridgy landscape from his description. Like so many of his kind, a part of him still lived out in those fields and ditches and hills.

When I got up to go I said I would like to come back.

Welcome

" You'll be welcome any time, but God only knows if you'll find me here ". Lapsing into vernacular banter, I said there were " years in you yet—without care ".

He laughed at that and observed: " We'll meet I hope, but it'll maybe be in Heaven, please God. I'm not afeared. I'm prepared. I know I can't last much longer ".

" You'll be here ", I told him. " Never fear ".

" Don't be disappointed if I'm not. An' thank you for callin' on me ", he added, when I was half-ways down the floor. He spoke again as I reached the door to the kitchen: " An' God bless you, *avick*, an' the height o' good luck go with you . . .".

Tradition

I thanked him and wished him the same, as tradition demanded, and went into the kitchen.

The woman of the house made me sit and take tea, and then hurried to attend to some chore outside. On a far hillside a man rested in his work to converse with a woman on the other side of the ditch: I heard her laugh. A youth was fencing a gap with slashed hawthorn thick in leaf.

I thought of the old man in the room, silent now, but no doubt living in his mind what I was seeing through the window, perhaps even imagining the talk and badinage of his neighbours.

I remembered the deep quietude of Donaghmoyne, and the wee lassie who had directed me to Barney, both a bit puzzled as to who and what I was: the memory touched a poignant, though indefinable relationship between youth and age and the dying wonders of the folk world.

Leaving the house I forgot about the cross dog, which ignored me anyhow: I was remembering so many other houses from Rathlin to the Boyne, where old men confined to their beds had spoken to me much as had old Barney, and I know they had meant every word.

A DEAL IN CALVES AND A WOMAN

" WAS Cox's man in yet? "

He was a heavily-built man in shirt sleeves and open waistcoat, a large head and a meal-dusted cap, a generous mouth with some bad teeth and eyes that vanished in habitual good humour. He could be sixty years.

He had come in suddenly through a door behind me in the spirit grocery in the County Monaghan village of Inniskeen; and when someone answered indifferently, in a brief negative, he went away. No one in the bar knew me, nor did I know any of the other drinkers—countrymen of varying ages in working clothes stained with soil or dung or tractor grease. Only one man sat on the seat fastened like a long stool to the wall, and he wore the uniform of a transport driver: I had mistaken him at first for a taxi-man, because a few men with a wedding party had gone out as I had come in.

The man in his shirt sleeves came back shortly and, as if building up his mood towards some joke, remarked that " it was workin' round to the rain ".

" It's tryin' hard all day ", said the man in uniform.

" It'll manage it this time then ", said the man in the shirt sleeves, as if enjoying that secret joke. He was given a pint of stout and reaching back-handedly between his legs, drew a stool to the bar and sat, legs splayed out, looking at everyone in turn.

All at once he took hold of the arm of a man near him and began to give an account of a marriage-match-cum calf deal: he had been sparked off by a reference to the wedding party just gone out.

" Did you not hear ", he cried, his eyes vanishing, " what happened me a while back when I was at home smokin'? "

" I never even knew you smoked ", said the man in uniform.

He affirmed quickly that he smoked only at night when sitting on his own.

" He's a deep one ", one of the men said with a touch of irony.

" Wait'll you hear the end of it! " the man in shirt sleeves cried. He even grabbed at my arm, and I saw that his eyes were a smokey grey before they danced behind the laughter-retreats of wrinkles.

He said he had been smoking at the fireside when a van stopped and two men came in, one of them a dealer from Crossmaglen in South Armagh. The dealer wanted to buy a blue calf, but he wouldn't sell. They had some further abortive bargain talk and " The Cross man " had said to him:

" You're sittin' nice here. There's only one thing missin': you need the woman. I can get you a woman with eight hundred of dry, solid money, forby what's runnin' loose in the land in cattle. Are you game if I bring her some night? "

He was game all right—anything to get a kick—and he added: " Anythin' at all to make me part with the blue calf ". And he shook with laughter, burying his head on bare arms folded on the bar.

He went on to tell how the " Cross Dealer " arrived one night with " this woman " and two men, one claiming to be her brother, and he described her:

" A big lump of a woman, not all that bad lookin', but every inch of her as solid as an anvil. Listen, now, listen ", he cried for the others were in laughter with him.

" What was her name? " someone asked.

His own face became strangely solid for a moment while he scratched his balding head, his dusty cap dangling from his fingers like a cockade. He drew it on again and said: " Damn me if I know now; but sure what odds. Listen—listen ". His eyes retreated once more behind the laughter folds. " But she was a woman of the Armagh country all right; I could tell be her tongue. We had some talk an' then says she: ' You'll have to come down to my place some Sunday '. Sure I said, sure—anythin' for a kick—yous know how it is. An' then the Cross fella tries to make another deal for the blue calf, an' the other fella with him carries in a red roan of a skitterin' calf in a bag an' tries to palm that on me. Nothin' doin' of course. Wait'll yous hear . . .".

He seemed to be able to laugh even as he drank.

" I went down one Sunday evenin'—for the hell of it. You never seen such'n a bluddy place in your life. Listen, now. Miles from anywhere, down a long guttery lane. I got into the house. One table first of all was full of brown paper parcels— you'd swear they were years in the thatch. Mind now, the Cross fella was there too, at the start, but he went out to see about some cattle she had. ' Begod ', says I, ' he's right; she's rotten with money '. Listen, will you—listen. She had two primus stoves an' went to light one, an' I got a decco into one of the parcels. Cigarette coupons—ould as tay. Thousands of them. Thought I'd think it was money. Listen, damn yous, listen. She lit a match an' lit a butt of a candle with the match an' lit the two stoves off the candle to make a bite to eat. That's as sure as yous're sittin' there—wait—listen . . .! " he cried as laughter from the others once more skirled around him.

" There was a lot of quare ould runnin' outside. An' a car or two. Miles from anywhere. ' A fella ', says I to meself, ' could be kilt dead here an' no one'd be any the wiser '. Oh, it's all right, but a man never knows what enemies he has. So when she asked would I want to go out to see the cattle I seen me chance, an' me out—an' through a hole in the hedge—an' as hard as the hammers of hell to the road where I'd left me bike. Hold on a minute but—listen . . .".

The door behind us had opened and a voice yelled:
" Who was lookin' for Cox's man? "

" I was ", said the man in the shirt sleeves, but the voice might have belonged to a different soul.

He drained his pint, slid stiffly off the stool and as he turned to go said quietly: " I'll be back ", and I saw that the laughter creases lingered on his face.

No one made any comment when he had gone.

Instead they talked of land and tractors, crops, football and the threat of rain. No one speculated on the sequel to the man's story, which was perhaps obvious anyway . . . or was it?

Some of the mood the man had created went with him as he withdrew, and when all the others had gone the mood was no longer comic but curiously tragic.

A lorry started up outside. Spits of rain dappled the window panes. The man did not return; and the only talk came like confessional echoes from customers in the grocery end of the place.

A BREATH OF SUMMER

OUT of the dusk on Clontifleece, in the County Down, some man on the road above the school near the copse was saying to a neighbour: " Aye, scorchin' hot the day. It's a pity the good weather ever done harm . . .".

" The country'll soon be cryin' out for a drop o' rain ", the other replied. " That was a wicked, weakening heat the day . . .".

Clarity drifted from the voices as if some hidden blanket of heat had wafted into the channel of sound. And even though the air was scented with the breath of first blossom, and the voices now relaxed, it was strange that one should remember that morning of mist just over a week ago.

Scotch mist

There had been no sign of the dry spell on that morning. " A Scotch mist ", as I've said, " that'd wet an Irishman to the skin ".

Nothing stirred, but the mist sometimes fell in a *smurl* of rain that wavered delicately like twisted spider-webs.

It filled the new leaves in the hedges and when they dipped to dislodge the moisture the movement caught the corner of one's eye as if a bird or skulking animal had flitted out of sight as quietly as the drop of the mist itself.

It enveloped the hills and the reaches of the valley falling away towards Carlingford Lough at Moygannon. It shrouded the trees, so that even those nearer hand in the flush of new leaf might have been fern or mammoth bracken screening a lake or an abandoned well.

Looking at Aughavilla and Clontifleece one remembered lakes where stone ditches slithered like fossilized grey eels down the shoreside fields into the water, to disappear in a mood oddly vibrant because of the association with some distant minds and will.

The mist brought something of the same mood to our County Down valley, because just above the houses on the hillside the ditches climbed to disappear, but vibrant in a different way.

They sported the resplendent green of untrammelled hawthorn leaf and carried like banners the rousing orange blossom of whin: when dimmed by the mist the whin seemed to glow as village street lamps had glowed one night of fog in Burren beyond the hill.

The morning wore on, but still there was no sound. Only the mind and imagination seemed active. This soft morning was the heavy breath of the spirit of summer, celebrating the fulfilment of new leaf and growing things; the sleep of a night of carousal bleared its eyes, and there was no pulse of bird-call to coax it from slumber.

No tractor chugged, no voice called a dog or yelled at cattle; there weren't even the usual morning cars yet.

At last, from the mist around the tall trees down the well field, the hoarse chatter of a magpie started, then went still.

It could have been a mocking lost echo of the raucous uproar of the rooks only a few evenings ago in late dusk; for this is June— the " hungry month ", when " no kind of meat will fill bird or beast ".

Homely plane

When the sound of the plane came, high above the mist, it might have been as apologetic as a guest moving among the sleeping hosts. But how homely now is the whirring throb of its engines against recollections of the arrogant whistle-whine sweep of a jet.

It seemed fitting to remind oneself that in the rush of progress the plane has almost become in sound like the lone thunder of our few surviving iron-shod farm-carts against the stoor and smell and bustle of the tractor.

A hare loped across the head of the field beyond the road. The cattle grazed on. Leaves dipped to dislodge moisture, bobbed and bowed and went still.

A field of oats, still bare enough, gave no hint of the future pageant of harvest. Even the smooth trunks of sycamore near the road glistened dully like wet macs; but one remembered the pattern of leaf-shadow capering on them in the first lights of recent mornings, sometimes in a shifting tracery that in turn made grimacing and whimsical old faces stare back from the bark.

No light came, and the mist stayed on. There was no chill, however, and this seemed to startle at first.

The mind was so apt to remember the extended rigours of a severe winter, and forget that this was a soft summer morning, unaware of the blazing days of sun ahead, with dusks where men could converse at leisure in shirt sleeves, while youngsters would come along when they had gone, to make a rook-raucous kind of fairy music thread its way ironically through those undulating channels of sound—with a modern transistor.

WATCHING THE MARE AT FOALING

SHE was carrying her first foal. Neighbour men had gone unbidden to " watch her at the foalin' " as we said those days in South Armagh. They were prepared to stalk her all night.

The mare was in a quiet field with mossy sod and stone ditches all around it: no *sheughs* or drains, no briars or wire which might cause accident or—God forbid—tragedy: a field near the bog that smelled sometimes dank, sometimes sweet in the June night under Slieve Gullion.

I would like to deceive myself now that I joined the men for an avowed purpose straight out of their folk talk: to salvage that umbilical item which, from a first foaling, made a charm to quieten any wild horse; or to watch and mark the exact spot where the foal would be dropped in the hope later on of finding the mystic wonder leaves of a four-leafed shamrock.

I hadn't heard that men were to keep a vigil; and there was a reason, inspired of course by communal anxiety. For when men were watching a mare to foal, people spoke of it in a hush, with eagerness, hope and apprehension in their voices, as in a kind of conversational prayer. So much could go wrong, they said.

" It's easier losin' a mare than gettin' one ", ran one traditional saying.

Dusk was on when one man quietly went down the fields. Later, when a single star appeared after the scorchings of the sunset had turned as grey as ash, another followed him.

I wondered what was up and followed timidly. Stray light seemed to linger and crowd on to the blossom piled on a hawthorn. The dew was sea-cold on my bare feet—we all went barefooted then by choice.

It was the wink of a pipe-bowl I saw first. Next came low voices as if from a sleepy murmuring of the very earth itself, like the tick of settling cinders in a silent room. None of the men said anything as I came up. None wore an overcoat. They were hunkered or stretched against the ditch outside the field where I knew the mare was grazing.

Outside other points of the ditches around the field other small groups of men were watching also, because now and then a whisper of their talk came to us; talk that seemed to be wafted in the wake of the rich, drowsy scent of whin blossom mixed with earthy bog breaths.

The men talked quietly on everyday topics: land and weather, neighbours, the progress and incidents of the work of the valley. When one of these incidents sparked off a rising phrase or a threat of a laugh, someone said immediately:

" Easy . . . easy . . . keep your voice down . . .".

At this one of the men would rise and squirm through the whins on the ditch and peer into the field beyond. I looked also, but could see nothing.

I could see a whiteness in the bog—blossom trapping the after-glow, a bog-hole perhaps. I heard a bog-fowl twitter and a duck made a splash and I half expected the men to utter rebuke. On the far ditch another pipe-bowl winked.

" How is she? " the man was asked when he slid back to rejoin the group.

" Up by the top corner . . . grazin' away ".

" Dammit ", another said, half in annoyance, half in apology almost. " I thought she should have shown a sign before now ".

" You can't tell to the minute with the best of mares, let alone one on her first foalin' . . ." another man added.

Suddenly the man on the ditch made an urgent gesture behind his back and said: " Move down . . .". Everyone got up immediately and in single file moved down along the ditch. From the corner they settled into positions and watched.

But the mare appeared to sense their presence and moved off slowly back the way she had come; her hoof clinked on a stone. One man stalked her, another followed, then another. I heard the mare groan, sniff, and heard her strike another stone as she moved off across the field.

" She's doin' her damnedest to beat us ", someone said. ' But they'll see her now . . .".

One of the other groups had her in view now; and later on, when a call came, the men seemed to find a youthful agility. " Hoigh . . . Come on . . .". They scrambled over the ditch; one man swore at thorns which jagged him; another cursed softly when a stone fell, with a kind of sleepy thud.

The voice said suddenly, taut with caution: " Not all of yous.
You, Francey, she knows you an' mightn't make strange. Easy . . .
she's gonna get up. . . . Easy, Francey . . . come on . . . she's lyin'
again. Wait till yous are called, boys . . .".

I didn't join them, but lay on the ditch watching, seeing
nothing except vague moving shadows, hearing their urgent,
swift words. No doubt the grasses stirred. I waited, however, to
hear the voice from the darkness, in triumph:

" Horse foal for you, Peadar, an' a dandy. The height of
good luck to you both in them . . .".

The mare had foaled. The June night had shed mystery, but
I remember only the chill of the dew and a grass-cut in a bare toe.

THINNING THE TURNIPS

ABOVE Warrenpoint, in County Down, I watched two
turnip-thinners on a hillside under the sun, and I recall
summer days when I was at the same job in high and low fields
under Slieve Gullion in South Armagh.

Every man went down on his knees to thin the turnips; even
men who, as seasonal farm workers in England, had used a hoe
along with the Connaught men and praised it for speed. But at
home in the hills those days tradition stalked almost every act
and thought, and it put us down on our knees to thin the turnips
just as it put us down likewise to pick potatoes from the pits
in March.

In our talk we used contrast the two jobs of work. There was,
of course, a difference in mood and tempo. When picking potatoes
in the open field, each man used a folded sack as a cushion between
the earth and his knees. When thinning the turnips, however,
strips of sacking were lapped puttee-wise around each knee and
bound in place with twine or " Red Ned ", grass-rope bought in
town. We crawled up a drill and yanked out young turnips as
fast as weeds, stones, the earth or the flies—and our abilities—
allowed us to thin them. I can recall the burning heat and the
warm, scented earth after a shower.

March and the priddy-picking were so different. Usually we could wear our jackets; even then we often had to erect a windshield of a winnowing-cloth draped over spades, graips and shovels, with the upended cart drawn into position as well. You couldn't draw blood out of a priddy-picker with a hatchet, as they said; but the clags sucked all they wanted from our arms when we thinned the turnips.

Priddy-pickers could have looked like forgotten followers of some old earth rite, fossilized in the posture of worship by a raw wind: turnip-thinners might have been sunstruck fools searching for shade in the open under a canopy of strumming flies. . . .

I remember the talk evaporating into dreamy silences; then someone would say: " Must be good huntin': no barkin' from the dogs . . .". A beetle or unusual spider a foot from your nose had new meaning. In masses of weeds and redshank smothering the turnips, one might see forests and clearings; stones could become blocks of buildings in ferro-concrete in a distant land. For talk came from pahvees, from sailors and from men who knew the Arctic woods and wastes and towns; men might remember jobs and incidents from days in London, New York or San Francisco.

And all the time the left hand was securing a weakling turnip while the right hand pulled away all living growth for about nine clear inches. The left thumb flicked the turnip prostrate, secured another and the right bulldozed again. All the time, too, the clags kept landing silently or when both hands were busiest; the bite—the swipe—and an in-sucked word far from prayer. " You're fair knocking clipes out of yourself ", the older men would laugh. One rarely had to wait long before tossing the jibe back to the taunter.

To pause in the crawl was only half-ease, because when you moved on again the stones and rush-roots seemed to jab or roll more wickedly than ever under the knees. There was always the heat; but the earth was alive and fragrant and warm.

In March the earth still held the dregs of winter bitterness and the clay slit and curled the cuticle at the butt of the finger-nails: " false-nails " as they called them. Talk at the turnip-thinning was airy and episodic, as inconsequential as the buzzing of the insects over a hedge after each shower. Talk at the priddy-picking was solemn, introspective, though tradition, of course, shaped many of the phrases heard in both.

Passers-by jibed at the turnip-thinners about the clags and tossed an expected joke:

" Say a prayer for me when yous're at it. It'll be a step nearther-er Heaven for yous . . .".

" Too busy catchin' up on our own . . .".

" I'd be a good boy, too. . . . But I've no turnips the year ".

Perhaps everyone would laugh then, and roll on to buttocks in the clay. Perhaps they would smoke, or idly finger a plucked and wilting turnip. Scales of clay on the sacking around the knees seemed to dry visibly. Talk, like the insects, would go high, buzzing hazy-headed. Perhaps someone's cattle with tails stuck out, would start to " bizz ", goaded by clags into frenzy. Or perhaps there would be in place a freshly whitewashed house, like untrodden snow, catching its best moment of light.

It is almost a tonic to recall the relief of taking off the sacking in the late evening. Newspapers were torn into strips and set throughout the drills, weighted with field stones. The hope was that the fluttering pieces would keep away the dawn crows, which could " make a slaughter " on thinned turnips, denuding perches in search of a certain grub.

The standard joke was that the newspapers kept them arguing politics instead.

A COAT OF WHITEWASH

THE last whitewasher using a bucket and brush I met was in the Glens of Antrim. He was a young man on a ladder at a roadside gable, and while I didn't know him I knew his job, even to the bucket hanging from a rung on a " S " hook made out of the handle of an old bucket itself. He also wore the some-what traditional outfit we used wear in South Armagh: a grass-seed pack with head and arm-holes rudely cut and reaching to the calves. A belt of grass-rope kept the folds of the smock out of the way of the hands; it kept folds of the sacking out of the bucket as well.

Even his hat had twists I felt I should recognize. He had made only one sensible concession to an era which prefers speed to taste in terms of a sprayer: he wore goggles. (Strange no one had thought of goggles in our whitewashing days, along wall surfaces, which were often snobbish dry-stone ditches with crevices where you could hide a boot—or the family fortune.)

A freshly-done wall was blindingly white in the sun, and I said, in deliberate vernacular, that it " would take the eyes off you ". He turned and squinted at me, the brush poised in his hand: he didn't know me, but I knew he was finding the talk oddly familiar. I then said: " Be sure and put the right side of it out now ".

" Sure if I don't ", he says, giving the rejoinder I had hoped for, " I can turn it when it dries ". He set his brush across the bucket and came down.

" I see you done somethin' at it ", he says, giving me a quick, probing look and then politely looking at the wall still dark with the damp wash.

" An' one rotten job ", I said.

" Still ", he said, " it must be done. It's nice lookin' when it's finished . . .".

I told him I knew a man in Armagh who likes to climb up Slieve Gullion at this time of year for the pleasure of looking down on valleys speckled with freshly whitewashed houses.

" It's well to be some people ", he said with a smile. Then he added: " Like ourselves, I suppose in your country the women give you no peace till you'd get at the whitewashin' ".

This was true, and men hoping for a breather between the final wind-up of spring sowing and the beginning of the hay used threaten to bring in cement and pebble-dash, as so many since have done. The women—well in advance of tourist appeals— used to urge them to have the place " clean and decent-lookin' " before the summer visitors (friends and relations) from England arrived. Even though eyes were blinded by lime, they used say the job was worth it; that they " liked the smell of it ". And you got no peace until you added a bordering of tar along the bottom of the walls, convincing yourself that tar kept away the rats anyhow.

There could be careless, tasteless jobs done with a brush, of course, ' slabber-dasherin' ' they called this kind of thing. When I

E

mentioned it to my Glens whitewasher, he remarked that indeed " there were fellows who would never make whitewashers ". I told him a story of a man who used to slabber the whitewash on with a tin. Says he: " He's not dead yet! I know people here that make their whitewash like poor-house gruel still—it could run a mile without barely leavin' a mark . . .".

There was the classic tale to tell: of the Liberal Englishman touring Ireland during the worst days of the landlords in order to help people in distress. He came on an old woman on the roadside outside her cabin of " one bay " and surrounded by a settle-bed, a dresser, a table and stools. He jumped off the sidecar and pressed a sovereign into her hand while he commiserated with her in her plight after eviction.

The old woman rose like a scalded crow. " Eviction . . .", she cries. " The whitewashin's goin' on in the kitchen an' as soon as the ould fella's done he'll evict these bluddy things back in again ".

Later that evening, when I returned from the Glen, the whitewasher had gone. He had finished his job and had swept the stains up neatly along the road. In a garden below the road a massive boulder showed a freshly whitewashed cross: I knew the boulder stood guard over the spring well. The last bucket of lime always touched up the cross at the well.

While it retained come colour it certainly helped one to find the well on a dark night. It retained also, of course, a touch of a practice older than Christianity; but like ourselves in South Armagh, I'm sure that Glensman never gave a thought to a tradition with a reach long enough to direct even the hand of the whitewasher.

DID GHOSTS REALLY WALK IN THE SUMMER EVENING?

THE public-house is midway between Newry and Dundalk, close to the Dromad forest flanking each side of the main road and near the beautiful valley of Ravensdale. But the bar has been changed since that Sunday afternoon. The windows were low; and it was in one of them the big Englishman sat with his beer beside him. Interested, diffident, but not aloof as he listened to us; a well-nourished man clad for summer, with open-necked shirt and sandal-like footwear—they were new then. His hair was freshly clipped, neatly parted and oiled. He carried a blackthorn almost raw from the hedge, and he would, as old Peter said later, " be kickin' it up tight on the sixty years ".

Old Peter wasn't really in our party. We were on our way to bathe at Rockmarshall on the Cooley coast, or to dig for cockles if the tide was right and pack them into the bags behind the saddles of our bicycles. They were the days (God be good to them!) when we talked of dancing and calculated our wealth in sixpences, and wondered if we could make a bargain that night with a decent doorman in the Adavoyle or Faughil halls in South Armagh.

It was hot, too, but the pace of traffic on the main road outside was much calmer than to-day. The Englishman watched it, or studied the green hill and the tented whins smothered in blossom rising beyond the far side of the road. Then he listened to our talk, a faint indulgent smile on his face: we were young, Irish, and not too wise. In a pause he asked something which startled us: " Where is the monastery round here? "

There was no monastery and, mutteringly, we said so.

" Not here exactly ", he added, " but further along the road. Back towards Dundalk. Near the end of the forest where the road dips towards Ravensdale ".

A Stranger's Tale

We wanted to oblige—without disappointing—the man, as most Irishmen do, but there was no monastery and we turned to old Peter to have his age assure the Englishman that he was mistaken.

" Maybe ", Peter began, not taking the jutting pipe from his mouth, " it's the Order of nuns above in Proleek, the gentleman means. At Mount Oliver ".

But the Englishman insisted there was a monastery of monks somewhere near by—white friars too; the nuns at Proleek wore a brown habit anyway. Unsure now, despite Peter's word, we muttered again, but insisted that there was no monastery. The

Englishman looked at us curiously, no doubt trying to analyse the form of this leg-pull, and he even showed annoyance. And then he told his tale.

A schoolmaster, a stranger, cycling in the dusk from Newry through Dromad, had to stop to let a procession of monks cross the road. When they had disappeared up the lane into the forest, he mounted his bicycle and rode on. In the guest-house where the Englishman was staying on holiday, he had mentioned the scene. The Englishman merely hoped to see the monks and their monastery somewhere at Dromad or Flurrybridge, near Jonesboro'.

Cave in the Wood

Old Peter remembered something then. " There's a cave in the wood there all right ", says he. " It's half-filled up, but you can crawl into it. An' when you go in you can stand up, and there's wee stone chambers on this side an' that. But there's no monastery. There was a monastery, they say, one time in the park in Ravensdale, where Lord Clermont's big house was—the house the boys burned down in the time o' the Trouble ".

I didn't know it at the time, but history confirms something of old Peter's tradition. In the year 1185 the Norman, Hugh de Lacy, granted the estate of Ravensdale to the Cistercian Abbey of Mellifont, and it remained the property of the Abbots until the dissolution. In 1599 it became the property of Sir Edward Moore, was later in a Chancery Inquisition taken at Ballymascanlon, near Ravensdale, in 1606, and eventually passed into the ownership of the Fortescue family in 1725. One of the Ravensdale Fortescues succeeded to the title of Earl of Clermont held by an uncle. The title became extinct, was revived in favour of one of the family named Thomas, but he died without issue in 1887.

Glassdrummond Church

Peter had that in tradition, too; no cock would crow, lark sing or hen hatch in Ravensdale Park; no heir would be born there. And the stones of the Big House, taken from the remains of the old monastery, he claimed, would one day go back into the building of a chapel. (Since then they have gone to help build Glassdrummond Catholic church in South Armagh hauled in a traction engine by my friend Donal Haughey of Forkhill.)

But the Englishman wasn't impressed, and went away more than a bit disgruntled.

In the same bar the other evening a man was whispering to someone about the monks: that someone had seen them walking late one evening on the roadside at Dromad, " near the loanan to the cave ", and he wondered. . . . Years ago his uncle had seen them. . . . He wondered, could it be true?

I listened, remembered, and even wondered myself.

THE MOURNE MAN REMEMBERED

IN a townland near Hilltown in the Mournes I had first met him. He was eighty years but still supple and mentally alert, always sitting upright in his chair with a hand on every knee as he talked to me across the hearthstone. Any time he had to move down his kitchen I liked the sound of his iron-shod clogs on the paved floor; for they resounded a firm but gentle sound which might have, onomatopœic-like, tapped out a sympathetic interpretation of the pattern and metal of his character. His face was pale but venerable in its beard, and he always wore his cap. His memory was phenomenal. He was, in short, an Irish gentleman of the people—simple and sincere, always dignified, never vindictive.

And he was always serious; indeed, his aversion to humour in his narrations is the only defect I can remember. He was what the conventionals would call, derisively, " a rusticated man ", rooted to his parish all his life. As far as I know, he was only once far outside it; and that is why I am writing this.

Essentially a simple man, he once made a simple gesture, and a natural one, and it has impressed me ever since.

He had many narrations of importance; but this was his personal experience of " duty days " spent at the residence of his father's landlord. " Duty days ", need one explain, is a sardonic term. They were not days at all but weeks of unpaid labour exacted by many landlords from tenants at busy periods of the year, regardless of the fact that the tenant's own crops were being necessarily neglected meanwhile, thus jeopardizing still further their ability to pay rent on irrevocable dates or else face the usual consequence of eviction. Whimsically, and with an eye on economy no doubt, tenants were again compelled to give weeks of labour gratis when they attended at the landlord's residence with the rent, extracted often for reasons which, in charity, one had better forget.

A Boy of Twelve

This is what happened to my old friend in the Mournes. He was a boy of twelve at the time, and it was a family council which had finally decided to send him along to deliver and pay the rent. They knew the risks, but the older members of the family and men folk were urgently needed at home; and only as a last resort were women folk sent along. He had a long journey to travel— from his home outside Hilltown to a townland near Dundalk in County Louth, where the landlord lived.

This is what interested me particularly, for that townland was in a parish adjoining my own in South Armagh and I knew the place and its traditions well. But I didn't know the man owned land in County Down. My old Mourne friend remembered well how two daughters of the landlord used drive down in a landau, for aggrandizement. An attractively-coloured calf might tittilate their fancy, or a brood of fowl, a few ewes and lambs; anything at all indeed, as well as observing that an abundant crop in a certain field appeared to justify an increase of rent. The ladies did not take their plunder with them, however, the tenants " be to deliver them "—and again yield " duty days ".

Sewn Into Clothes

My old friend told me he was afraid when he understood he was being appointed to go; but he would not refuse. As all rent had to be paid on the appointed day, they made preparations the night before. They described the type of country he would pass through, and where it was especially dangerous and noted for robberies—in the woods near Ravensdale Park in County Louth adjoining the Armagh border. The rent was sewn into his clothes, food was prepared for the journey and, accompanied by his father and uncle, the trio were sent off with the blessings and fears of the household.

He remembered the route from his own home well, although it had been his first and last adventure in that direction. They crossed over the mountains and arrived near Warrenpoint; then down to Narrow Water and over the river. From there the way took them up the steep Flagstaff Hill and into Clontigora and on to what is now Flurrybridge. He remembered that at this spot there was a public-house on the road, the main road between Newry and Dundalk. Here he was given his final instructions and set to walk the road alone. But on either side his father and his uncle stalked along through the woods giving whistling signals at periodic intervals. When the woodlands ended they whistled him farewell, and would wait in hiding as long as possible lest they hear a cry of alarm from him on his way further south. But no one molested him and he reached the landlord's residence.

The Climax

He described it intimately to me, even to the pattern of the gates and the drive to the house. He paid his rent and was bidden go to the kitchen to work for the cooks. One was kindly to him, gave him plenty of food and warned him to get to sleep early because of " the ghosts of the dead and tortured " who had been killed around the place.

As he talked of these episodes, narrations I had heard in the district itself came to my mind: of men being scourged and then wrapped in brine-soaked linen from a nearby bleaching green and cast into cellars.

His " duty days " exacted, he was released and returned home himself, gleefully welcomed by parents and friends and family. Twice his father had gone hoping to meet him, but always keeping at a safe distance lest he be spotted and roped in also for further exaction. But my old friend said little of that or of his reaction to the memory except, typically, a phrase half in charity, half in prayer: " It's gone, thank God, and cannot return ". Not at all a vindictive man, but a fibre, nevertheless, of that almost indefinable moral power which sustains every resurgence.

Then came the climax. He asked me quietly again if I *did*
know the place. I repeated that I did, and recounted some
further data: incidents and achievements of later descendants of
the family. He agreed that that was so. And then, quite simply,
he asked me which of the descendants of who was residing
there now.

I paused, sharing the anticipatory triumph as I said to him
across the hearth:

" Nuns . . . of the Order of St. Francis! "

Those hands on his knees went very still. His face in its white
beard became intent as he fixed his eyes on me.

" Say that again ", he said to me.

" Nuns of the Order of St. Francis ", I repeated. " The place
is now Mount Oliver Convent ".

He stared, but only for a moment. Then he stood up, took off
his cap, crossed himself solemnly and sat down again, in silence,
looking into the fire.

For he was not a vindictive man, but simple, sincere and
always dignified.

RETURN OF THE YANK

I HAD caught the Cookstown-Omagh bus where it passed
through the parish of Greencastle. Omagh was about twenty
miles away, and as soon as the bus pulled into the stop in town
I saw him, his attire unmistakable American: square-toed black
shoes, the high-crowned hat in a light blue tone to match his shirt,
the close-fitting overcoat swinging open to reveal a cardigan
much too ornate for a man of his seventy years as I guessed
him to be.

He stood between two large suit-cases which rested on the
pavement, both plastered with labels: one was outsize in blue
and white and read plainly: " Wanted In State Room ".

He watched until every passenger had alighted, then picked
up his cases and went into the bus station.

He walked like a man who might never have forgotten the drag of wet soils or clay-sheuchs. . . . Even his face, under the shadow of that hat, had a touch of colour unusual in the American complexion.

How long since he had left?
Later in the evening I saw him in a pub, alone. He looked like a man somewhat bewildered, as if searching for someone . . . or something . . . and oddly silent and nonplussed at not being able to find either. How long, I wondered, since he had left for The States? Was he confused by youthful memories, trying to reconcile the new reality with the image of an unchanging land and scene, which some Irish Americans carry for a lifetime, so that upon return they speak and meander for weeks like men in a dream? Or was he now afraid that finding the town changed, the buildings much smaller than he had imagined them, he would find the people changed, too, recognizing him only after long, involved explanation . . . or simply dead and gone?

He was already in the Greencastle bus when I joined it that evening on the run home. He turned slowly and stared at me, as he stared at each passenger arriving, but apparently saw no one he could speak to. The bus pulled out.

At that time I had been doing a socio-folk survey on emigration from Greencastle parish. No doubt the data was fresh in my mind; and I wondered if his name had cropped up in the accounts of locals who had gone to the United States, some to settle, others to return; some to disappear, a few to reappear at the close of their lives.

Many of the old people in Greencastle had emigrated to the States in their young days; but it had made little social impact: the traditional life and outlook of their glens might have been capes or cloaks, from which they slipped their arms, thrusting back in again when they returned, and living and thinking as they had done before emigrating.

This man seemed to be true to type. Everything in the countryside caught his eye, and he kept turning this way and that, looking back once to get another fleeting glance at a team of horses working in a field along with a tractor.

The bus stopped at the pub in Lislap and he peered hard at the tavern, hat-brim to the bus window. In the Gortin Glens, with their wraps of new forest, he tried to look down into the ravines as the road twisted sharply first this way, then the other. Gortin itself appeared far below through a gap in the hills, suddenly, like a town in a legend which rises out of a haze.

The remaining thatched roofs

He looked at everything while the bus stopped; the remaining thatched roofs, the pub where I remembered meeting a ballad-singer and some local native Gaelic speakers. Would the old American remember something like that? Or Mullacarn, now wearing a scarf of evening smoke from a fire?

The bus moved off. Near Greencastle he noticed a man cleaning a *sheugh*. He cried out some words and began to wave madly; but the man in the *sheugh* didn't notice, for although he had looked up, he immediately resumed his work of shovellfng. I knew the man, too, a good traditional story-teller. And I wished, that by some extraordinary feat of sense and sight, he could have recognized the old American. I almost felt like explaining to the old man why the other in the *sheugh* could neither see nor hear him clearly in a speeding bus.

A minute or so later we stopped at Greencastle. The two cases were left on the roadside grass and the old man got out. I was close behind; and I was going towards the pub when I heard a voice speak to him:

" Aw, how the hell are you, Johnny? I didn't know you at first ". There was a curious lack of excitement, even enthusiasm, in the voice. But then two young girls came running up, crying aloud in wild happiness and welcome.

I was in the pub when he came in, smiling now, and the youngsters seemed to drape themselves on to his arms.

" Glasses o' gin for these cutties an' two stouts for us ", he cried.

Didn't make him a teetotaller

" I'm glad to see America didn't make a teetotaller of you, Johnny ", the barman said as he set up lemonade for the youngsters.

" No odds if it had ", said the American, " for all yous ones will give me ". There was more laughter. Then he said to the young girls: " Come on. Get it down yous. They'll think at home I'm lost or somethin' . . . or away back to America ". I learned later that he had been less than a month away, on a holiday, visiting some members of his family.

RENDEZVOUS WITH A TYRONE MATCH-MAKER

IT was Fair Day in the small Tyrone town of Carrickmore and the Matchmaker stood alone watching the ritual of a deal over a calf.

" Are you for home? " he asked, as if his thoughts were moping among a cloud-cap on the distant Sperrins. When I said I was he told me to ride on and wait till he overtook me. He then hurried into a pub.

As he wasn't a drinking man really, I assumed he had gone to collect a parcel. I left the town and was sitting on a ditch some miles out when he rode up and joined me. He had no parcel. Suddenly he said:

" You can't put your foot on the neck of good luck; an' if luck's with me I stand to do a right decent man a good turn the day. I'm on a bit of a tedious mission ".

I understood at once, for he had pointed out houses to me where he had been on " tedious missions " making marriage matches between partners who sometimes hardly knew of the other's existence.

We must have been sitting fifteen minutes when he sprang from the ditch and dragged his bike up along with him.

" A car . . .", he whispered.

It was a car, overladen with men from the fair: the head of a curved cane, the side view of a hat, punched with personality, and a few flushed faces grinned at us as the car went by.

The Matchmaker looked after it, muttering, then sat down again. I knew now he had been on preliminary intelligence work and was clearly expecting a certain car.

When one came up and stopped at a branch road the Match-maker was already on his feet pretending to light his pipe. A woman got out, then a girl, one leg first.

No Lark's Leg

" Uh huh . . ." the Matchmaker murmured, " no lark's leg thonder. She should wear well an' stand a bit of abuse ". A basket and parcels and some incoherent banter were handed out, the door slammed and the car drove off.

When the Matchmaker greeted them solemnly only the woman answered. She was in dull black attire that found neither bump nor curve to interrupt its curtain-drop from shoulder to shin. The girl, butter-fresh, looked as if she were savouring the echoes of a welcome bout of teasing.

The Matchmaker fell into step beside the woman, talked of the fair, the weather, the crops, asked who lived there, who thonder. All seemed as natural as rainfall.

But he was tactically probing for the mode of approach. I watched how he hung back to look the girl up, down, over and across. The girl herself kept her eyes on the road and said nothing.

The Only Girl

Too abruptly, I thought, the Matchmaker said: " Would this be a daughter of yours, ma'am? "

The woman said she was.

" She'll be twenty-five-six or seven maybe? "

" Maybe you're right—maybe you're wrong ". The woman gave a wee dry cough.

The Matchmaker's lips tightened, then squirmed as his tongue prowled around inside.

" Have you any more like her at home? "

" None ", said the woman, as if the word were scalding hot.

" Pity . . ." he said. This could have implied flattery or merely a laconic word-drop ordained by tradition to win time. A false move could blunder it all. But his face revealed nothing as he went on:

" Providin' she's not bespoken to anyone, would you think of partin' with her? "

" I might if it fitted her ".

His pause showed pleasure.

Then he asked: " What does the girl herself say? "

Dry Cough

Down in her throat the woman gave another dry cough and said: " She's neither deaf nor stupid, sir. Ask her ".

" I'd far rather you asked her yourself, ma'am ".

" I'll not then ". And she bobbed her head. " I'll neither put to or from her. She'll have as much bother refusin' as you'll have askin' ".

" Understand, ma'am ", he cut in, his arm out to stop her, " that I won't push this for myself ".

" What odds. No one has tramped on anyone's luck yet ". Body-swinging her basket she pushed his detaining hand aside.

The hand came away as if bitten in rebuke. " True . . . there's no harm done yet ". He drew a pompous breath. " Well, ma'am, the why an' wherefore of my askin' is this . . . since it's gone so far. A decent man with no encumbrances, sound in lung an' mind an' limb, with no one to call at his door for tuppence of debt . . .".

For the first time the girl looked up and over at us. Her eyes fastened on me. Alarm somersaulted from my stomach, and stirred the ghosts of the hair under my cap. We hadn't topped the hill—but I thought it wiser to leap on my bike and ride on.

Which was just as well, for he made a match of it in the end.

WHEN OWENY CUT HIS HARVEST WITH A SCYTHE

OWENY had said the night before:

" Well, boy, be up gay an' early in the mornin' if it's good an' we'll make a start. There's nothin' much comin' over it yet, but by the time we get it all cowped it'll be ripe enough. You'll be up? "

" I'll be up ".

" More power to you ", said his father. And as I left he called:
" Leave your head now where you'll find it in the mornin' ".

Oweny always cut his harvest with the scythe, and although
I both lifted and bound the sheaves I didn't mind. He was an
easy mower, and you got time to feel the harvest spirit take on a
touch of perspective which elated all the ancient grandeurs and
traditions in the harvest mood in the hills. Above all Oweny,
like myself, was the type of man who found time to have a smoke.

I was with him gay and early. What a morning it was! The
country was aflame in the early light with ripening fields, the air
soft with dew. Oweny's little fields gleamed at the foot of Slieve
Gullion against heather already a dull scarlet.

Near Oweny's loanan I fell in with our neighbour, Paddy,
winkers on one shoulder, dish in hand with its fistful of oats to
coax and catch his horses on the grass. This, I mused, was no
day to follow a reaper if Paddy was in a working mood—and his
laconic greeting and scowling countenance told me that he was.
In the field I smiled when I heard him roar at the old mare for
eluding him. Turning up to Oweny's I saw the red-leaded handle
of his scythe, the *sned*, hanging on the trim hedge, the dew-swished
blade gleaming.

Already I could see it wet with evening dew: the glamour of
an old-world harvest, touched with starlight on rows of stooks in
regimented rows (" to a hair in the water " as he said) filled mind
and imagination. There would be the coming home in the dusk
(" duskus " to us in South Armagh) to tea under the lamp, the
old man in the corner at the bellows wheel asking how many
stooks we had cut, promising to try to give a hand on the morrow;
and then recounting tales and adventures of his own early harvests
as a *gothan* up in County Louth or with a squad from the valley
in Cheshire and the Fens of England, my own father among them.

Oweny was filling his pipe at the doorless cart-house as I got
to the top of the loanan.

" You brought the good weather with you, boy ", he sang out.
" Away in an' get somethin' to ate. Oh—I say? " He finished
filling the pipe, topping it with dottle, pressing the notched tin
lid on top of the bowl. I used one myself at the time. In a low,
almost uneasy, voice he said:

" I had Tam up last night, an' Paddy's cuttin' for him the
day with the reaper ". I hadn't surmised. " Would you care to
give the old boy a hand? He's mad lookin' for help. You know
how it is, everyone lookin' help at the same time ".

Hiding my disgruntlement I said I would.

" More power, boy. I'll nibble away myself at thon ripe
patch for a day or so. Or maybe I might have to run over to
him as well. The help's a divil ".

On my way to Tom's I looked back at Oweny's fields pushing
boldly against the heather. You were out of the world up there;
you could work and dream at the same time, for the wilderness
of heather, rock and whin threw a daring note of drama on to
the scene in the corn fields. When all had been cut there was a
sense of true victory in mowing the *Cailleach* in the last sheaf, even
if a drifting mist came down off the mountain and crept along the
massive stone ditches: years back every stone had been dug out
of the land and hoisted up on other, as wide as a country loanan.

For all that you couldn't dodge realities. I knew Tom's
fields, having worked both for him and Paddy. And I knew that
last man to reach the harvest field got adroitly stuck in the spot
thick with buck thistles. Going down the street Paddy called
from the barn where he was stitching a britching; the reaper sat
before the door, the horses already tied up. I replied that I might
as well dander down to the field, which was beside the bog.

When I got there Tom, as I suspected, had his area already
marked off and knelt like a sentry on guard, on one knee, smoking,
and ignoring me after a word of welcome and with barely a
glance: he knew what I was thinking and that as it was his own
field honour dictated that he should let his workers pick the sides
they would work on. Three other men and two girls sat on
sheaves thrown into briars where Tom had opened the field
around the ditches for the reaper. They talked and laughed and
speculated about a dance in Forkhill Hall that night.

" 'Pon my sacred sowl ", says Tom at length, with one langled
chuckle, " an' if Paddy gets his way all the dancin' yous'll do this
night will be harmless. Glory be ", and he got to his feet, " here
he is an' me only has the bleddy pipe lit right ".

" Whoa! " That was Paddy's semi-military wail (he had spent some time in the Irish Army) as reaper and horses clattered down the incline of a gap and into the standing oats, where the old mare artfully snatched a mouthful. For that she received a reprimand that had even more echoes of the parade ground.

A cloud shadow sliding over the field might have brought a wry smile to the oats. I could smell the scent of shorn under-grasses; but any flight of imagination was literally cut off as Paddy ran the wedged knife into the fingers of the bar of the machine.

. . . The rhythm of scythe mowing and the harmony of muscle; the singing of the blade as it swung into the oats and leaned each cut against the ledge of standing corn. The intimacy of the thing, wielding a scythe set for oneself, measured for oneself, part of yourself: then stooking in spells to vary the toil, not as when following the reaper where you didn't stook till the whole field had been cut, and the sight of the myriad sheaves was enough to dismay.

" Hop off! Lily! Hop off! Daisy, damn you, come 'ere. Hop off. . . . Go down, ponies. Go down ".

Drowning Paddy's cries came the road or the reaping knife. He was doing two men's work himself, both driving and leaving off the sheaves with the rake, the reins around his neck.

Coats came off and were flung into the briars. The girls threw off scarfs. At the gap where Paddy had begun another tier, a woman in her seventies, was already tying her first sheaf. Tom saw her and barely grinned. He cast a significant glance at the others, as each ran to gather their first sheaves for tying. He groaned as he stooped for his own first sheaf. I bent for mine, my eye alert for a sight of the thistles.

We would tie the sheaves around the field for the first few cuts before allocating ourselves to stretches where we tie to meet another tier on one run and the other tier on the next. We kept passing and re-passing one another. As I passed Tom he said:

" There's an odd thistle at the bottom ". That, I knew, meant hundreds, including ones we couldn't see.

The fragrance of grasses rose like a mist each time you bent to tie a sheaf. Stoop, gather the mown oats to you, whisk a band with the right hand, tidy your sheaf with the left; straighten quickly to fashion a " harvest band " for the binding so that none of the grain forms part of the knot; stoop again and half bind from the top; scoop up the sheaf in its band and bind as it comes up to finish on the knee, tucking in the twist-knot with the thumb; toss it aside under the left arm as you clean it of loose straws. A matter of seconds. Cotter (or rake with the fingers) the stray heads as you hurry to the next sheaf.

" A few days of this weather with this help would leave me well on ", Tom remarked. " Paddy has his own to cut—it's rotten ripe. Aw hell, me back . . .". As he stooped.

Before long you know you will feel the first twinges of the harvest *thaala*—the swelling of the wrist from the thumb on the hand you tie with.

Out in the oats a thistle bobbed like an ornamental shaving brush on a chemist's pedestal. I hurried on, tying as fast as I could to get as far away as possible. Tom understood my move.

" Bad luck to them thistles, an' I thought I pulled them all ". Tom said that every year. He added, by way of diversion: " It's goin' to be one real scorcher this day ". Already the sun was blazing.

The clatter of the reaper was muffled as it went up the far side of the field like a giant grasshopper.

" Bit quicker than with Oweny ", a tier said as he scooted past.

" He won't cut all with the scythe, will he? " another asked, a young fellow.

" Every head ".

" Horse's work ".

" He likes neat work ".

" An' nice tight tidy sheaves. Easier to save ".

" Hop off! Come 'ere—Lily—Daisy—Down, damn yous— Go down! "

" Glory be, he's not comin' down the cut already? "

He was.

" Spread yourselves out ", someone called, hurrying forward, in a stoop. I saw the eyes flick over the uncut oats: watching for those beds of thistles.

F

Paddy came boring down, roaring at the horses above the metallic roar of the reaper. He needed speed; the undergrass was heavy and that knife could clog. He didn't give us a break until he had to stop to clear the finger-bar and oil the glistening spots. We lie full length on the fresh stubble. The old woman stands with hands on hips. Tom is down again on one knee, the pipe in his gob, cap tilted over his eyes, studying the oats.

I muse. Oweny will cut all with the scythe. He won't hurry. Maybe the weather will break and he'll lose his placid temperament. From shelter in the harvest field he'll scan the valley below.

" Thank God. I see one field still to be cowped. If only we weren't cocked up on the mountain for the world to see. As soon as the weather mends we better open up a bit, boy ".

That made me smile; it was his excuse. For the old belief was that all the bad luck of the harvest sneaked like a hare into the last field. There the *cailleach* hides, the mythological spirit of harvest. Accidental or otherwise, how subtle too in psychology were some of our work superstitions!

You wonder, as Paddy roars and drives off again, will they cut late. Half the tiers will make excuses and leave the stooking to us. They always do. The sun will sink. Slieve Gullion will gather about her that cloak of shadow. The few clouds like kite-tails on the rays of the sun out of sight will become illumined scrolls fringed with gold. You remember once when a solitary cloud became a celestial fleece out of the folk-stories of the fireside; then, as the dying sun bequeathed its wealth of light it turned into a transparent urn crammed with magic gold.

The old man had the *cailleach* that evening, smoking contentedly as Oweny and I stooked. I remember his scythe blade turned a dull bronze as he hoisted it to go and the heather was a dim purple mist in the skidding light. You remember . . . .

" Hop off! Come 'ere, Daisy! Lily! Go down, mare. Hop off! Hop off, damn you! "

And you would rise from the stubbles, the dream gone, aching already in every joint of the first day of the harvest.

Then you find you've landed yourself in a nest of thistles.

WET HARVEST INTERLUDE

T HE meal had been quiet and she had cleared away the dishes. Everything that could be said about the weather had been said. There was nothing to do except sit and drowse and look at the rain falling steadily on the harvest fields.

Jackets with the sleeves inside out steamed on chairs before the fire. To beat the chill some of us wore overcoats. No one spoke. Only now and then did someone sigh wearily, groaningly, and re-light a pipe or cigarette; or fingers drummed listlessly on the chair between outstretched legs; or a hand reached frustratedly for a newspaper or woman's magazine already scanned and thrown aside half a dozen times.

Past the window, against the dark hedge, or past the door against the hillside fields, the rain slanted ceaselessly like quivering wires.

You believed sometimes you could hear the taut strum and hum of it, for there was no other sound, except the whispering gush of her outsize rubbers as she went about the kitchen. Even the flies on the clothes-line across the kitchen seemed to have been caught in the mood of drowse.

Abandoned

I looked at the harvest fields. One had lodged and had been half-mown with a scythe, with stubborn patches abandoned here and there as pockets of beard on an old face elude the razor. Dark streaks told of upright, defiant thistles.

Beyond the shimmering grey gauze of the rain before the door was another field. Three weeks it had been cut and stooked; and the hood-sheaves had twisted, slipped, or slumped forward like wounded riders after a mediæval affray, caught in a vision of still life.

We, too, were still, like men stupid from deep sleep, sitting and squatting here and there in dis-association through the kitchen, smoking, saying nothing.

Some primordial instinct might have recognized the symbolic ritual and reverence in grain harvest and looked upon this rain as sacrilege; the world of sustenance and profit and loss seemed far away . . . in the future.

The road fell away outside the gate, and none of us saw or heard the blue van arrive till its horn was sounded and a voice cried: " Herrin'-Oy . . . Herrin'-Oy! Want any in there? " And the call seemed to be peppered with the rods of rain.

" Herrin' man ", someone said, and the heel-shod of a boot scraped as a leg was withdrawn to make a sound like an old throat being cleared.

By then she had grabbed a plate, had given it a quick and unnecessary whiff of her apron, had picked a rain-dark mac from a nail near the door, and, swinging it over her head, was on her way out.

" Shockin'. . . . Desperate harvest weather ", someone said, as if answering a remark made an hour before; and then we heard herself outside:

" Oh, lord! Away without any money ". Her voice was nearer as she called back: " The purse is on the fireboard behind the clock ".

Spluttering

From a stool he dragged himself to his feet and lifted the clock. The kitchen was dark under the spill from the fleece of ashen cloud. He lifted this and lifted that. He pushed some knitting aside. There was a quick disturbance by his fingers like a mouse scurrying among safety-pins.

" I see no purse, woman ".

" Hurry up before I'm drownded ", she called. She was standing outside the door under the rain and spluttering eave.

" Ah, here! " and his hand groped in his trousers pocket, " this should cover the damage ".

" Hoigh, boy ", the herring-man called. " Are you not out cuttin' oats? " He didn't reply, for by then she had reached the gate. We heard the herring-man say: " It'll tell a bad tale if it doesn't take up shortly. I seen oats growin' in the stooks a week ago . . . a week ago, mind you. It'll tell a bad tale ".

I saw himself on the doorstep look up at the sagging clouds. Like old sheep caught in briars they hung about the hills and the harvest fields cowered. " It's not waitin' to rain ", he said as he came back, stood for a moment irresolutely on the floor, and then sat astride the stool again.

Outside we heard snatches of talk and a complimentary laugh, the slam of the van door, the clash of the gate as she slammed it behind her and ran; and I looked to see the blue van slide away silently.

Wild night

" He always has some crack ", she began. Everyone looked up as if permission had been granted to rouse ourselves. She saw the expectant, inquisitive glances.

" Oh, about some man an' the woman an' son an' a servant boy one wet harvest. The man was tellin' it after this wild night on the oats. ' I never closed an eyelid ', says he. ' The woman never closed an eye, nor our Larry never closed an eye. But the flamin' servant boy snored '."

There were chuckles, stares like reproval, a muttered word or two, a stirring. A mood had been broken. She asked would we take another drop of tea and looked around.

No one spoke; so she put down the kettle on the fire and again turned the wet jackets. There was talk now. And the red glow of the fire, like a sunset after rain, caught the thinning upward twist of vapour from the drying jackets.

Outside, the rain continued to fall. Once, when it seemed to gasp in a breath of wind, a spatter like a fistful of pebbles dropped on to the corrugated roof under the trees. Then the rain was falling as before, quivering like strummed wire.

And the harvest fields stayed miserable. The Corn Spirit of the folk-rituals, like a termperamental artist, might have been brooding over the interrupted pageant, deprived of that final curtain scene of death and reincarnation amid the glory of dry, sound and golden grain.

MAGIC IN THE HARVEST MOON

A HUNDRED years one's eyes might watch and never see the like again, or soar to the glory of its thrill, as when I saw a harvest moon on the crest of Slieve-na-Bola. Slieve-na-Bola ends the fort of hills which, running south of Slieve Gullion, dip towards the Gap of the North at right angles to the Carlingford range.

This harvest spell always makes a pageant of thought, lifting remembered things out of their trivial occurrence and giving them a moving significance. From the moment the oats were fully shot, making a green mist of the corn fields, this mystical presence was abroad.

Fancy awakened to ripening fields as the mind of a musician responds to the symbols of a famous melody. The chords swelled as the harvest approached, so bewitching and eternal that they seemed to have been playing for ever, seeking a climax—till you thought one intruded from the realities of the current day—and the melody stopped for another year. Yet the mind, unequal to this art, felt a glowing of the spirit and a strange content.

It was an exciting thing to walk out into an early harvest night and feel all that; for when fancy touches harvest thought it is reality that is illusion, and illusion a reality. That is why, on houses and fields, you saw more of a tension than a quietness. The rustle of a grain made music, while the hills, in vague outline, were roused from the stoicism of disgruntled gods to the revelry of a new and annual majesty.

High on their shoulders or hacked from their hips, a harvest field held back the heather, lustrous in the morning light which cannot find an unfriendly tone, and glowing in the dusk, a badge of victory. You knew why the man with his patch amid the whins shared the same glory of spiritual fulfilment as he who could boast a thousand acres.

For a reckless moment, your spirit clings passionately to that sense of peace and melodic harmony of man with his environment. The echoing loneliness and spiritual self-sufficiency of the thrill plays with the notion that here you might elude the artifice, sham and sick convention that contaminates the mind of the world.

But awe, just then, dignifies your thought. For time is surely an imponderable illusion, deferring artfully before the poetic irony of harvest airs. Loud as man is in his cries of frustration, he must always abandon his plunder and guns, his flights of vanity and tinkering with atoms, and return to the grain-field where he is really king, a real triumph about him, stooked in the afterglows.

Even that August platitude of harvest reflection made way, as I walked along, to more enticing signs of the spell. Like actors they were, watching their cue, restless on the edge of the mind for the call to the pageant played on the stage of memory.

Not a soul was about, not even a straggler; yet the night was alive with echo. The world is resting under the tension. Lights in the houses had that rousing gleam of harvest, and the stars jigged with the touch of frost. Kinship comes again to men, and a mellow fellowship warms the mind.

The glow from the rising moon at first surprised me, for a rash of the sunset still inflamed the north-west sky. Slowly the moon crept up, till beyond the thronged fields of the valley a patch or two of corn on the western hill captured the light. Somehow you thought of violins.

A little cloud appeared then, a bit of curtain which swaddled the moon. No man could move in such magic. The light came down in gauzy columns which visibly lost their slant and swelled to a billowing lace, fondling the corn fields till they became like enchanted lakes.

Then I met the student, home on holiday, and gladly stayed to talk and watch the moon. It sat now like a luminous egg between two rocky crests on Slieve-na-Bola. A hundred visions crammed the stage of imagination, fact going hand-in-hand with fancy, as if trying to soar into one gigantic expression of feeling that would for ever crystallize these moods of harvest magic of today and yesterday.

Its drama, its scene, its hungers and hopes, played through history and fireside story—the spectre of the Famine and the cries of patriots holding hands with harvesters from the Fens, walking the hills from Greenore boat to their homes in the valley and their own harvests.

And just then it happened. The student never said if he had seen it, but I was bewitched, and he was silent too; for a hundred years indeed your eyes might watch and never see the like again. A thousand images were struck at once and orchestras played in the stars. And one image stayed with me, and always will: that allegory from fairyland of the Frustrated Spirit of Man trudging blindly past the entrance to a Golden Age.

For some man had trudged past the big and brilliant moon, down one slope of the crest, up the other, and then was gone.

IN AN ANTRIM GLEN

EIGHT days out of ten, it seems, the blast through the Red Arch between Cushendall and Waterfoot takes me off the bicycle. It roars over the cliffs of Lurig and the Glenariffe mountains, down through Waterfoot (windy Waterfoot, where the blast tumbles the wild-cat and the wires are always screeching) and streams through the Red Arch as it must through a wind-tunnel where they test jets.

When it takes me off I usually light the old pipe, look around and reflect, as I did the other day.

Hedge-school

The tide was in. Before me, each breaker hit the wall of Red Bay Pier, spiralled into foam, threw up a ballet of spray; and then, like a young dog trying to get its teeth into the moving wheel of a car, it ran along the entire pier till it petered with a slash, another dance of spray, and a watery boom that was a frustrated growl of defeat.

Spume was picked out of the waters as if ash had been dumped on the Bay, and farther out I watched a " puffer " battling towards Carnlough.

Behind and above me in the sandstone promontory was the cave. It was dark with secret personality, for I know the story of every one of them now, every rock on the shore, almost every inlet.

There had been a hedge-school in that cave. Away over the road I saw the low outline of the new modern intermediate school. I pondered . . . and felt a hint of poetic justice.

H-bomb

Then something like an ice-demon lit on my face and died there with his dart; then another . . . and then a mauve bit of rain cloud, thin as nylon, fluttered over the hip of Lurig and, losing the touch of hidden sun, turned as grey as the waters.

I was still there when a woman came round the bend; a small but compact woman in black, plump apple-red cheeks, and carrying a handbag. We greeted each other and she stood to talk.

Two girl cyclists in shorts, pig-pink legs and " trams " pedalling in rhythm of their capes, whisked themselves towards Cushendall.

My wee woman in black says: " What's to become of the world an' the people? "

I thought she was referring to the flash of extra nudity just gone by. But no. " It's wild what spuds have yet to come out ", she says. And without a breath: " Their bluddy ould bomb blew the roof off the world an' nothin' else ".

Imagery

This is the sort of crack that agreeably helps the ignoramus, tutored by modern tempo to draw the supercilious grin from ear to ear. Did my wee woman believe there was a roof on the world?

God help their foolish wit (and they won't believe she said that either); she was only being graphic in an instinctive, Gaelic way.

Gaelic is a language of imagery. Now that some atom scientists seem to believe that their fireworks *could* have had a guttery effect on the world's weather, how else would one wish to describe a consequent atmosphere of turmoil which seems to spill rain eternally because man made a wee sun of his own and split an Age wide open?

Before she left we talked of schools. Scholars at the new school were putting in a bit of physical recreation making a bank with spade, pick and barrow.

" *Myxo* "

" Maybe learnin' to be navvies ", says she, typically, and then, quick as a wink: " An' divil the button of harm it would do some of them ". (I had memories of days when our own Master did the same.)

Next she talked of myxomatosis.

" There's a bit for everythin' in the world. Feth ", says she, " the weather destroyed more in a week this year than all the rabbits would manage to do away with in a twelve month ".

I had been waiting for that from this wee woman; it came off an angle of philosophy that goes to the root of the race.

When a car came along and gave her a lift I rode on towards Waterfoot. Near the village, which always strikes me as if being undecided whether to stay by The Acre in the shelter of Lurig or march on to join Cushendall (God look to me if it should be vice versa!) I passed a tramp on crutches.

Glenariffe

" It's no use flyin' in the face of Almighty God, master, now is it? " he was saying to someone, one foot poised, his old waterproof stained like a camouflaged army mac, bound down with twine, and as billowy as a pumped balloon.

I knew him. But beyond Parkmore, where Glenariffe folds her cliff and roof-steep grassy sides like the end of a drill where you've run out your plough, there was a gathering darkness in the sky. That wind seemed to be stirring the makings of another dirty evening.

Sheep clung like maggots to the slopes above Ardclinis, just as they had done in summer when the hillside fields might have been drooping leaves. Dead rabbits lay along the shore road. (A little over a hundred years ago our people lay like this; again, much the result of a man-made manœuvre designed to reduce numbers.)

Snow

Turning up the Glen the wind seemed to decrease, but it still thundered among the cliffs above, the rush and throb of sound mingling with the fall of waters. For on both sides of Glenariffe

the waterfalls drop. . . . In summer, the forgotten ribbon of a
festival beaten ragged by rain. . . . But now, like saliva down old
faces rutted rock-deep with character.

I was just home when the snow-shower came like a fanstasy.
With the dark cliffs of the far side at Kilmore for backcloth it
seemed one was actually watching the very cloud open: in a slow,
suspended descent the whiteness fell, bunched like bristles in a
brush, bending and drawing over crag, slope and hollow. . . .
Then all grew as dark as night.

But when the brightness came and the shower was over a
rainbow bridged the Glen; and the dark head of Lurig, now in
a border-cap of white, might have been a wise old woman
remembering eternal things before the evening glow of her
winter fire.

THE GLENS FAIRY WOMAN TALKED

A T the time I was living in the Glens of Antrim in the townland
of Layde, a headland overlooking Cushendall and Red Bay.
I was there for the Irish Folklore Commission—now absorbed
into the Department of Irish Folklore at University College,
Dublin—and the Commission's Honorary Director was the late
Professor Séamus Delargy, himself a Cushendall man. I had done
research throughout Ulster for six documentary programmes for
the BBC in Belfast called " The Fairy Faith ", which proved to
be both popular and a revelation about the traditions of the
fairy tribes.

So Delargy wrote that he was sending me to a young American
named Richard Murphy, a graduate of Harvard, then doing work
in Oxford, and an anthropologist. He wanted to be introduced
to people who could tell fairy tales. He wasn't, of course, the first
American anthropologist to visit Ireland in search of such material
which, to them, was simply " evidence " of the nature, attitudes,
cults and culture of our pre-Christian ancestors whom we came
to know as " fairies ".

Richard Murphy arrived; a very pleasant but serious young man standing at least six feet. I wasn't surprised to learn that his father was a Kerryman with a physique like that; but he mentioned that his mother was German, and of the Lutheran faith, as was Richard himself, but he understood the rites and practices of the Roman Catholic faith of his father.

This was interesting information to me, because I had first of all arranged to bring Richard Murphy to a household where the brother and sister were of different religions. Dan Hyndman lived in the townland of Cusskib near Layde, and he was a Presbyterian, and a bachelor. With him lived his sister, Biddy McAllister, who was a Roman Catholic. As was the common custom in their day the person marrying a Roman Catholic became a convert to that faith: and as was common, though not invariably so, children of such a marriage—both in Antrim and Tyrone—shared the faiths of their parents: if the man had been Roman Catholic any sons of the marriage were brought up in the Catholic faith, the girls took the faith of the mother. This arrangement worked out amicably in all the instances I came across, with no friction whatsoever, and the household was visited now and then by the respective clergymen and made very welcome.

This was the background I etched in for Richard Murphy as we walked to Cusskib. Dan and his sister Biddy were then in their seventies; Biddy's family had grown up and left home to make their own lives. Dan and Biddy were a very happy couple, but Dan suffered severely from asthma. Both, however, were fervent believers in the existence of fairies as manifest beings that could be seen now and then and they respected faithfully all the taboos that the fairy tradition imposed on the mortals who lived among them. Richard Murphy was very interested.

Biddy and Dan made us both welcome, especially the American visitor. Tea had to be made first. True to the courtesy and obligations of a Glens welcome Biddy sat down next to the American, while poor Dan crouched in the fireside corner. He had been a farmer and noted horseman and fowler and kept his gun. A man, too, with a fine sense of humour which came out in the telling of folktales, but never in the narration of fairy tales, which were to him and Biddy part of a tenet of secondary faith, a belief; the folktale was for wonder and amusement, and still only a tale.

The folklore collector does not approach his source like the journalist, but talks to make talk with sympathetic and under-standing lead-ins. When such came up I mentioned the fairies. Both Biddy and Dan had told me all the fairy lore they had heard, of course, and I commented on one tale which I knew would interest Richard Murphy particularly—the seeing of and talking to the fairies. At that mentioning Dan seemed to crouch lower, and sagely and with some apprehension shake his head. Biddy was somewhat more outgoing, though none the less sincere, and I got her to tell a favourite tale. It ran like this:

One day her mother was busy in the kitchen where we sat when there was a polite tapping at the door. The call to " Come in " was ignored, so she went to the half-door herself. Standing outside on the threshold was " a wee woman " and she was begging a bowl of oatmeal and a wee can of sweet milk. Biddy's mother went to the bin and filled a bowl of oatmeal, then filled a small can with sweet milk and brought the charity gifts to the wee woman. The wee woman thanked her, and then said that she would " leave the bowl and can on the stone going down to the well in the fort ".

This fort was in the Hyndmans' land and just across the road, but unless one knew the district one would never suspect that a spring well existed there. The fort had its lone whitethorn bush— a relic of pagan tree worship which can still be seen throughout the country in the survival of lone hawthorns in fields, or a dead bush at a house no longer suspected.

Biddy's mother looked hard at the wee woman but couldn't recall ever having seen her before; so she asked how she, a stranger, knew about the site of the spring well. Says the wee woman:

" Sure I'm your nearest neighbour ".

She thanked her again for the meal and milk—the main ingredients of sustenance of the people of the late Bronze and early Iron Ages—and went away. Biddy's mother watched her take the pad, or path, to the fort and said " the wee woman disappeared at the Lone Hawthorn ".

There are between thirty-five and forty thousand " fairy forts " in Ireland. They were the original farm dwellings, and most of them—though not all—have a souterrain or " cave ", as the old people called them; entrance was through a stone slab which could be fitted in once the person was inside. The iron weapons of the Iron Age invaders decimated the bronze weapons of the denizens of the forts, which then had wooden stockades around a clay and wattle house. While the men defended and were slain by the superior iron weapons women and children went into the souterrain, a culture evidently not known to the Iron Age people. They burned out the " fort " and stock and assumed all other living things had been consumed. When the wave of invaders had moved on, the people emerged and looked for the food—oatmeal and milk.

With Richard Murphy I had discussed this theory, which I give briefly. But he was impressed more by old Biddy McAllister's tale of the wee fairy woman meeting and talking to her mother. I cannot recall if he had met any tellers of fairy tales before coming to me in the Glens of Antrim; but he seemed to be somewhat taken aback by Biddy's open sincerity with no tongue-in-cheek sense of apology—as so many people still do in deference to an ignorance really derived from the slave-minded sense of a subservient inferiority complex.

As an anthropologist I could anticipate his query when Biddy had finished telling her tale: but I did not anticipate old Biddy's reply. After a pause Richard Murphy said quietly to old Biddy:

" And did your mother really believe she had spoken to that wee fairy woman? "

Biddy almost glowered at him. Then she prodded him in the chest with her forefinger and said:

" Young fella: my mother seen and talked to that wee fairy woman; because my mother was a damn good Presbyterian that wouldn't tell a lie! "

The phenomenon of the racial memory enshrined in fairy lore and reaching back unwillingly to events of four thousand years ago wilts before an assertion like that of old Biddy

McAllister's. As far as I recall my anthropological visitor, Richard Murphy, said nothing then or afterwards. Coming from a rather serious-minded old woman then fifty years a Roman Catholic must have set him reflecting, though he may have been unaware of the socio-historical-religious complexities the statement brought up. In her day as a mother of a young family Biddy would have set the tongs across the cradle before going to that well in the fort to protect the newborn from the malevolent designs of abducting fairies, especially if the infant were a boy: the souterrain people had to replenish the blood and the male stock of the tribe; but since they dreaded fire and iron the fire-tongs combined elements of both which made a potent and menacing counter-witchcraft to their own.

Biddy and Dan are both long dead: but a few years ago I sat again at their fireside with my friend, the Ulster poet, John Hewitt, who knew them both. Then, to an assembly of notabilities which seemed sometimes indulgent, sometimes bewildered, I told the story I have just recounted. I confess, however, I was more than a bit bewildered myself, for it was an occasion when for the first—and no doubt last—time in my life I experienced a real sense of physical ubiquity which is a common enough motif in many fairy tales. Before I left the Glens I had sat at that fireside and looked out on the Antrim countryside I had come to know so intimately; the last time I sat at the same fireside I looked out on the landscape of County Down. They were miles apart. It was in the grounds of the Ulster Folk and Transport Museum at Cultra, near Hollywood. Stone by numbered stone the house had been taken down, transported to Cultra, and re-erected, and is now known as " The Cushendall House ".

THE HARE ON THE HEARTH

I WAS told I would find him in the Low Hotel, as the older folk call the Glens Bar in Cushendall. Half the crowd inside were coursing men; even before I went in the talk might have been an echo of the shouts of encouragement to this dog or that.

The rest were locals and an English party of three, including a middle-aged woman in puce slacks, as well as the Poet and Himself and the hare.

The Poet was a big man, full and benign of face, smoking a peculiar pipe cupped in one hand, his other hand supporting the elbow. Before him on the bar lay his walking-stick, a wriggling thing of strange and fascinating personality like the elongated fossil of a lauchraman.

Himself was wiry and slight, all in black, his shirt neck open. I think I remember the peep of a tattoo.

The Poet kept turning his head slowly, first this way, then that, beaming like a lighthouse through the haze of tobacco smoke and the torrents of talk.

Himself stayed beside the hare, gesturing and talking, now snatching the cap from his head and adroitly tossing it on again, or tossing it under his leg; as lithe and active as if the very spriteli-ness of the hare in death had got into his bones. Still and stiff, as dead only as myth and legend would allow it to die, the hare lay full stretch across the hearth, with Himself between it and the blaze.

I paused in the doorway. Himself was entertaining the English people, who looked as if unsure whether to accept him as the genuine article or suspect a new version of Stage Irishman pulling their legs.

Then he saw me. He bounded into life, waving and cheering to make himself heard. " Hoigh, Mick, hoigh! See what's here at me feet—the ould blade herself—the Cailleach, Mick. Here's folklore, Mick. Hoigh, I say! " And he gave a kind of skip before he stooped, and the hare came on to his forearm as if it had run there.

" Blast you and the hare. We've had enough of the hare! " someone admonished, but the backwash of the phrase was swamped by a new wave of talk.

" They give wild fortunes with women in Donegal. They must be anxious to get rid of them! " (They were teasing the barmaid.)

A disconsolate young man, who seemed to speak only when the occasion called for wit, said to an Englishman: " Cinema

Thrah-hook or rope-twister

Twisting a grass rope, Clontifleece

The late James Loughran of Ravensdale, near Dundalk, with a " pannel " he made

here? Sure, Hopalong Cassidy has a stable at the back. If he hasn't, he should; he's on often enough ".

". . . Jugged hare. . . . Jugged hare ". The Poet was declaring to himself through the tornado.

The hare was now back on the tiles, full stretch. When anyone came in they stopped and looked at it, and Himself started all over again.

Something as airy as fantasy seemed to come over the scene, as real and intangible at once as if all the myths and legends of every hare legend I had heard were cavorting around me, as if the scene were being suddenly blacked-out, as suddenly re-lit, the characters, hearty men one moment, symbols of another era the next, toasting some vague triumph in liquor which, against the light, burned with every glow of a summer sunset on a bewitched hill.

The babble of talk had become the raucous chant of celebration borrowed from a jubilant, primordial day. The Poet might have been toast-master or chief: he was quoting some lines of his verse—quite good, too. And Himself? Himself in his antics was a whimsical Antony come to orate the Cæsar of animal myth in a *rann* of famous banter:

" Hoigh, Mick! How much will you give for her? Puss! Look! There's hares an' hares, but that's *some* hare. Now isn't it? What'll you give me—pot of soup? Did you ever have roast hare, Mick? "

" Jugged hare. You always jug a hare, sir ", the Poet cried merrily.

Himself kept on: " Don't bid me till you hear what I'm only askin'—I'm giving it away, Mick. I say . . .". And the hare was back on his arm, a potent thing even in death.

Talk drowned his voice again. Someone was speculating, the voice coming and going amid the babble like a lament. " Many a time that girl stretched herself across Crebilly, I'll swear. Aren't they strange lookin' things when you study them, too? "

" We were across the Border, you know, in a car, and we had a bottle of brandy—not that we went for that—"

G

" I know. I know. But why pass a well with an empty bucket if they want water at home? I know ".

" Is that a South Armagh one? Well. On the road this side of Limavady—wild, lonely, worse than Cary—we run over this hare. An' as sure as The Maker made me, comin' across Cary we run over another.

" I wouldn't let them get out to pick up the other one. But nothing would do them but I go out for the second one.

" An' as sure as I have my God to face—I'm not tellin' a word of a lie—I was stoopin' for the hare when the bluddy bottle of brandy fell out of me pocket an' went in a thousand pieces on the road. Up on Cary mountain between here an' Ballycastle ".

" Jugged hare! " the wit cried, and haunched himself.

" Jugged hare your granny. We should have lifted thon first hare. They're not right an' never were right. Sure, take a good look at that thing on the hearth an' you don't have me to tell you there's witchery about them somewhere ".

And the hare on the hearth lay stiff and still . . . as dead as only myth and legend would let it die.

A MAN WITH A CHARM

WHEN I was collecting folklore around Ballycastle a point came up which baffled every narrator I knew. Then an old friend thought he knew a man in his home townland who might help elucidate. So that evening both of us were driven out to him.

My Ballycastle friend spotted him on a hillside picking potatoes from a pit, and he shouted and waved him down. The priddy-picker was longsome in leaving, and my friend groaned; he was bad with pains, and to take the weight off his feet lowered himself on to the roadside bank to wait.

The other came, a small can in one hand, and holding a sack with a few stone of potatoes over his shoulder with the other.

A lively sort, when he saw my friend he let the sack slide to the road and ran over to greet him, shaking his hand in both his own. My friend wanted to get to his feet to introduce me, and had to haul himself up, with both of us giving a hand.

Instantly, almost feverishly, the other says to him: " Is it the pains you have, John? " John said it was, and began to curse them in a mild way. " Hold on—hold on now ", said the other.

Whether he was objecting to the language, or eager to get explaining I don't know. He told John that he had a " charm ". John looked more alarmed than astonished, saying nothing. As we listened we heard of an emigrant in America writing home for the " strainin' thread " to cure a friend " wild bad " with the pains.

We heard how " the American doctors were bet ". He explained that " the thread " was either of flax or wool, not platted in any particular way, but simply twisted into a cord. And all the time he was searching his pockets.

He asked John had he " a bit of cord on him " and John somewhat tartly said he hadn't. Then he asked me. I would have taken the lace out of my boot rather than miss the demonstration, but, as it happened, I had a piece of elastic which was useful for improvising a delicate lever-spring on the carriage of my portable typewriter. He said it " would do rightly ", and without attempting to twist it into any kind of traditional " thread " began there and then the ritual of the charm.

First of all he held the elastic at full stretch from hand to hand, telling John to stand still. Then, suddenly, he whipped off his cap and thrust it between his knees. " Your cap ", says he, " take it off ". A bit balefully, a bit apprehensively and without sign of hope, John did so.

The other bent forward slowly. I had the impression that every nerve and muscle in his body had begun to twitch and strum, maybe because of the posture he had struck—cap held between knees, shoulders hunched, head bobbing, with the " thread " of elastic again full stretch from the fingers of both hands. Without looking up he said urgently: " Say the Lord's Prayer ".

It was a sunny evening; I seem to remember the distant height of Knocklayde in a drowsy mood, like some ancient clansman, watching us wryly, having seen all this when it was, no doubt, part of a druidic rite. To save John embarrassment, and for purposes of diplomatic association, I took my cap off also.

They were facing each other on the narrow road. Then the man with the charm put the " thread " between his lips, starting with the left side and moving it slowly through his lips in an anti-sunwise direction, which was valid enough according to the laws of folk charm.

But as he moved the " thread " he seemed to munch it in rapid bites—I was wondering why his head kept bobbing—and I saw he was reciting something under his breath. When the " thread " had gone full distance he started all over again, and finished after a third movement. Old John, toothless gums tight and jaws bulging, was watching the other uncomfortably—but now tolerantly.

Next, the man with the charm dropped on one knee on the road, startling both of us. Without a word he stripped John's ankle bare, wrapped the " thread " around the foot and knotted it. He went on to squeeze the ankle, his hands hurrying, twitching, and, finally, gave a breezy rub to leg and knee, stood up and put on his cap. Only then did John put on his.

" Walk ", says he, commandingly. John limped a few steps, turned, and limped back. " Do you feel it any easier now? " John hesitated before answering: " Well, it's no worse anyhow ".

I tried to induce the man to tell the words of the charm, although anticipating his reply:

" I daren't; I got it from a woman. It's handed down from man to woman an' from woman to man. If I told you the charm, it would be lost. If you were a woman I'd tell you since you've asked, an' you'd have it an' I'd lose it ".

Old John laughed most of the road home, and laughed louder when he recalled a Ballymoney " charmer " who did it more thoroughly. But we'd forgotten about our original quest, and only now do I remember that I never learned what John did about that bit of elastic round his ankle.

THE OULD LAMMAS FAIR

At the Ould Lammas Fair, boys, were you ever there,
Were you ever at the Fair in Ballycastle O?

IN Antrim the Ould Lammas Fair is held on the last Tuesday
of August. I first went thirty years ago, but that was too
late to meet the wood carver, John McAuley, who made the
famous ballad about his native town.

Only Puck in Kerry can stand with the Lammas Fair (dare
I suggest which out-rivals which?) in a boast of a feeling for
festival, tradition and a birth dating far back in history. They
don't crown a puck at Ballycastle; but they remind you that the
ruins of the renowned Franciscan Friary of Bun-na-Mairge are
just outside the town, close to Dunaneeney where the original Fair
(which, within living memory, lasted a week) was held before
the site was moved to The Diamond in the centre of the town.

And any Glensman can tell of the rock off Ballycastle shore
where the Children of Usna landed with Deirdre; of Sorley Boy
on Fair Head, a tragic figure, listening impotently to the cries of
his people being slaughtered in Rathlin Island four or five
miles away.

Clay pipes

The Glensman can link the funeral of Sorley Boy to Bun-na-
Mairge with the comparatively recent days when the Jura and
Islay Gaels came to sell their bundles of fish. They lodged and
camped along the shore, and often brought their womenfolk with
them over the Sea of Moyle. And the men always carried a stock
of curved French clay pipes; before they tried to sell you fish they
whipped the old cutty clay from your mouth and replaced it with
a new one.

I first cycled to the Fair from Cushendall, through Glen-na-
Corp, skirting Cushendun, up through Cregagh Wood and over
the long hill to Carey Mountain with its vanishing lake; the
Lougharema immortalized by Moira O'Neill. I remember the
heather on Carey like a festive spread in a dew of amazing purple.
Hay lay ungathered in the lap-cocks in the fields further on and
the oats were colouring.

This is where Casement used let the side-car go on alone by
the road; he preferred the lonely walk through the heather,
re-joining the car near Ballyvoy. And lonely it was that day;
everyone seemed to be in or going to the Fair.

In the town people streamed towards the shore to watch
" the shores " or breakers; others were moving up, among them
some of the islanders from Rathlin. One could linger; for Ballycastle is a town of people who seem to brood if they feel they have
not been neighbourly.

And so to The Diamond. The streams of people seemed to
move in a whirlpool. Hails, cries of the " Kent-men ", the talk and
chatter and shouts of greeting came over stalls and " standins "
from a throng packed like herrings in a barrel. Good humour
flavoured every voice and most expressions.

" *Yalla Man* "

" Hoigh, Maggie! Where'll we get a post office to post these
souvenir cards? "

" Dulse an' Yalla Man . . . Dulse an' Yalla Man ".

Dulse is an edible seaweed and Yalla Man a brown, rock-hard
toffee broken with a claw-hammer and chisel. I'd been told to
watch for the rope-seller. He was on the back of a lorry like the
deck of a ship with coils of rope. In shirt sleeves, his face sweat-
red, he was yelling at the top of his voice:

" Damitskin I'm givin' it away! Come on. Real Manilla.
Have yous nothin' at all to tie up at home? That yous mayn't
be right home till yous find every four-footed bayste about the
place loose an' in harm . . . that yous mayn't be able to lave your
hands on a bit o' stray rope . . . barrin' to hang yourselves . . .
here, you . . . take your hand off that half-crown in your pocket
till I make me livin' . . . here . . .".

In a corner near the church a group of grey-clad men tried to
make themselves heard singing hymns from small, black books;
flanked by stalls stacked with pyramids of apples and plums,
doled out by men in paper hats bearing the catch-cries of jazz:
" Howdy, honey ", " Sez you ". Somewhere a loud-speaker
blared a rag-time. The cattle and sheep were out of sight down
the hill from The Diamond.

Ballads

There were two ballad singers: one I'd seen before in a June fair in Gortin in Tyrone. The other wafted here and there singing of " Sweet Ballyvoy ". Once, the rope-seller bawled at him: " Shut up an' go home an' sell one of your streets o' houses in Ballymoney ".

The traditional mind shaped the lines of mock harangues which flew from stall to stall when customers thinned: " If brains were rubber you wouldn't have enough elastic to make garters for a snipe ".

An enraptured man played on a saw. A countrywoman appeared from a cave of a tent where fortunes were told, showed panic and cried: " He was here afore I went in with his nose buried in an ice cream cone. Would he be wi' our oul' fella in one o' the pubs? "

On the pavement, with a card-table that should have overturned a score of times while I watched, a fellow with a southern accent was selling awls in a flat, repetitive banter. When I looked again the awl-seller had reversed the cloth of the table and was giving: " Four to one the Green . . . Red Rover . . . Red Rover wins again ".

And all the time, everywhere, the friendly crush of the pushing, trudging throng.

In one moment of extraordinary quiet a white butterfly flew its startled, stumbling flight around The Diamond. It might have been the spirit of the Old Lammas Fair, a bit bewildered by the new trimmings.

A BAD RUN ON THE SHORES

AFTER they had seen the Rathlin boat safely away from Ballycastle Pier on its voyage back to the Island, the group of men moved to the " Quay Yard ".

Here they seemed to cluster by traditional concert and settle into an almost ritualistic quiet amid the boom and clamour of the " shores " or breakers: a compact group drawn together by a skein of instinctive concern, its voice psychologically camouflaged by banter and idiomatic phrase.

They stood shoulder to shoulder—except for the aged Englishman, a visitor, who had now followed up and was standing rather self-consciously, significantly apart and leaning forward on his stick.

To one side of the group the surrealist effigy in The Granny Rock threw a stubby shadow. Before them, the Rathlin boat was now running up a sail. Breakers threatened and a wet spot showed where one had reared and slobbered the wall.

Outside in the Bay, and in the Sound of Rathlin, the sea was inconsistently placid, a splintering mirror that shimmered under a fretful, dull sun. And beyond the waters the remote rise of Rathlin Island itself. It might have been drowsy with myth.

The Englishman, content-looking, bent a little further over his stick. He studied that shore-line seven miles off as the gull flies, but nine miles for the boatman. Perhaps he thought the others were studying it as well for he said suddenly and mildly:
" Is the Island inhabited? "

The group didn't seem to have heard; they were still watching out to sea, away now from the direction the boat had taken. Distantly, youngsters were cheering.

One of the group, exchanging idiomatic monosyllables that nipped in to mutual comprehension between the thunder-thuds of the " shores " beyond the wall, turned courteously to the old visitor to reply.

Before he could speak someone interrupted, unexcitedly, almost boredly:
" Look at thon ones now ".

They fell quiet as if awaiting some climax. A gull alighted on top of The Granny Rock and again the children were cheering. As if finding breath once more one of the group said:
" I never saw the shores so bad ".
" Not for this time of year ", affirmed another.

The Englishman, if he had heard, may have been nonplussed as usual, but didn't show it. Nor did they explain.

For they were watching a " bad run on the shores " from the cliffs off Church Bay down to the point of The Rue on Rathlin . . . and the Rathlin boat was growing smaller . . . smaller.

The distant surf made fantasy, a ballet of thrill and stealthy menace. Watching it made the Island seem as distant as the birth of myth itself.

Sometimes one burst of foam danced alone. Sometimes it shot up in recurrent runs, like witches in a crazy procession. And sometimes another lone burst made a flying wraith of the lighthouse itself down on the point of The Rue. They must have been running to sixty and eighty feet.

The Englishman was being succinctly enlightened about the life of Rathlin when a " run " started off the Pier before us. Shallow valleys seemed to form; then the waters heaved in long, curving wriggles, slithery as a serpent.

I thought, allegorically, of the folktales I'd collected on Rathlin of the famous monster of *Slough-na-morra*, that whirlpool of tide and current out there in the Sound.

I remember one calm crossing when I had seen a pattern like circling bubbles—disconcerting to me, but as fascinating as the legendary lure of the multi-eyes of the fabled sea monster itself. Fantasy became entwined in reality to portray new origins of the wonder-talk of a winter fireside.

But there was no fantasy about these rising " shores ".

The men in the group seemed to be counting, identifying the run of the breakers yet to form. The group moved back a pace. In a moment or so there was a wet thud and spray squirted up. They moved further back.

The next one made a rush and a boom and spray splattered over the wall on to the concrete with a delayed slop of flung dishwater, but hissing as viciously as spilled ice. Now, as if by concert again, the men moved past The Granny Rock and paused at the top of the Pier. The third " run " was on its way up.

It made spectacle. Off the head of the Pier a fabulous seabeast might have been thrashing the way the waters heaved and swelled. It was angry now.

Then it charged and seemed to gulp, missed the Pier-head and split itself in two; but pouting an octopus snout that ran a malicious lip all along the top of the wall, spewing water and foam spray. When it burst majestically with a bash of power, seaweed rose and fell like debris after an explosion.

The Rathlin boat was almost a speck now, out in the Sound. And beyond the Pier, between the boat-slip and the pile of cut stone from an old sea-wall, the youngsters were cheering and squealing with delight.

Over there, in a tiny bay, the walls of water of the " shores " were petering out, top heavy with carnival foam, thundering out their lace patterns under a fall and a splash and with a chuckle of pebbles.

The Sound remained inconsistently calm. For a moment or two longer the group of men talked and speculated as to when ' the shores would go down ". Then they walked away, scattering to their work.

Gulls suddenly rose from somewhere and swooped like chips of falling limestone thrown up by a breaker . . . and a woman with an empty basin walked back from the edge of the water.

Beyond, on Rathlin, the " shores " stayed up. I left the old Englishman with his own musings and walked back to The Granny Rock to watch that menacing ballet of wave and surf on the distant rocks at The Rue.

ON A RATHLIN ROCK

HUNDREDS of feet above the Sea of Moyle the struggle took place between the landlord of the island and a noted rock-climber; a focusing into personal conflict of an upsurge of that agrarian discontent of the last century when clashes exploded into assassination—or attempted assassination, such as this event turned out to be on one of the cliff-faces of Rathlin.

The background, says tradition, was the familiar one: oppression and extortionate rents. A plot was hatched, lots were drawn and two men selected to carry out the elimination of the landlord. But on the night before the attempt was to have been made one of the men died suddenly. In the superstitious mood of the day— on mainland or island—this death was then interpreted as being an omen, a " sign " either of disapproval by Providence or as a warning that the attempt was bound to fail, followed by consequent disclosure of the plot and the usual penalties for those implicated; death or imprisonment or eviction—or at least banishment from Rathlin.

Island people anywhere, including resident landlords like the one involved in the struggle on the cliff-face, are necessarily a more integrated people than any other community; so fears, superstitious and sensible, about the outcome of the plot were understandable and feasible. On the very day of the proposed attempt on his life word was indeed brought to the landlord as to what had been planned. Instantly he challenged some of the men involved and they admitted their parts in the plot and left themselves at his mercy.

The landlord, however, called his Island tenants to assembly and announced a reduction by half of every rent imposed on every rood of ground. Pressure on land in Rathlin was then intense, the Island being mostly in rundales, with stones and sticks or lengths of rope—to save arable soil—as marks of the divisions between each family's few acres.

It was on one of these cliff-faces that the struggle took place between the landlord and the climber. Like the climber, other islanders had to go over the cliff on a rope to collect the eggs of rare birds for the landlord, who preserved them. There was, however, what we might call a " black market " for such eggs to be found in Coleraine, with a better price paid as well. It is not mentioned by tradition whether, in fact, the landlord paid at all.

A tale is told on the Island how this climber once went over the cliffs himself in the dark to get a bird's egg. He had overheard an islander tell of seeing a rare bird make for its nest on a certain cliff and was looking for the usual help in the morning to get the egg for the landlord: a climber required the aid of at least one dependable man to handle the rope on the cliff-top before he could descend, and later ascend, the cliff. That market, however clandestine, in Coleraine was tempting . . . but to enlist help might result in disclosure.

That night he brought his own horse to the top of the cliff. Here he tied a rope-end to one of its hind legs, put the other end around his own body and, by shouting directions to the horse, went over the cliff, secured the egg and climbed up again, and was off on a boat across the Sound of Rathlin before dawn.

This was the calibre of man who attempted, single-handed, to eliminate the landlord on the rock-face. Whether this attempt took place before or after the abortive plot is not clear. But it seems clear enough that both landlord and islander were men who respected each other for fearlessness and interest—however conflicting—in the wild birds and their eggs. So that when this climber went over the cliff one day on a special quest for the landlord, the man who handled the rope was the landlord himself.

It was a cliff-face known to both of them; the landlord knew of the ledge further down out of sight—on which the climber would find his first footing, and from which he could crawl to the nest. He let the climber over the cliff and the rope went taut as soon as he was out of sight. It would go slack when the climber reached the ledge. The roar of the seas would be in their ears, for it is continuous at that point on Rathlin. The rope was still taut: the climber over-long in reaching that ledge. Then the landlord heard the terrified cries of the climber.

He was shrieking that he had slipped and over-shot the ledge and was dangling in mid-air. Hundreds of feet below lay the sea, with pinnacles of rock jutting through the foam like vicious fangs, hungry for death.

The tussle began. On the cliff-top the landlord hauled on the rope. But not a foot of it could he draw back. The climber had, in fact, landed safely on the ledge, had secured his footing, but kept a pull downwards on the rope so that the man on the top, out of sight, imagined he was dangling in space. The climber was actually trying to pull the landlord over the top of the cliff and hurl him into the rocks in the sea below.

The tussle continued—one man struggling to haul the other up, the latter struggling to pull the landlord down. In the end the climber gave in and allowed himself to be hauled to the top and to safety. And then the climber noticed the landlord's fore-arms. " From the elbow to the wrist ", says tradition, " the arms were in raw flesh—the blood was comin' from under his finger-nails even—an' he was drowned in sweat ".

Afraid that the rope might eventually slip through his tiring hands, he had wound it around each arm in turn.

Tradition has nothing to say of any sequel. But it is significant that for years afterwards the climber went over the cliffs on a rope handled by the same landlord, secured the wild birds' eggs for him, and was hauled to the top again without incident or accident.

THE HOLLY AND THE HAZEL AND THE FLAILING OF THE HAY

IN the pub in the village of Meigh in South Armagh I sat at one end of a long stool. A yard or so away, with the window to our backs, sat a man from the other side of Slieve Gullion. Like me he was listening to four men at the bar talk of threshing. They were in shirt sleeves, the youngest wearing a beret flecked with hay-seed. The sound of their talk almost had an echo of the clamour of the machines they discussed—threshing mills and balers, and the merits of this and that particular set.

Their talk, appropriately, was couched now and then in a rush of a car speeding along the road outside.

" This is all right ", said one of them, finishing his drink. " But this won't get the work done ". And he went towards the door.

There was laughter and badinage from the other three, and jokes about the great yield of hay-seed: that " it would buy the ring " and leave over " an ould rusty pound " which the fellow might as well kill now. They left and drove off in a car.

" Changed times ", said the man from the back of Slieve Gullion. He was lightly built with a thin, shy face under a hat and he wore a light raincoat. His speech was slow and his voice soft. " Not much word now of thrashin' hay with the flail ".

I remarked that the younger fellows wouldn't know what a flail was.

" Why ", says he, " do you tell me you swung a flail yourself in your time? "

How many years, I mused, since I had last swung a flail, in Loughinisland in County Down? Four? Five? But not to thresh a single sheaf. A Scots phonetician brought me to the house of James McLeigh, he to annotate the sounds and nuances of the local dialect, I to unearth some folklore. It was he who revealed that James still preserved two flails, and had mentioned this fact as if announcing the discovery of a rare survival. So James and I demonstrated for him how the flails were used.

" It was heartenin' to hear the flails ", my companion in the bar was sying. " One crackin' here, there an' everywhere on decks through the fields of the country ".

How it was done

That afternoon in Loughinisland our flails made no cracking rhythm on a deck of boards; not even on a door lifted off the hinges and laid on a winnowing-cloth of sacking. Our flails merely thumped on tufts of grass at the end of the street, simply to show the visitor how the job was done.

James, understandably, let me begin first, and his sister, watching in alarm from the threshold, called out in alarm. She cried out again as James, facing me now, timed his stroke and swung in, the excitement of the swift rhythm and vigour of the craft catching both of us.

" Aye, it could be nice work ", the Slieve Gullion man was saying in his slow way, " if you had a good timer thrashin' with you. Many a one I seen left with half the eye-brow hanging' off them at the thrashin'. You need a good timer. It's the other fella's soople still on the sheaf on the deck does the damage when your soople cracks down on it ".

Not for the life of me could I recall, off-hand, if the Loughin-island vernacular called the striker of a flail a " soople ", but the hand-staff, an old pitch-fork handle, bore the same name as our own.

Absent-minded

Only then did I realize that, while musing on the demonstration in Loughinisland, I had been absent-mindedly answering the Slieve Gullion man as well. Now he was chuckling.

" If you were ever gettin' it stiff ", he asked, " did you ever hold the hand-staff right, instead of lettin' it go round in your hands with every blow? That broke the midgelin that ties the soople to the hand-staff at the *caabins*, an' you be to stop an' tie a new one ".

" It let you draw your wind ", I said.

" There's tricks in every trade, surely ", he said, still chuckling softly. Had I been more attentive I might have wondered if his detailed descriptions were meant to imply that I had never swung a flail at all.

He went on to tell that hazel made the best soople for threshing hay, while holly had the weight for threshing oats or barley. He also described the leather eyes tacked and sewn with waxed-ends on to both hand-staff and soople, and again referred to these, idiomatically, as we used do, as *caabins*. The tyings or midgelins, he said, used to be made from strips of calico or a flour sack or from the tow of flax.

I found myself wondering, habitually, about the names for these fittings in the dialect of Loughinisland, knowing I had noted each but still unable to recall the terms off-hand. This always annoys me but, obsessively, I went on thinking.

Brave long road

The Slieve Gullion man got up saying he had a brave long road before him and he'd better be making it short. I wondered then if my behaviour had puzzled him. But as soon as he had gone I wished I had asked him if he had heard the folk story about the thresher courting the girl who, because she favoured him as a suitor—and he her dowry as well as herself—gave that traditional advice ever since quoted to every thresher with a flail: " Two sheaves and a clean deck ". He had to impress her father with his knowledge as well as his prowess.

And why, I wondered, did they always jibe the bachelors that the grass-seed would " buy the ring " ? But maybe I had heard that, too, and forgotten, as I had almost forgotten that afternoon four or five years ago, when I swung a flail in Loughinisland in County Down.

POTATOES FOR HALLOW EVE

THE hay bothered the old people, the harvest worried them, but saving the potatoes meant suspense.

Just as they were anxious to have the last seed-potato set by May Day, the last of the new crop had to be out of the ground and safely in their earth-battened pits or bings by Hallow Eve, or they bewailed the fact as if it were an event foreboding famine.

" Let yous put a spurt on now ", they'd cajole, " an' not let Hollantime on us an' priddies still in the field—what sort are yous diggin' now ? " We'd try to be whimsical and remark that the pits would remain in the field anyway.

" Ah, less o' the codology ", they'd retort. " The frost'll be on yous an' not an eatin' priddy safe. Make them secure first an' never mind the pigs' priddies ". Any brand of potato, however readily marketed, was a pig's priddy if not the kind they regarded as eatable.

Famine was a reality.

We met that with a wry satire and they became quite vexed. How thoughtless of us not to realize that the spectre of the Famine was a reality to them, whispered by souls who had smelled over a mile of ground the stench from a pot of Famine potatoes—not whole ones either, but the best pieces cut off and left to be edible.

Subconsciously anyway, we still regard Hallow Eve as a deadline; and just now in every potato field the workers are busy. After the mystical excitement of harvest moods, with its butterfly caperings of fancy, this work in the naked soil might be the silent labouring of ants.

Harvest scene—Reaping oats: Slieve Gullion in background.
On the reaper: The late Paddy the Racker (O'Hare)
Going to tie a sheaf: The late Johnny Babe

Stacks of oats preparatory to threshing at Clonallon, Co. Down

William Carleton's Cottage,

The year, of course, is ageing and the airs brood. On one headrig, still shackled to its plough, a horse drowses. Sometimes the crows collect in silence in a field and when you look again they have gone, maybe whirling like a tickful of emptied feathers—and as silently—about the potato fields.

Everyone stops to gossip

In other fields where, like ourselves, spadesmen dig a set of two drills at a time, the potatoes in their rows create a liveliness as incongruous sometimes as crocheted ties drawn over the cardigan design of the rows of weeds.

Everyone passing the road stops to gossip about potatoes. Our crop is poor; but he is a rare spirit who says so to your face; he waits till you make the reference yourself.

" Ah sure ", he comforts, " the blue ones are a poor run everywhere the year. How are they keepin' ? "

" The very best—hardly even a damaged one in a drill. I see you're fairly cloutin' them out anyway ".

" Ah, it's the getherers. Yeh can't get getherers. Well, Good Further to yous ".

White cloth on the hawthorn

The day is calm, not much brighter than a dusk. Far away a threshing-mill moans. Unlike the harvest day, a shout now attracts your attention. You wonder will we complete the second set before dinner-time and sling a glance towards the house.

And then the day brightens. From a house you hear a call: " Yoo-hoo! Hoigh! " An arm waves. From a field someone brandishes a spade and, poor as the light is, it flashes like bronze.

" Our sign's out ", says one of the children. Sure enough it is—the white cloth on the " kurk ", the tended sprout of haw-thorn which looks like a bush superimposed on the hedge itself. You stretch your back in relief, out of the arc of movement to which the work restricts it, lest you lengthen the ache.

The children gathering the potatoes upset their buckets with a clatter. At the bing, a bucket goes on top of a spade-shaft,

H

while at another a coat is draped around a graip, all in the habitual hope of scaring off the crows. Trudging deliberately, we pause to assess the progress among the neighbours.

Seagull on the pit

" Holy fly! Tommy's walkin' through them. Maybe we should try the plough after dinner, what? " Then he says: " Still, he can't be gettin' them all an' get over yon scope o' ground ". We go to our dinner confirmed in the virtues of spade work.

After we come out, the day seems chillier. The crows have pecked some potatoes on the fringes of the pits; and now the dog is clattering through the stalks, falling over the drills, while the crows rise tantalizingly almost from his nose and alight at the other end of the field. A seagull, like a sculpturing, perches on a potato pit.

We linger over our smoke, and then he suddenly picks up three potatoes jooking among the dug weeds. " Hoigh! I say! " The children, coats tights and faces pinched, hang around the pits as reluctant as ourselves to start; but they jerk at his shout.

" The crows'll get their fill without leavin' more ". To emphasize his remonstration he flings the potatoes towards the bing, and the fool of a dog, barking, follows them.

Silence and whin smoke

But the lethargy has been broken, and as we delve for our spades he says: " She'll freeze the night ".

Sometimes a crack compels us to lean over our spades; but sometimes we dig for an hour without a word. Like your humours, the season is prone to sudden silences. The valley seems full of an odourless whin smoke that muffles sound and turns thought inwards. The children gabble and boss each other, and then seem to weary.

You come out of a reverie to be astonished at the amount of work you have done automatically—and hardly sliced a priddy in the set. Thought here is a dreaming that makes a mental wine. But you are amused to see that the children are running their bing crookedly.

Like ribs in a fawn hound

And then, alarmingly, there is an overhead noise as of the ripping of silences. Even the dog, now curled on your coat at the bing, looks up. The children are exclaiming, too. It's just the crows, diving crazily in twos and threes with the agility of swallows, while the dignified gull looks on.

"Wind? Or a spell of good weather, what?" You nod.

Maybe the evening odour off the fresh earth revitalized us, or maybe the careering crows suggested a release from the lethargic airs of the day, but we work with a free and facile zest. The spade seems lighter. The murkiness might be caressing sound—of a spade on a stone, a man whistling, the laughter of a group taking tea in a field.

But the dusk comes early. Out of the murkiness matronly beams reached to tuck its shade about the hills; and to probe among the heather and high grass lands between the whins for the furrows which show like the ribs in a fawn hound. They are undug ridges. . . . The autographs of Famine.

I FOLLOWED THE THRESHING MILL

I HAVEN'T "followed the mill" since the year I pulled the breast out of Larkin's thresher in a haggard at Dromintee under Slieve Gullion. The "breast" is that portion of the thresher containing the chutes which spill the threshed, cleaned and graded oats into the sacks.

You "followed the mill" in two ways. Threshing was a co-operative task: I go to your threshing, whatever the equality or disparity of various acreages, and you come to mine. If I can't return the labour I pay someone to go.

I was paid half a crown a day to "follow the mill" round our part of South Armagh—and that isn't as many years ago as some social statisticians would like us to believe either.

There was, then, a third way you could "follow the mill". This was the adventure of the wageless vagabond, a contemporary spalpeen, drawn from his father's farm by the carnival thrill of a steam-threshing set as more urban spirits are sometimes tempted to follow a circus.

In the days when a cask of porter was an essential item demanded by tradition to be " killed " at every threshing, whatever the bulk, there were sometimes as many louchers " following the mill " as could carry the two parts separately.

But, as an unfortunate piece of vernacular has it, " the porter quit " before I began to follow the mill; and as far as I know has not been restored as an item of tradition.

I usually " followed the mill " with an ancient pitchfork. It was sheer mischance that I was " at the bags " the day I yanked off a fourteen-stone sack and took the breast of the mill along as well. Knowing my attachment to the ancient fork it was hinted that I was destructive on purpose, hoping to be banished to " the straw " with my fork, perhaps hunted from the haggard altogether.

But the charge was not true. For reasons which are clearer to me now than when I hauled heavy sacks up to a barn I certainly liked being " at the straw ". But I did not like my old pitchfork.

A conscientious old man for whom I worked, and who understood more of the unpoetic character of threshing, always insisted that I take this fork, although he possessed other newer and better ones.

No one would ever dream of " lifting " *my* fork, for it was as much an embarrassment to me as a shadow-sticking relation who insists on dressing out of age, decorum and season. It was, in fact, becoming a legend.

I used to be glad when the whine of the drum of the mill gulped the first sheaf and the threshing began. Unless I was there early or lucky enough to beat someone in a scramble on to a stack to pitch sheaves I always discarded my old pitchfork, took a good, idle fork, and " went to the straw ". My old fork, with two daubs of red lead on a shaft rough as bark, and secret filings of identity no longer necessary, used to stand untouched against the hedge till I reclaimed it.

I loved being " at the straw ". In cascading bundles the glamour and glory of harvest fell and spreadeagled and piled. From your turn in the row you watched it pile . . . and pile.

With my ancient fork I would come away from a body-delve into that straw with about as much as might nest a hen, and my boss knew it: " Let whoever likes bust themselves the day ", he used to warn me, " you stick to handy wee forkfulls—an' don't go on the ladder! "

The spirit of a robust carnival gathering at a threshing could swoop inpulsively to serious horse-play: half a gapful of stones in a sack of oats to be carried to a loft or butting a heavy forkful of straw to " bring a man down off the ladder ".

When the rick got too high to be reached from the ground a man went on a ladder, took your forkful of straw and dumped it over his head on to the rick; your fork was then returned. As the rick rose higher a second man went on the ladder. It was muling work that could strangle you.

It was the bottom man they tried to " bring down ". Unable to hoist a heavy forkful over his head to the next man he would struggle or drop the forkful if he were wise; but he might be jeered then and told to come down. Or he might lose his footing. The mystery is that accidents were few.

There was, of course, a remedy. If your appeals for " smaller forkfuls " went unheeded you took the heavy forkful, rattled the end of the shaft among the rungs of the ladder, yelled aloud— and let her go. The forkful swung outwards, helped by your hand, and a handy fork was snapped in two.

That usually " brought you off the ladder " alright!

THE AGELESS ONE

AS I came out of the old G.N.R. station in Belfast he was coming in, hurrying as I'd sometimes seem him at Slieve Gullion when late (Lord forgive us both) for second Mass in Dromintee; hurrying as if caught in a stumble and relying on speed to take him out of it.

His face lit up when he saw me and he grabbed my arm in both hands but didn't stop; he even pulled me back a few paces.

" I haven't time to talk let alone take the curse of the town off us over a drink. I have to catch this train back to Newry ".

" You're late, then. She's just away ".

Wealth of hair

" Holy fly! No! "

Only then did he let go of my arm which felt as if it had been squeezed between buffers; and then he did what I thought he would: he took off his cap.

Hair like a pressed mesh of rusted wire sprang over his face; and not even that wind—born among icebergs—lifting the corners of the penny-weighted newspaper bundles like feathers on the backs of a row of geese, seemed to shiver one hair.

Twisting and twirling, yanking and pulling, he got the hair back into captivity under the cap.

" Ah well, it might all be for luck. We can have a drink now, anyway. Come on. There's an edge on that wind would peel a crowbar. I heard your ould fella was down in Antrim seein' you. You'd be seein' him away, but you would . . .? "

Embarrassing memories

We stopped to let traffic pass, while the wind planed the street of a shaving of paper, a cigarette carton and an old man's hat.

" Your ould fella stands his years powerful well. You stand the times bravely yourself. You've put on condition, but why wouldn't you

" Where'll we go for a drink. Mind . . . mind that flamin' bus! You'd die afore your time here or go home on a crutch ".

Safely across and going into a pub he took over from the incessant blast outside.

" It's the age of an ould cow since I seen you last. You were toilin' with Tam an' Owney an' Paddy then. Mind the time you used to go to Faughil Hall, boy? You an' Paddy. Do you mind? "

A little apprehensively I minded.

TV ignored

" A right pair you an' Paddy. As God made yous the divil matched yous surely. I mind seein' you in Faughil Hall many a night in a hairy coat an' a clay pipe an' your hair out through holes in your hat.

" I used to take me end at yous actin' the kaltherer before the Newry girls. D'you mind the night you had them spellin' out the dance posters for you? It's a wonder to the world you ever got a woman to bother her head with you: when you got married there's hope for the worst of us. Do we try a half-one or go for a big pint a piece? "

With our pints of porter we went to an off-shoot and sat down. Above us squatted the idol of the latest electro-mechanical fervour, a television set; but now a silent and immobile Buddha impelling no one's attention—unfortunately. For I had taken off my cap.

Weight of years

" Holy fly ", he cried, drawing glances from the bar, " you're not goin' bald, are you? "

Again he whipped off his cap and bent the wiry head towards me.

" I could give you fifteen years at least, boy, an' look at that. An odd grey one maybe, but she's all there ".

Well, under the old Gaelic code even kings suffered deposition for a blemish. But having given me the dig he must now caress to take the harm out of it.

" Ah well, you never see an ass they say without a heavy coat of hair. You can't have hair and brains ".

" Still, it's a poor roof of scraghs isn't worth its thatch ".

He was never a man with a noticeable smile and he hadn't improved.

" Divil the hair you need care, boy: you have your markets made ".

The flower, having attracted the bee, has no further use for bloom. And then we believe the idea in reverse was born among beauty barons keen on dividends!

" How many of a family have you now? "

I told him, and was glad of the chance to ask him when he meant to do the big job himself.

He tugged at his cap and took a swill of porter.

" Ah, you may well ask me. When a fella lets it run to my time of day he hasn't the same heart for the wee janes somehow— ould courtin's coul' courtin'.

" Not that I'm for givin' up the notion. Oh, not on your sacred life. Some early mornin' I'll take a wild flitter an' tie with me tongue what you don't loosen with your teeth, boy. Maybe afore another winter's on me ".

It was a traditional flow of banter, but tired and as worn somehow as the pattern of hearth and field culture he represented, its bluster no more than a pathetic echo of the robust, virile expression which embarrasses the straight-laced garb of a new respectability. Next he talked about land.

" I have to break up thon wet bottoms of ours the year an' I dread it. It's pure slavery; but sure I don't have to tell you. You were a damn lucky man to get away from rootin' in the bluddy land. What is this folklore you're after anyway ? "

Long céilí

In a vernacular both elliptic and idiomatic and bamboozling to outsiders I tried to give a resume.

" I heard a fella on the wireless one night call you a druid. There used to be a druid's altar in Padraig's Whinny Tops till they pulled it away to build the new ditch. They hadn't an hour's luck since ".

I had a bus to catch for the Glens (" They must be good to you down there, boy ") and as we parted he says: " I'm at home all the time now y'know. Be sure an' make a long céilí with me next time you're up ". I said I would. " An' if I die between then an' now don't forget but come to the funeral at self ".

" If I don't ", I said, " sure I can send offerings. Make it a weddin' and I'll come up with a present ".

He worked again on that cap. " Aw, I doubt me an' the priest'll have to make do with the offerin's, boy ". We laughed.

But whether because of the wind, cold and scornful as any modern breath, the bantering sounded as lugubrious and insensitive as it does to those sentimental people who take the rural scene and its people at a literal surface value.

SENTIMENTAL JOURNEY IN THE SNOW

FROM half-way up Glenariffe to the town of Cushendall is no more than seven or eight miles there and back. But with a white world ennobling mountain and brae and the road as slippery as new oil-cloth, with birds to pursue and caves to explore— the distances must have been at least half as far again.

The wee man who led me was not yet seven. A cut at the side of his mouth (from someone's rusty knife, he had just admitted) was giving bother. But only when his elder brother had gone to school did patience give way and we decided to let someone else see it.

How would we go? The bus had gone; we might get a lift. We would have to walk. " Walk. . . . Walk! " The fellow was leppin' to go. I took down a vagabond ash-plant, which could now find its way round half of Ulster, and followed him.

We were passing the school at the foot of Glenariffe when he turned on the first of the sentiment: "If only Patrick knew we were here. He'd be wild mad! " And with a skip and a slip and a sprinter's start he was after a thrush that hopped before us like a bouncing ball.

Threshing Mill

Already I was back in a school-room at Dromintee, in South Armagh, on a late autumn day of lazy light. Beyond the bog in a haggard a threshing mill was throbbing, the engine billowing smoke. I had been promised a free day when the mill came to that house, but it had come since I had gone to school.

Something in my soul cried quietly all that day. I raced home. But only the muddy tracks of great wheels through drifts of chaff soiled like dirty snow remained when I got there.

Another thrush was hopping just ahead of my leader. Even his shrieks could not allay its cold and hunger. He caught it under his cap, fondled it excitedly, wondered would it eat some tit-bit he had. He marvelled at the speckled breast . . . then opened his hand and it flew towards the shore over strands of barbed wire. Some gulls rode the waves of the full tide.

White World

Barbed wire, rusted and grey as the gull and the sky. Kintyre beyond, dim but white with a russet tint, like hope. There were weals in the sky as on a face aired and scoured by this black breeze from the sea over the white world of frozen innocence.

A car went by, waltzed at speed, then slithered back. I remembered flashy dancers who used to jazz the length of the floor in Faughil Hall at Slieve Gullion, while we in uncouth hobnails, sat tight and cynicized. Still, I thought that dancing as dangerous then as these cars speeding on packed snow.

Waterfoot was quieter than ever: a village that seems to be awaiting some cue. Above was Lurig, now a marble pedestal, awaiting, too, some fabulous bust. Then we were at the caves. My leader whooped and disappeared like a raindrop down a pipe and only his shouting to his own echo came out.

In one a famous smith once kept a forge. In another a woman kept an equally famous sheebeen (in Northern phonetics as " sheebin " and " shibbin "). She used sell the water that goes with hard liquor and give the elixir itself free while the law stood by—flummoxed. I well believe it.

In the early nineteenth century at Parkmore, where Glenariffe spirals like a sea-shell, a shepherd was paid £2 by the parish to maintain his side-line of poteen-making because he afforded relief to travellers snow-bound there after the Ballymena market.

We left the caves and their icicles of dragons' teeth. The wound was seen to. In Cushendall frozen snow overflowed on to the pavements. And a woman, who is unofficial guide to the town and district, and whose disposition holds tourist and you in a drift of good nature, made much of my leader and even gave him a hazel stick to "see him home".

Off in a coach

Leaving the town I thanked heaven he had missed the folky and famous " Stoney Loanan ", which goes by Bradley's Hotel. But further on, at the barrack brae, he would go up. Near Gortaclee a dog lay in the snow on the road, waiting forthrightly, but wanting to come home with us. Then we met a friend.

" We're gettin' nothing compared to out of here. We're getting off in a coach ".

Appropriate word: this was part of the old coach road. Coaches bogged in sentimental snow. A live rabbit—a rabbit that could run—sprinted across the road near Crookanarvick.

Here the road loses girth like a corkscrew as it winds to the Coast Road at Red Bay. Here the coaches used drag-horses and travellers used to get out and push. If I remember rightly Thackeray mentions the point as well.

Now that I remember, Thackeray mentioned the house where he dined in Cushendall—the very house where that good woman had given my leader a stick so that he might be as good a man as me.

He was, of course, much better; he walked the feet off me on that snowy road home through the caves and Glens, leaving me to recollect another snowy walk with my father when I was his age over the South Armagh hills, as barren as the ribs of rock which showed through the snow on the braes above Farusklin.

TURKEYS IN THE STRAW

THE woman in the Newry bus was telling her crony that the turkeys were a heart-scald and that she would " redd the place of every track of them the year ".

Though I didn't believe her I knew what she meant; and I recalled that year when Tam and I were in a bog field under Slieve Gullion opening " shores " to drain off the floods of approaching winter.

When Tam said that the wind would skin fairies we cleaned our shovels on wisps of grass and went home out of the bog just as the late bus turned the corner above with a roar and went off towards Newry.

A scrawl of fowl, humpy with cold and hunger, were clustered around the doorstep when we got home. They squawked resentfully as we waded through them while Tam swore and called for the dog.

" It's a wonder you wouldn't fire a fistful of oats to this curse o' God regiment of fowl ". Tam began as he pushed his way through half-and-big door.

Bog rushes

There was no one at all inside. A stained pinafore lay over a chair, a dish-cloth half-hanging off the table piled high with unwashed delph, a bucket with a dish on top. A big pot, with brown sudsy sacking under the lid, blubbered over a dismal dying fire.

Tam scratched his head a moment. " See is she about the house or in the garden ". As I went out he took off his cap to lift the big pot off the fire.

Once more I waded through the fowl, closing the doors behind me. I toured the byre, the stable, the hen-house. She was nowhere; but everywhere I went the fowl followed; up and down, back and across, like the slither of coloured grains in a sand-glass; their claws pattering in the clabber might have been the sound of the rise and fall of the breeze in the bog rushes.

I was in the garden when I remembered I had forgotten to look in the barn, and came back just as Tam himself—fresh soot-marks on his cap—was striding towards it like a man bent on murder. He yanked open the top half of the door and was reaching for the second when her voice came out of the gloom inside:

" Now you've done it, clooty! Didn't you know right well that openin' the door like that would scare the turkeys off their meat ". A hen tried to fly up from outside and was rudely knocked down. " Close that door can't yous. . . . Come in or go out. . . . There, look't. . . . Scared them again ".

She tried to clear the hair from her eyes and dabbed herself with gruel; and when a turkey-cock began to throttle his brother she told me to come in and separate them. I saw blood on her wrists where a claw had struck. Suddenly she asked for the door to be shut and as Tam withdrew he breathed venomously: " The divil strike a hump on Sebastian Cabot ".

" There's language for you ", she said and clicked her tongue. " What sort of luck in bird or beast could follow language like that ".

The reference to Cabot was an illusion to a note in an almanac in the kitchen window. Cabot was said to have been first to introduce turkeys into Europe.

We were back in the gloom. Now and then a turkey-head reached into the slotted light from the closed door, took a delayed peck of gruel from her hand, looked as if it had choked itself, and when about to take another would withdraw snake-quick into the dank shadows near the bins and bags and tubs of pigs' meat. A cock had moved up.

Mannequins

" Blind that flamer of a cock with a skelp of your cap ", I was told. Then she called the turkey-hens to eat. " Pee-Pee . . . Poor Pee, come on. . . . This is my last year with youse anyway. I've pains fit to kill two or three. But sure him an' his shouting would put anythin' off its meat ".

All the turkeys were in the corners now, wandering into the light near the door like mannequins suspicious of a dull spotlight. Without straightening from her crouch she followed them, grotesquely, gruelly hands outstretched. They ignored her.

I heard hurrying feet first, heard the hens squawk and heard him curse them. Then the top half of the barn door was pulled open and Tam leaned in.

" Tell you what, woman ", he began with angry irony, " I'll take out your shawl so's you can roost with your turkeys—or would you rather have a blanket an' bed an' board? "

And he filled his cap with corn in a bin and threw it broadcast on to the street. " Fill yourself on that ", he said as the fowl flew in a gust.

" No wonder the big bucks roast them ", he grinned. " Make soup of a turkey, an' some old woman was sure to shout to fish him out afore he got wet. Come on in. I have the kittle boilin' ".

A QUIET RAMBLE ROUND THE ROADS

ONE meets an old man, stands for the usual crack, and then he asks: " Where have you been puttin' yourself lately? " I suppose I give evasive answers.

Then he laments: " Do you ever mind the country bein' so quiet an' dead? A body could be got dead in the house. No céilin'. No young fellows with a box "—vernacular for accordion. " Why, dammit, it's as long as I mind since I heard a fella whistlin'; an' as for a song? I don't know what's come over the country at all ".

Somehow I feel responsible, for my own area anyway. Other old friends have been saying: " An' what did we do on you that you never made a céili with us all winter? We never see a soul at all ".

Is the house haunted?

And because that was true I was a little puzzled, then somewhat stunned. Of course there were reasons. One old soul almost explained a main reason when she said with a guarded sympathy: " Lord protect the people—an' if it's no harm to ask—how do you stay in thon house at all? " Having what people think are peculiar ideas about our standard of housing, I luckily asked why; for she said:

" It doesn't suit a body to be talkin' these times; but our ones was sittin' up with the cow calvin' for a few nights; an' at three or so in the mornin' they allowed there was light in your window, an' they coulda sworn the door opened a' closed. For any sake don't say I mentioned a thing, but since I could read A B C I heard thon place was full of quare lights. There was always something seen *there* ".

A Druid People

When I laughed she saw my amusement as bravado and didn't look too pleased. I could explain why I was making a ghost of myself, but one hesitates; and a moment of realism sees these itchings of curiosity for what they are, innate and cautious as ever, blarneying their way, maybe, to possible gratification.

One hesitates, because while the old social pattern may lie shattered between the laments of the people, an old code of clan preservation, as subtle as instinct and as dogged as an inhibition, seems to edge out the writer who has arisen from them and the wee stony fields.

Country people are terribly conservative in their philosophies; and the writer is a potential informer who betrays to the world old faiths and secret thoughts hidden deep within mind-springs which haven't yet dried up since the Druids tapped them.

And how was I to explain to my friends that I had come to feel I was abusing the purpose of the spontaneous homely visit? The moment a bit of folklore trotted accidentally out of their speech the habit of mind haltered it, so to speak, held up the crack while it led it back for grooming, for harnessing in the specific detail of the locality, even if sometimes the harness was the worse for wear.

Echoes in the Mind

We have a patient and hospitable people. But this can frustrate the writer. Collecting folklore can become an absorbing task, but the good collector dare not let his imagination play upon the turn of phrase, the incidents or the theme, while they are being narrated. There is nothing to stop him doing so later (and indeed this is one of the purposes for which the work is being done). But while he is actually collecting he must discipline his imagination to the point of constriction—and that can become a habit.

So while I had taken a walk or two around our roads, it wasn't my heart which hindered me from lifting the hasp off their gates. There was one hasp stiff with rust, with a big stone behind the centre bars of the gate, and, maybe, starlight streaking a window-pane. No dog barks. No talk or laughter. Not even the stir of a bit of junk to mimic the living sound of foddering in the stable or byre. Nothing except mind echoes crossing memory's floor.

The Good Memory

He had great stories and lore; and while watching, with the quiet hissing in my ears, the mystery of this pondering touched greater things far beyond the reach of dream to excite strange chords in the heart and mind. Grass rises eagerly behind departing feet and breathes an air more forsaken than the whistle of a breeze through the teeth of mountain-top heather. Still there is a sense of elation, of satisfaction and worth in the knowledge that you have recorded most of his tales, although not for the life of you can you recall one in detail there and then. How blandly we overlook their feat of memory—art? The good memory is still a fine faculty.

Looking around the valley you commiserate sentimentally that you have no good storytellers left. This isn't so true. One can never safely say that a custom is dead. Nor can one tell where tradition has taken refuge. People, particularly younger people, withhold lore for a score of reasons. Still, when a strong voice has been silenced it is sad to try to pick up its echoes.

The Trick of the Heart

Here one courts an even wilder risk. You are not disappointed when he has no stories to tell. He will have bits of lore, limping on good crutches of an unpretentious telling and that rare turn of phrase caught in the flash of an active imagery.

But ten chances to one he is the type who will drop something which does the trick, unexpectedly as always. That trick of the heart, the mind and the emotion, and something vividly spiritualized from all three and yet too delicate to define, but which seems to switch on bulbs of a witchery of mood hidden within the national consciousness itself.

This is the old story of the missing mood; the vanished atmosphere; the vague charm and spirit of another era, all sailing into the modern hour with the thrill and magic of vision. Time and again one has dismissed it as juvenile impression and adult sentimentality.

And then comes that word; or an idiom now out of use; a custom maybe; or a peculiar arrangement of light and shade on a glen or a gable. Normal, petty, even accidental flicks of existence which electrify the ends of the broken tradition till they garner the threads of a mental fabric which emotion reshuttles into its old pattern for the swiftest of moments.

THE GHOST TRAIN OF SOUTH ARMAGH

PART of the country through which the express from Belfast to Dublin passes in South Armagh has a legend of a ghost train. To the folklorist it is in a way a unique story. It is the only ghost train I've heard of in folklore, and it is a tale of good realism, without any of the terrifying fantasies of the old favourite ghost vehicle—the ubiquitous Dead Coach, drawn by headless horses and driven by headless men.

Unlike other tales, it was hardly known even in general terms outside that particular area. It is a country rich in tradition and folklore, and I've often wondered whether the legend was the omen that some of the people claimed it to be, or whether it was a first instance of folk imagination assimilating the wheeled magic of the age into its wonderland of story-telling. The folk mind is a conservative element, usually reluctant to let a breath of modernity trespass on its preserves of enchantment. That is why the legend holds an unusual interest.

As far as this ghost train is concerned, only those in the immediate locality appear to have seen it.

The townland is Aghyallogue, in the parish of Killeavy, in South Armagh. The parish comprises one of the mountain valleys of Slieve Gullion, a beautiful run of hill and moor, of rich vale clustered with white houses. Visitors glory in the stretch which flows like a lawn towards the wooded slope of Slieve Gullion, where wistful reaches of land mingle with the woods, and where fields cling precariously around the pigeon-cote houses.

It breathes the very charm of old lore, and caught in the rich depths of winter light, one can imagine an old-world scene of a bright fire, a clean hearthstone, a door latched against the wind, and shanachies unfolding their kingdoms of a wild winter's night.

The ghost train was first said to have appeared about sixty years ago, and the story was told to me by a person born and bred in the locality. First to see it was a man attending to one of the railway gates. Sitting in his cottage, he heard a train approaching from the North, and believed it to be " a special ", as all the scheduled trains had already gone for the night.

I

It was his duty to be outside at the gates with his hurricane lamp when the trains passed through. He went out and saw the train, a " passenger ", well lighted, coming out of " The Wellington " cutting in Killeen, but when it came to Barney's Bridge it disappeared. He left the level crossing and went up the line to the bridge, but saw nothing.

Next day he told his story. But who would believe a story of a ghost train? The person who told me the story said that their family actually heard the train that night, but thought it was a " special ", and " passed no remarks of it ". Everyone said that the gateman was just making up a yarn.

Said my storyteller: " But that was all right until a night or two after we heard a train puffin' in the Wellington. We were more than childer at the time, but divil the out would we go— nor would the oul' people let us out, either. An' it didn't pass Barney's Bridge ".

One can easily imagine the topic of awe which all this created, especially in those days when the folk world was a living reality. Many a night a " special " did come along, and much relief was felt when it did pass Barney's Bridge.

People were disinclined to believe the gateman's story. There was nothing extraordinary about the appearance of the train; it looked like any other train, and sounded like one. But it disappeared at Barney's Bridge. Old men recalled that, during the construction of the line, a number of workers had been killed in an accident at Barney's Bridge, and this—a familiar thesis in folk tradition—was held to be the cause of the ghost train. For why should a *whole* train appear?

The gateman's cottage was, of course, a great ceili house where men gathered to chat and talk or pass the hours " with a hand of cards ". Traditions of ghost-watching abound, and perhaps they " hung on " in the hope of catching out the man in his story. And they were, says legend, rewarded.

After all the scheduled trains had gone one night they heard another. The gateman got his lamp and turned up the wick as he prepared to go out. The " ceiliers " looked through the window, saw the lighted carriages draw out of the cutting and

come down the metals. But at Barney's Bridge the train disappeared. Some said it seemed to crash; others that it went out
as "you would snuff a row of candles".

The story took on new life now. There was verification. In
time, the immediate residents appear to have grown quite used
to it. There is a further adjunctory legend which says that a local
prophet (who said, during World War No. 1, that "soldiers
would go into it with weapons that would be no more use than
pot-sticks afore they'd come out") disclaimed the popular origin
of the ghost train, and declared instead that it was an omen of a
coming smash—a sort of mechanical wraith.

"After that", said my storyteller, "our hearts were in our
mouths every time a 'special' came out of the Wellington at
night".

And then the ghost train appeared no more, and the legend
was almost forgotten. But when the "trouble" broke out in
Ireland the Republicans blew up a troop train—as the local ballad
has it: "Within a mile of Adavoyle". And thus, they felt, was
the prophecy fulfilled and the reason for the appearance of the
ghost explained.

Adavoyle is a station roughly a mile south of the spot where
legend said the ghost train used to disappear into the bowels of
the earth.

THE TWO HAWTHORNS

"YOU won't fall out with your company up there", they
used to say when they heard where I was working. That
was in early spring when I renewed acquaintance with the two
hawthorns growing out of a dry stone wall—or ditch—of split
boulders separating two stony fields at the foot of Slieve
Gullion in South Armagh. The ditch itself is as wide as the old
mountain road.

That was over fifty years ago when I worked as a half a crown
a day farm labourer and when, to paraphrase again that couplet
from "The Kerry Recruit":

" I buttered me brogues an' shook hands with me spade
And went following fairies instead for a trade ".

(I did so at the request of the Irish Folklore Commission;
and even though folklore collecting is no longer regarded as the
pastime of eccentrics the popular notion persists that the quest is
still exclusively concerned with the study of fairy lore.)

After traversing much of Old Ulster I am back in South
Armagh. I now view the hawthorns from a spot on the Dromintee-
Forkhill road, over a distance of five intervening fields. They
don't appear to have grown an inch. But because of the new
forest skirting Slieve Gullion they are not as easy to identify any
more. The other morning a fog bank lay between the hawthorns
and the mountain and they stood out in sharp outline; all the
poetic symbolism and imagery they used to engender came
trickling back.

Self-consciously, they sported pongos of green like two young
girls going hand in hand by entwined branches into the year of
new life, lively, shy, but hopeful. Later they'll sport head-scarfs of
blossom, until in Autumn they became rosy-cheeked ageing
women in garbs of lichen-grey under the blush of haw, helping
each other towards their destiny. In winter I recall them trans-
formed into the images of two old colloguing men, wry and limb-
twisted, hawking in the embittered winds of memory, even
cynical with the weight of a wisdom that epitomized the rise
and fall of life and the irony of trying to formulate a message that
would not only pass on—but stick.

In early Spring enough of the gnarled winter image lingered
to enable me to identify my old boss with the hawthorns (I don't
think, had he known, he would have been amused). He was
Long Barney O'Hare (A'Hehir to us then in the Gaelic phrasing).
Tall and massive-boned, carrying not an ounce of spare flesh;
cap peak over his eyes, leaning on a blackthorn as inelegant as
himself, his face craggy in a perpetual grimace with mouth agape
to show the few discoloured bars of teeth, he was a kindly, under-
standing, unimaginative man who admired good farmers of any
degree, and in rush periods some of the small-acre men worked
for him, like myself, for wages.

I don't own a yard of ground on or around Slieve Gullion, but my possession extends over every hollow and height, ditch, boulder and hawthorn bush: a poetic insight into the spirit and moods of the entire landscape that is ever inviolate and which requires neither legal lease nor title deed and is trespassed now only by the imagination.

From the road the other day it went trespassing again. My first Spring job usually took place in one or other of the two fields of the lonely hawthorns, which afforded a wind-break shelter in a shower, and a shade when one sat to take the meals out of doors. One task was known then as " a spadin' round the lea ". You dug this along the ditches of stone walls and tossed each sod out on to the land being prepared for ploughing. A stroke or two of one's spade went to split each sod.

Until confined with his stick to the yard at the house out of sight two fields down, Long Barney used to visit me.

" Sound man, Mick. Draw your wind. We'll take a smoke ".

We sat on the split boulders under the lonely hawthorns and smoked pipes fitted with serrated lids. He would recall days of his own Spring work in those fields; winter days too when with his father and a worker like myself they " riz " boulders out of the field, all by hand with the aid of crowbars and planks. Edges and faces of the blue whin-stone here and there showed the smooth half-groove mark of the drill, a long steel chisel, which one twirled in the hands after every stroke of heavy sledge wielded by a partner; eventually the boulder was split into manœuvreable lumps by wedges known as " Plug and Feather ".

As he rose to go back home Barney used to prod and perforate with the end of his stick a sod I'd cast on to the hard lea; his subtle way of telling me I should chop the sods smaller. He was a placid man.

Sometimes while sheltering or resting there I would find a rusted pipe lid, even an old clay pipe itself, and once a very rusted knife. Barney remembered when he or someone had mislaid them and would talk about the men who had used them, one a namesake of mine. I came to look on the boulders as personalities and believed each had a story of its own.

The hawthorns told their own tale. Growing out of the centre of a ditch was unusual. There had been a house there at one time, as there had been houses in fields along the butt of the mountain, their gables of stone and blue or yellow clay discernible in the ditch: they had died out in the famine years but their names were remembered. The hawthorns would have been at a gateway, or end of the house or bottom of garden, and looked on as semi-sacred: the afterbirths of calvings dried into nothingness on such branches; the churn-staff was allowed to freshen there; and the " dead beds " of the family were emptied there of their chaff and, if not set alight, carefully allowed to rot and never tramped on. But that gable-end was immersed in the split boulders dug out of the fields.

More rocks and boulders still remained in the fields, most of them out of sight. Barney knew the sites of them as well as he knew the callouses on his mighty hands as if he had infra red sight. This knowledge was passed on in the field itself and at the fireside at night; yet, I've watched his son, Oweny, ploughing those fields with horses and iron swing plough—no wheels—and the earth-polished mould-board like the bow wave of a canoe shooting the rapids as he seemed to cling to the handles rather than guide and control as the plough heaved over the skull of a sunken boulder, skimmed another with shoulders showing, sank back into the earth, and then sometimes the sock, or ploughshare, struck the corner of a hidden rock. It wasn't The Angelus one heard then, however monosyllabic; for once a ploughman relaxed in the handling of horses and the guiding of such a plough when it struck and reared in his hands in an arc the handles could catch him in the ribs like a blow from a sledge.

My job was to follow with a spade, tap the sods back around the edges of the rock and fill holes which would swallow seed; every foot of ground counted in those days. It was a relief when someone brought a meal to the field and we sat and ate beneath the hawthorns, with little mood for dreaming or fantasizing. We worked often till the light left the sky over Forkhill and maybe a star made a pin-brooch for the top branches of the two hawthorns.

Picking the potatoes to clear the fields for Spring was more like an earth-rite of obeisance than a job of work. The long, conical pit or " hole " was first stripped of the clay. (Harvested potatoes were once actually buried in a hole or pit to secure them from winter frosts.) With a folded sack we knelt alongside each other and filled other sacks and were glad of the shelter of the tall, broad ditch of split boulders. It was a job of long silences, of startling confidences, but it was deadly on the knees, the back and the fingers which prodded out the potatoes as tightly wedged as stone cobbling; a co-worker who had travelled was a God-send, like the man who first told me of seeing the canoe shoot the Canadian rapids, and a man, or woman, with folklore, was to me better still. Neither Barney nor Oweny had much of either.

" Do you remember ", said a woman to me the other day, " the great lively times we had settin' spuds in Long Barney's upper fields ? "

As well as paid workers like myself neighbours came to give a hand, the women to " drop " or plant seed potatoes. The meal under the two hawthorns was a festive affair, the banter invariably about courtship and marriage, and the older the bachelor the better he enjoyed it.

" As soon as all the Spring work is redd. You'll see me take a flitter, boy. I'll never let another winter on me ".

" Old courtin' is cold courtin'. Better buck up, boy! "

Some of them did marry, some never did, and most have now " gone to their reward ". So when the lands dry out later in Spring I'll maybe make my own way back up there, on the stick I now carry, as Long Barney used to carry his. I'll try to recall him up there last time we were together with all the Spring work finished and I was repairing or " brerrin " fences of stone ditches with whins to keep out the marauding mountainy sheep. The ditch there dips and rises on the head of the field where Slieve Gullion sardonically edges under and in. No doubt it has extended its terrain of heather, fortifying its grip on land impervious to any " jumper " or crowbar. Barney would inspect my work and with his stick might pat down a whin or add a weighting stone of his own, indicatively; but then without a word, look back down over the wide flat valley of fields set in contented, rising crop, with the first of the white-washed houses gleaming as bright as daisy petals.

Then in a murmur: " The country looks well, Mick ". He
admired the cropped fields for a minute or so. To-day there is
little or no crop, while one field may carry as many grazing cattle
as once were spread over a townland. (" Isn't it great to see your
money makin' walkin' the land? " I heard a young man say
recently, and seriously.)

Barney wouldn't have approved, I think. He could also
admire the tidy houses as well as crops, with the tarred bottoms
of the walls setting off the white-wash; it deterred the entry of
rats they said. To-day, that young man seeing that tidy farm
would likely say:

" Man, that place would bring a quare penny the day if she
was put up for auction ".

Values and standards change and often, insidiously, deter-
iorate. There can be an odd sense of communal starvation of
spirit and soul about the landscape. But the two lonely hawthorns remain the same in their rising Spring garb of quiet,
colourful life. The thought, anyway, of our materialistic day fits
more the mood when the two hawthorns make a sex-change and
become wry, fatalistic and embittered symbols blasted by winter
winds. It's enough that at the moment the two hawthorns bear
again the life, the hope and the promise of youth; and who knows?
Youth may yet agreeably surprise us all with a new worldly
wisdom of its own.

SLIEVE GULLION, MYSTERY MOUNTAIN OF THE NORTH

THE visits last summer of two Scottish geologists to Slieve
Gullion in South Armagh have now become associated
with the claim that the mountain and its area are rich in mineral
deposits. More will be heard of this. But enough is already
known to vindicate the folk beliefs of minerals in the mountain
and, once again, Slieve Gullion has crept into the news.

It always does, sometimes almost superstitiously, and always with mystery. Mystery and mysticism have always been the traditional breaths of Slieve Gullion. Few writers from Staudish O'Grady to " Æ " have looked at it without having to say afterwards: " Mystery . . . Mystic . . .". Even its magnificently domed summit suggests a temple of secrecy. The lake on the top between the cairns reaffirms it—The Cailleach Biorra's Lake to us, and Lough Liath to O'Grady. Ancient people lived on that dreaming summit. Druids held their mystic rites there and on every hill-top around the valleys below. Tales of the Fianna are woven around it. Saints walked it in early Christian epochs. A temple it might be truly, stored and scored with the remnants and tokens of almost every turn and phase of our country's history.

Slieve Gullion is off the official route of the tourist; but the scenery of the area is unequalled. It breathes a mood found nowhere else in Ireland. The very displacement of the fort of hills, as the eye travels along, suggests omnipotent arrangement and mystical implication. The hills might be guarding Slieve Gullion, and the land is cultivated even to the shoulders of high-flung rocks. To look on the wide valley from Slieve Gullion top presents a sight that quickens the mind in an extraordinary way. The valley is thronged with little fields and sprinkled with houses as thickly as wild cotton on the bogs themselves. There is a magical air of the miniature Ireland over the scene, and a sunset can suggest a fantasy that might be a dramatization of that spiritual wistfulness so characteristic of the whole Irish scene itself.

Rich in Folklore

It is an area rich in folklore and custom; a land of tradition and one of the northern fastnesses of the Gael. One hears the old tongue still on the lips of an old person—particularly when, under the stress of emotion, the English language is apparently inadequate and lacking the power and colour of the expression sought. Traditions die hard in these valleys despite the fact that the people have been great travellers, known throughout the world as "Pahvees", or pedlars and dealers of one kind or other.

But all seem to be drawn back again to Slieve Gullion. It might be more than the old *gradh* for the home place. Mystery and mysticism never emanate from a place without proper reason, and Slieve Gullion has reason in plenty. The lake on the summit, most tangible perhaps of its mysteries, is an eerie experience—more than a sight—on any day. I've sat beside it at all times of the year, even in mists which confused me. Eerily mocking our modern minds, its water turf-tinted, but still not brackish, never drops below level. Stories and traditions about it are told *go leor* in the valley and one is the Fianna classic of how the Cailleach Biorra brought age to Finn by tricking him into diving within it to retrieve her supposedly lost ring.

Who Knows?

The two big millstones can still be seen beside the lake, and who knows the real story? Folk legends abound of efforts to remove them. History suggests that corn was ground on Slieve Gullion's top in the time of Concobhar, when the heaps of stone near the cairn beside the lake were the *bó-dun* or shelter of the cows of Uladh. The summit commands a view of many counties spreading over the plains of the south beyond the ring of foothills, no larger looking than cassocks from the top.

The chief cairn on the summit is a little distance south of the lake. It is one of the most important in Ireland because of its identity with similar copula cairns in Portugal—a Milesian link, perhaps, when thorough archæological excavation looks at it. It was explored in 1834 and in later years. The account of the excavation of 1834 added that it was the burial place of Cualgue, Milesian chieftain, killed in a battle at the mountain foot, and referred to in a poem by Ossian. Other very important cairns exist on the lower hillocks of the mountain and on the slopes below. Every top of the surrounding ring of hills has its cairn. This plainly is territory that was held in reverence by our early forebears and probably as well known in the Ireland of that day as Dublin or Belfast is in ours.

On the slopes of Slieve Gullion, too, Cuchullain earned his famous name. The grey of Macha, the legendary water-steed, was said to come out of the Cailleach's Lake, and to this day one can hear living tradition of water animals in Camlough Lough, lying in a beautiful setting at the foot of the mountain.

Any rocky rest on Slieve Gullion affords an overwhelming panorama of scene and history. The cycle of epochs turns before the mind's eye as the living eye rests on some associate sign or relic of the period. Carnagore, the hill to the south, is where Deirdre is said to have sung the birds to a jealous silence when in keeping for the pleasure of a king. The winds of Glen Dhu keen her sorrows to this day, and from there one sees the prettiest sight of Slieve Gullion between two epaulettes of rock, with the distant Mountain Road worming its way tremulously on the heather. Somewhere on Slieve Gullion lies a forgotten wishing well.

A Battle Ground

Now a Dublin-bound express on the other side of the valley wails a valedictory sound to the Gap of the North as it goes through. The very stones proclaim their history here. From mythological times to Edward Bruce this was an Irish battle-ground down to the defeat of the O'Neills in 1600 by Mountjoy, who built the castle, the keep of which remains.

On the hill beyond—the last—is Faughart of Saint Brigid. And here on the slope of Slieve Gullion itself the Well of Saint Monnina of Killeavy, or Blinnia, as our own people say. Over-looked in the Gap of the North is Kilnasagart, where stands the earliest inscribed Christian monument in Ireland. And Clough-innea, at one's foot, most mystic townland of all, with its religiously-inscribed boulders and cashels on the slopes. Hardly a century passed but this land saw some event which added another respect to the spiritual passions of the Irish soul.

This is but a glance at the country of Slieve Gullion, at its mystery, its lore and history. " The Gentle Mountain " our grandparents called it, meaning The Fairy Mountain. Old tales record that a fairy palace, called Sidh Finnchaidh, lay on Slieve Gullion, and from which sailed Aillen Mac Midna to burn Tara each Hallow Eve until Finn killed him with a magic spear. And the magic seems to be there still on our Most Mysterious Mountain.

SOUTH ARMAGH'S OUTLAW POET

CELEBRATIONS to honour the South Ulster School of Poets of the eighteenth century have already commemorated Séamus Dall Mac Cuarta in Omeath and Peadar Ó Doirnín (" the sweet-throated singer of Ulster ") in Urney, beyond Forkhill village in South Armagh. Celebrations took place in Creggan, where Art MacCooey rests along with Séamus Mór MacMurphy.

Inseparable friend of Ó Doirnín, MacMurphy may have been minor in gifts to his contemporaries; but his tragic story—once told and sung from Rathlin to the Gates of Dublin, to Mayo and Donegal—assures his memory a distinguished position in any recounting of the famous school at feis, function or fireside.

This verse is still recited:

" On the peak of Slieve Gullion the feast was prepared,
And Seamus MacMurphy presided at the celebrations:
He who would refuse obedience to the English-speaking churls
But reserves all loyalty to the wandering Rapparees of Ireland ".

That meeting was held in 1744 and was convened to prepare the people for the expected coming of the Pretender. Séamus was then aged twenty-four years. He had been born in Carnally, near Silverbridge, his family, the earliest known chieftains of The Fews, being of the same stock as the O'Neills of Ulster. He aided agents of the Pretender, recruiting in South Armagh for the disastrous Battle of Culloden in 1745, and returned to Carnally to find himself outlawed by the notorious Johnston of the Fews, a man whose name is still execrated.

With Peadar Ó Doirnín, also outlawed from his school by Johnston, he founded a School of Poetry in Dunreavy Wood, which at the time extended to Forkhill. Séamus's direct lineal namesake, the late James Mór Murphy of Carnally, could point out the site of the school and the house on his own premises where Séamus had been waked, as well as the Mass Rock where he had been acolyte to a French priest acting on behalf of Prince Charlie.

(His ability to speak French was brought against him at his trial.)
In his poem, composed in Armagh Jail, Séamus could recall:

> " In wild Carnally of the patch field of corn
> There stands a Mass-stone;
> Would that I had knelt
> In humble prayer that August Lord's Day morn
> And for my sins repentance felt . . .".

" If ever ", wrote the late Father Larry Murray, to whom we
are indebted for much research on the period, " we have an Irish
Shakespeare, he will find, in that scene enacted in The Flagstaff
ale-house that August morning around 1750, material of even
more dramatic possibilities than was available for ' Macbeth '."
The late and still lamented Malachi Conlon, M.P. for South
Armagh, wrote his play, " Dunreavy No More " on this theme.

The Flagstaff in Fathom, in South Armagh, overlooks
Carlingford Lough in one of the most breath-stopping panoramas
to be found anywhere in Ireland. Séamus's " dark girl of the
mountain glen " lived on the Flagstaff. She was Molly MacDacker,
believed to be half French, and the daughter of Patsy, a carpenter
and brandy smuggler who ran a shebeen.

At the time Séamus was about thirty years of age. According
to both historic and traditional sources he was the tallest man in
South Armagh, an outlaw with the statutory fifty pounds on his
head. Rich planter farmers in Armagh, Louth and Down knew
who was behind the pistols stopping their coaches when this
bantering, sardonic hail rang out:

" Come out! Come out and meet the handsomest man in
Ireland! "

But tradition also agrees that both Ó Doirnín and MacMurphy
were over-fond of the brandy bottle and the feminine caress;
Ó Doirnín, in fact, is still quietly reproached in tradition for an
alleged vice which cost him a school. Both used to frequent the
shebeen on The Flagstaff together.

One evening, as a love-tease, Séamus roused Molly's jealousy
and was aided by his lieutenant, Arty Fearon, who secretly loved
Molly himself. Eventually they concocted a plan to betray
Séamus Mór. Alarmed at the organized efforts of Séamus Mór,
Johnston of the Fews requested a peace pact; he would cease

beheading Séamus's followers, and Séamus would undertake that no more satirical poems would be made on the Head-hunter of The Fews. As one of the kin of Johnstons of Annandale, he was of the Scots Gaelic stock himself, and feared the scourges of a poet's lines.

Molly invited Peadar Ó Doirnín to visit her, set him drunk and persuaded him to compose a mercilessly cutting poem called " Heretic Headcutter " on Johnston: for whether " sweet-throated singer or not " Ó Doirnín could turn out the blistering verse: one such poem of his actually banished a rival school-master named Maurice O'Gorman from Forkhill.

The poem on the " Heretic Headcutter " was brought late at night to Johnston in Roxboro, in The Fews, by Molly, who swore it was MacMurphy's composition. Johnston was enraged. Together they planned that she would set Séamus drunk the following Sunday morning in her father's shebeen. Séamus was asleep when Johnston and his men seized him.

" Alas! that my hand had not been crippled
My leg broken,
Before I started drinking whiskey that Sunday morning:
My hat stolen—
My pocket plundered—
And to my eternal disgrace I let them take me alive ".

He was tried in Dundalk but the jury refused to find him guilty on what were trumped-up charges of, firstly, stealing a hat, then a sheep, finally a horse. Under armed guard he was transferred to Armagh Jail, tried and sentenced and was hanged on Saint Patrick's Day. From the prison he wrote:

" Alas! that I am not on Ardagh Hill in Omeath,
On the high Fathom Peak,
Drinking from the glasses in my loved one's parlour . . .
Ochone, maiden of the white throat
It was you who left my mind troubled . . .".

He was carried home to Carnally to be waked and was then buried in Creggan. Arty Fearon was killed on his way home from Armagh. Patsy MacDacker went at night to collect the fifty pounds reward, was paid in " red pennies ", which he carried home in a sack, and this, untouched, was found by his dead body near his home in Fathom.

Ó Doirnín, supported by Molly MacDacker, tried to confess the truth, but was refused a hearing. When the verses became popular Molly lost her reason and was found drowned one morning in Carlingford Lough. She is buried in an old monastic cemetery at Ferryhill in Omeath, opposite Narrow Water.

Ó Doirnín made his peace with Johnston, and in 1769 was found dead in his school close to Forkhill.

THE LAST SCORE IN DROMINTEE

THE last score thrown in Dromintee at the foot of Slieve Gullion in South Armagh took place one Sunday afternoon in 1945. It was an unusual event for two reasons: it was not intended to be a score but rather a demonstration; in other words—as we then phrased it—" a throw of bullets " which developed into a score.

Professor E. Estyn Evans and John Mogey, both then of Queen's University, Belfast, were in the Dromintee district with a party of students, several of whom were from various countries on the main Continent of Europe. Professor Evans then asked would it be possible to organize a " throw of bullets " for the benefit both of the students and himself. I believed I could muster enough bullet-throwers but the problem was where to get a bullet; and although we favoured the stone bullet in our area and I had helped to make them myself, I doubted if I would have the patience and skill to produce one in time.

The late Myles Mallon, a good thrower himself, eventually unearthed a stone bullet in the safe keeping of Stephen Murphy of Dernaroy, past whose gate the score usually went and indeed sometimes ended there. Rumour of the score got around and no mustering was needed; bullet-throwers of all ages came along. As far as I remember I played in partnership with Myles—and we won the first score! The visitors looked on me as veterans around

Armagh City might adulate " Hammerman " Donnelly or Red Crowley from Cork: the fact was that singly or in partnership I had never before won a score in my life! I was never better than indifferent; but my late brother Owen still has the reputation of being an able bullet-thrower among the old stagers in Dromintee. (The under-arm throw did not impair the prowess of his change to the over-arm as a cricketer when later he worked in Liverpool.)

John Mogey took the photographs of that last throw and later told me that while the moment of delivery of the bullet from the fingers came out in a blur, he had been able to get speed-cars clearly at the same shutter speed. Among those he referred to and who were throwing that day were old men like the late Tom Dunne of Dromintee (an able folk storyteller, too) and the late Jemmy Ned Murphy. Peter Nugent of Dernaroy, Dromintee, now dead also took part; he was also a noted thrower up to the late twenties before he emigrated to Canada. The game, in fact, died out about that time, not only in Dromintee and the townland of Ballinamadda, but in Faughil also. It would appear to have died out earlier in Clontigora, in Killeen, and earlier still in Killeavy.

Incidentally, the stone bullet used in that last score is preserved in Queen's, and I was able later on to unearth another which I presented to The County Museum, Armagh.

Iron bullets had been used in local scores also, of course, but players appeared to prefer the stone variety: I have heard them complain that an iron bullet, due to hard impact with the rough surface of a road, developed scollops which could lacerate the fingers upon release from the hand. Just the same, I remember a few of us when very young using a hacksaw blade in the clouds of night on the round bulb of a water-pump handle at Francey O'Hare's on the Dromintee Old Road; we never succeeded in making more than a trace of impression, the idea was to saw off a bullet!

Blacksmiths made iron bullets in earlier decades, and one smith named often was called Finn; his real name was Eddy Woods. I remember him as a very old man with a venerable beard. He used make both types for the Ballinamadda players, including my brother Owen.

(A humorous item about Finn and his bullets. Two young cousins of mine, John and the late Larry Campbell, were brought home from Liverpool about the same time as myself, 1922. A RUC man stopped them one day and in his northern accent asked if they knew were there " any Sinn Finners around ". Larry pointed out where one lived—Finn—and added that " he made bullets ". The raid on Finn's which followed was more in the nature of an inquiry in force; I don't think they confiscated any bullet old Finn may have been working on.)

The term " bowls " was unheard of in our area, though I think someone had to use the word to explain to the police when they were being informed of the planned last throw for the students. Neither did we ever apply for a " closed road " permission: someone kept a watchful eye out for any sign of a RUC man in uniform or out and the game halted if he were spotted: as it did similarly when the Sunday newspaper seller on his bicycle came along from Newry: his customers were mainly in the barracks. On one occasion, however, enthusiasm could not be restrained (bullet throwers anywhere will understand this impatience). He was walking up Jemmy Ned's hill when the speeding bullet " left the road " and hit the pedal of his bicycle to send it spinning. " Was that a rubber ball? " he asked. He was told it was!

The same enthusiasm accounted for the few accidents in our area during bullet-throwing. Before young boys could be cleared from a roadside dunghill the bullet came " lofting " over the corner, sped, then left the road and hit a young fellow in the chest. He was knocked out but recovered without any ill-effects. The same enthusiasm almost resulted in my brother Owen seriously injuring, at least, my friend Mick McCrink of Ballinamadda. A steward (as they'd say now) at the foot of Mick's loanan waved frantically to Oweny: it was the signal to throw. Mick, with his father and mother, were coming down the loanan in a pony and trap and mistook the arm signal as meaning to hurry; knowing the eagerness of players to get on with the game he whipped up the pony. He swept out on to the road as Oweny threw the bullet—and it grazed the side of Mick's head. He was knocked unconscious nevertheless.

K

Accidents with fatal results appear to have ended the game elsewhere, as in Hilltown in County Down (Patrick Brontë was a noted bullet-thrower in his era) and in Omeath when bullets were thrown on the Bavan road.

No gambling took place at scores as far as I recall. Players simply paid stakes of a penny each to the owner of the bullet: if it were lost he retained the stake money. (It was not unknown for a youngster to find a bullet which had " bogged " in a *sheugh*, plank it quickly under a stone or big sod, recover it later, freshen it up with a few tappings of a hammer, and claim he had made a new bullet!)

Bullets were also thrown in Newry, and old people still know the route of the score as " the bullet road ".

The only other area outside those mentioned where I found a reference to bullets was in Monaghan. A field near Scotstown is referred to as " The Bowling Green " but there is no living tradition of participation in a game called " bowls " or " bullets " having been played on the green or along the roads.

But an account does survive. Harry Smyth of Scotstown quotes information told to him by his father. His father gave him a stone ball and said it was " a bowl ". He said it was one of many introduced into that area by a Captain Starling of Scotstown. Starling used " gather all the musicians and blind fiddlers of the country to his house. He'd keep them there: and my father said he gave out these stone bowls to them and they'd be throwing them along the road in a kind of game ". Unfortunately no knowledge of the form or nature of the game appears to have survived, but it would seem to be related at least to our " bullet throwing ".

WHO BANISHED THE BANSHEE?

ONCE we turned down the lane which led to a popular bar in Warrenpoint we heard his voice from behind the closed doors. The words were indistinct and were followed by that kind of expectant pause which awaits an answer. None came.

Hardly had my companion—a former neighbour from Slieve Gullion in South Armagh—gone through the door ahead of me when the voice, with appeal in its query, came again:

"Answer me one of yous if yous're fit. . . . The sixty-four dollar question. Who banished the Banshee out of Ireland?"

He said "sixty-four" to the exclusion of the thousands in the common by-word, and was standing alone on the centre of the floor as we moved to the bar to join a few others. They sat on high stools, well spaced out, one reading the racing page of a newspaper, the others apparently staring at the shelves of bottles behind the bar. They could see the speaker in the mirror behind the bottles, but no one seemed to care enough to say a word.

"Who banished the Banshee out of Ireland?" the voice said again. "I'd like to know".

There was a stirring along the bar and my heart sank. My association with folklore is so well known, and folklore itself still so erroneously and exclusively misinterpreted in terms of the popular myth of fairies, that I waited for someone to direct attention upon me—as they have done: almost as if demanding that I detail the genealogy of every fairy mentioned in local tradition.

But no one spoke. They shuffled but showed not the slightest interest in any of us.

I looked at the speaker. He was no townsman; the way he wore his cap told me that, apart from the overcoat, which swung loose in a casual, careless fit. He would be in his late fifties, and his countenance held an extraordinary expression: there was either interest and real concern in the eyes and troubled brows, or else he was a wit, hoping for someone to bite. There was no hint of belligerency in the voice and the barman who set up drinks behaved as if the man on the floor had no existence at all, even when once again he demanded an answer about the banishment of the Banshee.

Not a soul moved until my companion turned.

"I know who banished the Banshee", says he.

The others in the bar showed interest now, and again my heart sank. My friend, who was a pahvee (that is, a pedlar of cloth, though no self-respecting pahvee would endorse such an

explanation in any part of the world, and they have been in most)
was the sort who could, as they say, cod a king and get away with
it. Lord, I said to myself, now *he's* going to pin this fellow's
attention on to me and then sit back and enjoy it.

" You know who banished the Banshee? " said the other.

" I do ".

" Then I'd like to know ".

By his reflection in the mirror I studied the man. He hadn't
moved, but he kept blinking slowly and his mouth had fallen
open. His voice, however, astounded me: it had dropped to a
soft whisper. The man seemed to be in earnest. " I want to
know ", he repeated.

" Why do you want to know? " my friend parried.

" You answer me first, friend, an' then I'll answer you.
I asked first an' fair is fair ".

" Do you ", countered the pahvee, " know who the Banshee
is in the first place? "

" I do ", says the other, as if surprised he should be asked
such a query.

" Who, then? " the pahvee insisted.

" She's a woman. A livin' woman that got took away be the
Wee Folk an' was never let back. Am I right? "

" Right ", encouraged the pahvee. " Go on ".

" She never really died at all. She was fit to come back an'
cry to let her own ones here know when one o' them was goin'
to die. I heard her meself. Years ago. But not now. An' she's
a miss-lee thing in a way. That's why I want to know who
banished her from Ireland. If you're fit to tell me ".

" I can tell you all right ", my friend assured him. He paused
and took a drink, replaced his glass and swivelled back on his
stool to face the other. " It was the Sinn Feiners an' The Tans
in the time of The Trouble ".

The other blinked again, wet his lips and said very quietly:
" If you mean that the shootin' an' blargin' scared her—then
that be damned for a crack ".

" I mean no such thing ", the pahvee assured him. They were
staring at each other, my friend's face dead-pan, the other's
showing that expression as if indeed he were a bucolic wit, full

of patience, merely waiting for the right moment to pounce and raise the roof in laughter with his retort. My friend asked: " Are there any old forts in your part of the world? "

" It's hivin' with them ".

" Well ". A pause. They looked fixedly at each other. " Isn't that where the Wee People an' Banshees were supposed to stay? "

" Correct ".

" Well, then. Who'd break a bush off a fort. Who'd go next or near them after dark? But once the trouble started, wasn't half the country on the run every night stayin' on them old forts. A breeze couldn't get through the throng. How could you expect ghost or divil, fairy or banshee, to remain after that? You might say the livin' people evicted them. That's what banished the Banshee from Ireland. Us. Me an' you an' others like us. In the time of The Trouble. What are you takin'? "

He didn't seem to have heard: only for a moment did the expression quicken and I expect a retort, or some remark like " I believe you to oblige you, though there's thousands wouldn't ". But he said nothing, and after a moment turned and went out. The odd thing was that after he had gone no one made a remark, not even the pahvee. I had never seen the man before and I haven't seen him since.

OLD LORD ERIN'S SON

" THIS is a story about a blacksmith. He was an old black-smith and he went under the name of ' Lord Erin ': a sort of nickname you understand. Well, Old Lord Erin was a blacksmith as I said, and he had one son—Oh, a lazy villain, a terrible lazy man. He'd do nothing but lie in the ashes all day and Old Lord Erin as they called him was always scolding him, but not a bit of use; no good. He never stirred. Old Lord Erin had two goats and one cow and a bit of land, I suppose, but that's all.

" Well! This day the son took some notion and begod he gathered himself out of the ashes and he went up to his father and he says says he: ' This place is going to loss and I think ', says he, ' I'll get meself a woman and see can we put some sort of shape on it '.

' In under God! You get a woman? ' says Old Lord Erin. ' What woman would take you? ' says he, ' and you never out of the ashes. Ah g'way outa that '.

' Oh, you'd wonder '.

' Wonder be damned ', says Old Lord Erin. ' You that wouldn't do a hand's turn. A man ', says he, ' that wouldn't as much as hold a horse for me till I'd put on a set of shoes '.

' Well, I think I should ', says the son.

' Where would you get money to get married ', he says, ' even if you got a girl to take you? '

' Well ', says the son, ' there's that cow out there, and I could take her out and sell her '.

' Sell the cow? ' says Lord Erin. ' By God I'll hold you you won't. Sell the only cow I have? ' he says. ' If you want money why don't you go away and hire yourself '.

' I need a shoot (suit) of clothes, too ', says the son.

' Well, away to hell and work and earn the price of them ', says Lord Erin.

" Anyway, the son was for going—he was a scholar too, a great scholar, could talk. Anyway, he thought on this Fair that was near by; so he shook the ashes off himself and got in a fair sort of trim and put on an old top-coat and tied it with a rope round and pulled an old hat on his head. He never said a word to Old Lord Erin, but he slips off this morning, taking the cow with him, and begod he sold her—he got rid of her anyway. So begod he joined (began) to count his money. Oh, a big wild sheaf of notes that he got for the cow. So first go off he bought himself a shoot. Then he got himself a shave. That was all right. ' I'm not finished yet ', says he. ' I need the guard '. So he bought a lovely goold (gold) guard for across his waistcoat and he bought a cane stick. Well, when he had all that done he looked at what money he had left, and it was light (very little).

' Aw ', says he, ' it's not much use going home to him with this trifle. It's no use offering him that. Ah ', says he, ' I think the best thing for me to do is to take the boat for England '. So he pays the boat (pays for his passage) and landed in England and off he starts to walk. So anyway he went to this place and got a mouthful to ate and off he started again on his travels, till he come to this big castle of a house, and man—there was a grand garden in front before the door and the grandest flowers of the world growing in it. So he went to pluck one for himself to make a button-hole. And he was just putting it in when this girl put her head through a window and shouted at him.

' Hoigh, there ', she says. ' What are you intruding in my garden for ', she says, ' or what do you want? '

" Oh dear a dear ', he says rising his hat, ' I'm very sorry ', he says, ' I seen the grand lovely flowers and thought I'd just pluck one for a bouquet. Oh, I'm very sorry ', he says.

' Who are you anyway? ' the girl says.

' Oh ', says he, ' I'm the great Lord Erin's son from Ireland '.

' Oh, is that so ', she says, and she slipped in to the old lord— he was her father—he was sitting back, man, in a big arm-chair taking his aise (ease).

' There's an intruder outside in the garden ', she says, ' and he claims to be the great Lord Erin's son from Ireland ', says she.

He looked at her. ' The great Lord Erin's son? ' he says. ' Oh, that couldn't be. Never heard the name before. Give me over that book ', he says. ' I'll soon find out whether he's telling lies or truth ".

" The book was brought to him quick enough and he joined to look through it. ' No sign of the name here ', he says. ' No sign of the name here. . . . What is he like? ' he says.

' Oh, a grand well-dressed gentleman ', she says.

' Is he good-looking? ' he says.

' Oh, a very fine looking man altogether. Grand ', she says.

' Oh then ', says he, ' in that case take him in till we see. There's no sign of the name in the book anyway '.

" So she went out and called him in and he was taken up and the old lord was still sitting back in his big arm-chair.

' Good day, sir ', says he.

' Good day kindly ', says Old Lord Erin's son.

' They tell me ', says the old lord, ' you're the great Lord Erin's son from Ireland? '

' That's correct ', he says.

' Are you long over here in England? ' he says next.

' Oh no, I've just arrived ', he says; ' just arrived '.

' And where might you be stopping? ' he says.

So he told him, mentioning some hotel.

' Oh dear a dear ', says the old lord, ' that's terrible. That'll never do ', he says. ' A man of your class mustn't stay there. There's bad characters and everything there ', he says. ' You must stay here ', he says, ' while you're in the country. Dear a dear I wouldn't for any money to have you staying in a place like that '.

' Oh well, my lord ', he says, ' I'm a stranger and I didn't know ', says Lord Erin's son.

' Well, stay where you are ', the old lord says. ' It'd be a great come down (indignity) if it was known that Lord Erin's son was in the country and staying in that place without my knowledge '.

" So he thanked him. And there was what they called a foreman (footman?) in the house, and it was part of his duty to tell the old lord all that he heard or seen or what was going on. So anyway didn't Old Lord Erin's son and the lord's daughter fall very much in love with other, and didn't this foreman see them embracing, so he daren't but tell the old lord. So up he goes to the old lord.

' My lord ', he says, ' there seems to be a little matter that's bothering me ', says he.

' Well, tell me praise be ', says the old lord.

' Well ', says he, ' I think your daughter and this Lord Erin's son are getting very much in love '.

' Dear a dear—can that be so? ' says the lord.

' I'm afraid, my lord ', says he, ' it is. I saw them embracing '.

' Oh dear a dear ', says he, ' send her to me at once '.

" So he did and the girl come in, and he put it to her and asked her was it true.

' Yes, father ', says she, ' I love him very dearly '.

' You love him? ' says he.

' Yes ', says she, ' I love him '.

' Oh, daughter dear by no means ', he says. ' By no means don't think of marrying that man ' he says. ' Have nothing to do with him till I find out if things are as he represented them to be '.

" So he sent for the foreman.

' Well ', he says, ' it's all true what you say, so before I can consent to let her marry him you must find out what sort of a place he has in Ireland ', says the lord till the foreman. ' You go to the boat. Take the steed and saddle her and take plenty of money. Ride on ', says he, ' and on to the boat for Ireland and take the steed with you ', he says.

' I will, my lord ', says the foreman.

" So he takes the steed and throws the saddle on her and off he goes, and he had leavings of money and he comes to the boat and he takes the steed with him. But before he left, him and Old Lord Erin's son come together and Lord Erin's son says:

' Now ', says he, ' do me no harm if you can do me no good ', says he.

' Oh now ', says the foreman, ' I can't help it. I have to do my duty. I have to do what I'm told. But ', says he, ' if I don't do you no good I'll do you no harm '.

" On the boat and landed in Ireland and he went ashore and threw his leg on the steed and began to ride off, inquiring where he could find Old Lord Erin. He was inquiring everywhere but no one could tell him, till this night he was inquiring and he had a loose shoe. He met a gentleman walking along and he stopped him.

' Excuse me, sir ', he says. ' Would you be so kind as to tell me where there's a forge around here? '

" So the gentleman stood a while looking into the ground.

' Oh yes ', says he. ' Do you see that old flow (rhymes with ' plough ', a soft or swampy place) up there? ' he says.

' I do '.

' Do you see that old cabin in the flow? '

' I do '.

' Well ', says he, ' ride up there and you'll find a forge ', he says. ' There's an old blacksmith lives up there ', says he, ' and he goes by the name of Old Lord Erin '.

("Man, that was good, what? He was right beside it ". Interpolatory comment by the story-teller.)

' Oh, thank you, thank you, but how am I to get up there? ' says the foreman.

' Up that green pad you see before you ', he says.

' Oh, thank you, thank you very much '.

" So he bid him good night and off he goes, up the pad (path through a grass field) to the old cabin in the flow. That was Old Lord Erin's you know.

" And man it was a lovely night. Oh, the dandiest moonlight ever you seen. Up he goes, and when he got to the cabin, here was the two goats up on the old thatched roof eating the grass off it. There was a wee window, and six panes in it, but there was glass in only one pane, for the others were out and stuffed with rubbish and rags. So he went up nice and easy and he peeped in through the good pane, and he seen the old boy sitting at the fire eating a lock of spuds: Old Lord Erin himself. He had six priddies (potatoes) in the ashes. He, the foreman, counted them! So he watched him till he ate five of them. Old Lord Erin was sitting on a big stone at the fire, and he had a grain of salt on another stone and the spuds in the ashes beside him; that's how he was eating. So he watched him, and waited till he had the fifth spud eaten and then he goes up and knocks the door.

' Come in! Come in! '

' I have a horse with me '.

' Take all in with you! '—Old Lord Erin, you know—' Take all in with you! '

" So begod he done what he was bid and he come in trailing the steed behind him and tied him up somewhere inside to the end of the *cooltyee* (in phonetics: a kitchen bed) ".

' Would you be so kind ', he says, ' as to drive a shoe for me? ' he says.

' I will, I will surely ', says Lord Erin, ' as soon as I finish these lock of priddies '.

" So he ate the last one; and he was very down-hearted ".

' You seem to be very down-hearted, sir ', says the stranger.

' I am kind of down-hearted ', says Old Lord Erin. ' I had one son ', he says, ' but he left here three weeks ago and there's neither hilt nor trace of him since. . . . Maybe in jail or dead ' he says, ' and damned the much loss. He took out me last cow ', he says, ' and sold her and cleared away to England '.

' That's too bad ', says the stranger. ' I'm very sorry to hear that '.

" So he waited till Old Lord Erin was done. And when Lord Erin was done he took up the skins of the priddies he'd ate and put them in a dish and rubbed his hands with them, and then he made his water (urinated) into the dish, and then he drove the shoe.

" He made a good job of it, and the foreman says ": ' How much have I to give you for that? '

' Oh, nothing, nothing. I never charge for driving a shoe ', he says.

' Oh, that won't do at all. Name a price '.

' Nothing now, nothing. You're a stranger ', he says, ' and sure maybe you'll be calling again '.

' Oh, you better take a something ', he says, ' for I have plenty of money '. " And he reached him ten shillings ".

' Oh, God Almighty bless you ', says the old boy, ' it wasn't my neighbour stood in need of it '.

" So he thanked him; and the foreman took out his horse and got on his back and away like hell for the boat. ' Now I have news for them. . . . Now I have news for them. . .'. On the boat and away like hell for England. And the bells all joined in ringing, because he was back with the news, because everyone knew about it. He arrived at the big house and in he goes, and the old lord was sitting back in his arm-chair ".

' Oh ', says he, ' welcome back, and what news have you? Let us have it here ', he says. ' What news? ' " And before he let him speak he took the Old Lord Erin's son and put him there— one side of the chair. He took the girl and put her there—that side. And he put the foreman another place ".

' What news? What news? '

' Splendid news, my lord ', says the foreman.

' Oh, that's great. Let us hear it '.

' Well, my lord ', he says, ' I got on the boat for Ireland with my steed as you directed ', he says. ' Arriving in Ireland I rode many roads and began to pursue my inquiries ', he says. ' I may tell you, my lord ', he says, ' that I met a very fine gentleman who directed me to Lord Erin's castle from the county road ', he says ' I rode up to this castle, my lord, and when I arrived there were two grenadiers on guard the finest ever I seen. I may tell you, my lord ', he says, ' that when approaching the castle I rode on the finest carpet ever I've trod on from the county road to the castle. Moreover ', he says, ' no money would buy it. And when I reached the castle ', he says, ' I found Lord Erin dining from a table a thousand pounds couldn't buy a leaf of it. (" That was his knee—Good, ay? "—interpolatory remark.) ' Moreover ', he says, ' he was eating by the light of a lamp and a thousand pounds wouldn't buy the wick of it (the moon). And moreover still ', he says, ' he had a pump in the house and he wouldn't sell it for love or money '.

' Oh, that's good enough. . . .'.

" And they were married ".

NOTES

This was written down by me in January, 1950, in the Glenhull area of Greencastle Parish in County Tyrone. The storyteller himself, a man of sixty-two years at the time of recording, was one of the best I've ever met; this tale is one of many that I took down from him. His name was Francis McAleer, or ' Francis Daniel ' as he was popularly known.

The tale has minor defects: there is some omission and a touch of confusion. These were inevitable since the storyteller hadn't told a tale for over thirty years until I came along: I've watched him in a kind of frustrated agony trying to remember dozens of others. So conscientious was he about his art that he wouldn't even try to tell one until he felt he had remembered it as he had learned it. This is what he told me:

".... It must be forty years since I heard that story told first by Peter John Bradley; he had a feed-all bag of stories in his head, in Irish and English: I knew no English myself till I went to school. But I learned most of my stories from James Netchy— McRory was his right name. He was a thatcher. McRory had this story as well. He heard them from Charlie Bann who was a terrible age—ninety odd—when he died. It would be all in Irish. McRory had Irish surely . . . and his house would be full at night, a low thatched house . . . but some would be playing cards. But I always took a great interest in the stories, me and a fellow named Dan McCrea; if he was alive he could tell them as well as me—but he couldn't tell them much better. For many's the time I went back to Netchy and he'd say: ' Well, have you it off now? ' And I wouldn't be far out. ' You're wrong in a word or two ', he'd say; ' you haven't that bit right '. I kept at it till I got them off be heart. . . . If only I'd known someone like you would be round for them I could have them better. . . . Lord God we never thought they were of any value at all or I'd have them all. . .".

" Old Lord Erin's Son " was, I think, the first full-length folk-tale to be recorded in Belfast by the B.B.C. The storyteller himself emigrated to England when he sold his farm in Tyrone, but returned later and died in Omagh, in September 1976 aged 87 years.

ANOTHER VERSION

In an Omeath version of the tale a girl is a servant in a " big house ". Son of the house falls in love with her. His father resents the prospect of a marriage between his son and a " hired servant girl ", but she says she has been " reared as well as any ".

Man servant sent to investigate. Girl is a daughter of a blacksmith who lives in an old thatched house with a " big puddle before the door with ducks slapping in it ". Goats graze on the roof. The blacksmith is sitting on his anvil in the forge eating " potatoes and salt out of a dish ". The man-servant returns and reports agreeably on his finds and the couple are married.

A County Cavan version is known as " Lord Benbow ".

POTEEN IN THE THATCH

FOR over an hour he sat at his turf fire telling tales of poteen and poteen-makers from his parish near the Sperrins, in Tyrone.

It was folklore really, because the illicit still—once as common as the three-legged pot of pigs' potatoes on the kitchen fire—had disappeared, been expelled in fact.

His next remark made me sit up: " Less than half a dozen yards from where you're sittin' on that furrom there's a drop of the best potyin ever run in these glens—there above your head ".

Wondering where the catch was, I looked at the thatched roof. The couples had been white-washed quarter-way up, intensifying the gloom of the rest of the roof which, in places, sagged through bramble-lathes like old earth pressing against the rods of a worn basket.

" Aw now ", he chortled as I got to my feet, " you didn't grow enough to be able to see it from the floor ". He was astride a stool himself, smoking, his back to the jamb-wall of the fireplace.

When I said I didn't believe him, he got to his feet at once, pulled a table across the floor from the wall and said: " Hop up ".

The floor was of clay, and as hillocky as a harrowed field. He steadied it as I clambered up, and then warned me to watch my head. I straightened cautiously, feeling embarrassed and foolish, and came face to face with the couple where the white-wash ended.

Beyond my nose was a world of slumber—black, silent yet alive. The breath of old thatch came dank and sooty like the tang of burnt weeds after rain. Ages of sleep seemed to cling there, and the ends of rod scollops were sticking through. It was like smelling a piece of ancient earth from underneath, roots and all.

There was no sign of any bottle.

" I've a flash ", he said, " but the guts of the old, done battery ate its way through in green champ. Strike a light, but for God's sake be more than careful. That ould roof would go off like the heart of a whin-bush in March if it got half a chance ".

I struck a match and held it low. No sign of anything but grime. I moved my hand, hoping to catch a glint, and saw the grime gather shadow and become as crinkly as the wool on a black lamb. In the weak shadows from the match the roof seemed to twitch like some weird being stirring from a stupor.

I struck a second match. Almost at once a glint winked, showing a wry eye as I moved my hand. I could see the butt of a bottle.

" That's it, bad luck to it ", he said. " That come off a run that was nabbed in Cookstown. The District Inspector of the poliss swore in the box it was the strongest stuff ever caught in Tyrone, an' the fella was fined thirty quid or three months in the Crumlin Road. He paid the fine, of course. It was in all the papers—sure thon District Inspector give him a better advertisement than Guinness or Bushmills. He'd 'a' made a wee fortune in no time if the bishop an' his reserved sin hadn't killed it. Don't! Damn your skin, do you want to send me to Derry? Don't touch that bottle. . . . Don't! Come down from that, quick! "

I was reaching for the bottle when his wild cry of alarm and rebuke came up at me. He dived for my legs at the same time: the table rocked, and I dropped the match and grabbed for the couple. Remembering the age of the roof, I let go instantly, and seemed to hang in mid-air with arms flailing madly for balance. Then my arms were around his neck as I bounced on to the table, and it almost toppled with both of us.

He pushed the table back against the wall at once. " Man alive ", he cried, " don't you know we daren't even handle potyin now in this diocese, with as much as a finger. Or let anyone else handle or harbour it either. One touch of the bottle from you and I was for Derry ".

When he calmed down, and got his breath he explained that " the reserved sin had done in a month what no ten barracks of poliss could do in a lifetime ". And while his interpretation of the episcopal decree may have been over-scrupulous, he was telling the truth.

Decreeing any sin to be " reserved " means that only the bishop of that diocese, unless by special delegation, may confess and absolve a miscreant penitent. And while a man will show pride in his bishop with genuine respect and obedience, he would tangle with a glenful of police any day rather than go face to face as a sinner before His Lordship in his episcopal See—in Derry or anywhere else.

PADDY THE PROPHET

IN South Armagh about a mile north of the hills where the border runs, is an unfinished road we know as Barra-wurrey (Bóthar Mhuire, Mary's Road). Originally, it was part of an older road which appears to have linked early eccelsiastical settlements from Carlingford Lough to at least Urney, near Forkhill, where the poet Peadar Ó Doirnín is buried.

In order to provide shorter access to the now by-passed-because-of-border station of Adavoyle, work was begun before World War I to widen and fence the road. But three-quarter ways along the first section the job ended abruptly to leave a veritable bottle-neck.

And here, since this is no political disquisition, is where Paddy Kearney from our side of Slieve Gullion, merits a word of resuscitation. (" An unlearned prophet " a Father O'Neill of Dromintee had called him when castigating that instinct which made a butt of any spirit that fell, rose or stepped outside the rough-and-tumble of conventional rural vision.)

Because even before Partition became a conjectural topic in political gossip Paddy had made this utterance:

" Ireland will never be a nation till Barra-wurrey's a county road. It'll be a border across the country ".

Tanks

I take my prophets, folk and otherwise, with a grain of respectful salt: yet I am sweetly intrigued to read that money has now been granted to the local council to complete the job of making Barra-wurrey a proper county road from end to end.

Blaeberry baskets made from rushes

Griddle, pot oven and three-legged pot

James McLeigh with flail

The fallen fairy bush.
" To cut or not to cut "

This council, incidentally, has a strong Nationalist majority. If only some wit of a Unionist would pretend alarm and try to stop the fulfilment of this job lest its completion fulfil the prophecy as well. This would be a better turn of incongruous fun that meeting Grand National winners with a brass band on the quays of Dublin.

Not that Paddy Kearney, I think, would appreciate that kind of lark. His temperament was generally morose, his best remembered characteristic a talent for political declamation. He was never egoistic about his prophecies and, in fact, never announced that he was doing anything of the kind.

" Boys, boys, keep your powder dry: there'll be war on wheels to the door—aye, an' to the bed ". This was taken to refer to the War of Independence; just as the First World War was foretold in: " They'll go in with weapons that'll be no more good than pot-sticks to what they have coming out " and was taken to predict tanks.

" Paddy might be a fool, but there'll be wise men yet ". Bare-footed, with one sleeve out of his coat as usual, and mounted on a porter barrel in the Hiring Ground of Newry, he used denounce the degradation of the hiring practice. " The Irishman in the clay-shuck to his knees and the big dog on the brow. . .". Hearing this kind of rhetoric, the hard-hatted Northmen come to pick up a servant boy or girl used respectfully pity and define him variously as " a brucken-down school-master ", or " a man that the larnin' be to go to his head ". Illiterate in English, but with a good memory and gift for paraphrase, Paddy was a native speaker of South Armagh and one of the best judges of cattle in the area. " Boys, boys beware: there'll be clumper-heads talking with two tongues. . .". South Armagh, remembering the idiomatic snap of that phrase, applied it unhappily to historical events and personalities over an unfortunate decade.

Maud Gonne

Yet one of his oratorical feats appears to contradict the basic character of much of his declamation. This happened when one of the first Sinn Fein meetings was held on the top of Slieve Gullion for the purpose, among other things, of symbol. (Séamus

L

Mac Murphy, the eighteenth-century poet and rapparee, also convened his meeting there around 1744.) Trains brought thousands from all over the country to Adavoyle; and among the speakers who climbed the famous slopes were, it is claimed, Arthur Griffith and Maud Gonne. (Maud Gonne, I know, had a special veneration for the mystic mood of Ireland's mystery mountain.)

But to detain people from making the ascent Paddy stood on the slope of Garriba along the mountain road near McGuill's, later burned down after an ambush. He talked, they said, " for near half a day " to a constantly changing audience that went on up the hill. But this delay-by-oratory was, some claimed, politically instigated.

" I'm a finger-post for everyone and I can't direct myself ".

Dozens of tales are told about Paddy's wit and power of disgruntled retort which revealed a tortured intelligence.

As stated, he was in great favour with the Dromintee curate, Father O'Neill, who had referred to him as " an unlearned prophet ". Father O'Neill knew Paddy liked a jorum of whiskey and especially on cold days when Paddy called at the Parochial House took him in, gave him a drop and a meal. He told a new second curate to treat Paddy similarly if he called in his absence.

No doubt curious about this new sagart, Paddy called one chilly day. The new priest made him welcome, took him in to the sitting-room, and then brought a bottle of whiskey from a cupboard. He filled a good " rozenor " for Paddy, corked the bottle and turned to put it back. Over his shoulder he said:

" Paddy! I forgot to ask if you take water in your whiskey? "

Paddy replies:

" I never take water in the first one, Father ".

Still quoted is his declamation at firesides or when walking the roads at night:

" Mammy jewel, I was the finest water ever washed till that bitch of a red-headed barmaid in Camlough put the blight on me ".

Love philtres, known in the vernacular as " coax-ee-lore-um ", were then taken to be fact, not to mention love charms with which the female—rarely the male—aroused an irrational love attachment by means of a ritual: this is still believed to be possible and effective even today in places!

One morning he was found dying near the house of one of the greatest-hearted women at Slieve Gullion. Her own father had taken suddenly ill during the previous night, and when Paddy's face and clawing fingers pressed in panic and agony against the room window she didn't recognize him and had bolted the door in terror.

Paddy, ghost and typical symbol in one, crawled back to the frosty roadside till strength left him . . . forlorn and dramatic as first footsteps in dawn snow.

HISTORY FROM THE MOURNES AND RAVENSDALE

COUNTY LOUTH AND COUNTY TYRONE

NARRATORS of folklore are now rightly recognized as having become historic personages themselves, though more discernible as such perhaps when talking from the category entitled " Historical Tradition ", a category embracing for instance lore on Orangeism and Ribbonism, Fenianism and agrarian secret societies, as well as the fate of refugees expelled by dispossession and pogroms dating from the seventeenth to the early nineteenth centuries.

In the latter context I particularly recall three events, one centred around Hilltown in County Down, the other in Ravensdale, County Louth. In 1944 I was sent by the Irish Folklore Commission to collect in the Mourne country generally and selected Hilltown as a starting point. I was walking: collectors with transport were using the cumbersome Ediphone but the tape recorder had not, seemingly, been invented at that time. I had never been to Hilltown before, but knew of it from tales told by hired servants, my mother and father among them. I knew no narrators in the area but had one fine and sensitive contact, the late Dr. Francis McPolin, a scholar and able schoolmaster, and a cousin of my own, John Campbell, who had been a hired boy there.

The second World War was on. Vehicles of war sped and clattered the Hilltown roads and their tank cannon shelled the mountainsides in practice. Sitting on a " summer seat "— a grassy ditch with a backing of hawthorn hedge—in the area of Stang I sometimes saw an old man staring across the road and apparently oblivious to the clamour and clatter of tanks and trucks. He did not seem to be the type who wanted to talk, but when forced by the dangerous convoys to get off the road I sat beside him. I found out then that he was blind; his name was John Murphy.

Over subsequent days we talked on the " summer seat " of the popular topics taken still to encompass the extent of all folklore—fairies, witches and ghosts, customs and so on. When I felt we had become familiar with each other and the bond of confidence established I got on to Settlement: was he native? If not where his people had come from, when and why?

No, he told me, his people were not native to the area; they had come from farther north in mid or north Armagh. They were Roman Catholics. He told of the Orange Lambeg drummers circling the house clusters at night to strike terror into the inhabitants—as such drummings were intended to do. (He told also that Roman Catholic drumming parties around Hilltown beat similar drums in defiance of local Orange factions until a priest persuaded them to stop the practice.) One morning a notice was found impaled to a door with a dagger: they were to get out. The whole community fled in a group towards the south.

John O'Neill of Bannvale had welcomed refugees from successive dispossessions. There were rumours of other similar areas where refugees were allowed to drain bogs and to reclaim mountainsides of whin, heather and boulder and begin life again. But outside Newry the refugees, the old man said, split into two groups: one went to the Mourne country around Hilltown, the other to South Armagh, whichever found the better sites for settlement would inform the other. They arrived in almost identical terrains and stayed. When John Murphy ran off family names of the Hilltown group he might have been reading from the parochial Dues List of my own parish of Drumintee at the foot of Slieve Gullion in South Armagh.

He asked, of course, where I had come from and noted my accent. When I told him he said he had been once to Dromintee many years previous to attend the funeral of a man named Pat Jordan whose sister Susan was married to " a far-out friend of theirs ". He had been telling me about my own grandfather, Oiney Murphy of Dromintee, and his wife Susan, my grandmother, who lived to be 103 years of age. I had been talking all the time to a kinsman. My father confirmed what John had told me.

The event in Ravensdale, County Louth, had a significance of a different kind. My great informant in Annaverna was the late James Loughran. His turf supply used to come from the top of the mountain which rose behind his house. James told how the turf had to be hauled down, not in sacks carried on one's back as we had had to do at Slieve Gullion, but in home-made rough linen sacks slung across the backs of donkeys or ponies on " pannels ". I associated the word " pannel " with a door panel and was completely flummoxed. He began to explain that the " pannel " was an article made of straw or hay, much in the shape of a horse's collar, and which sat on the animal's back; it obviated a heavy sack chafing the flanks of the donkey or pony and prevented the sack from falling off at the same time. From inaccessible houses, pork for the Dundalk and Newry markets used to be hauled down to the main road. That was in 1961. " Pannels " ceased to be used about sixty years previously. He explained the manufacture of the article but I couldn't envisage it and its position on the animal's back. He then said he would try to make a specimen for me, but from hay. I was greatly excited.

Dr. A. T. Lucas, then Director of The National Museum, was equally enthusiastic about acquiring the specimen. (Since 1942 I had been collecting articles of material folk culture ranging from simple rope twisters to slide-cars of Antrim and Tyrone and the huge Lough Erne cotts from Fermanagh: all, I deeply regret to state to my personal chagrin and our national shame removed from Kilmainham Old Hospital, the projected site of the National Folk Museum, to be dumped in a derelict boys' reformatory in the midlands. Only those articles of similar specimen in The

Ulster Folk Museum at Cultra are safely housed and on display. Kilmainham is to be diverted to a site for an EEC apartment and office block!)

James Loughran duly made the " pannel " and it reached the National Museum. In the *Louth Archæological Journal* of 1961 Dr. Lucas wrote an account of how welcome it was and called his paper: " A Hay-rope Pack-saddle from County Louth ". After a detailed description with meticulous measurement and the art of structure he went on:

" The local name for the saddle is ' pannel '. The only other Irish context at present known to the writer in which this word occurs is a passage in *The Montgomery Manuscripts*, describing the triumphant return of Con O'Neill, Chief of Clandeboye, to The Ards, County Down, in 1605, after having obtained a pardon for himself and his followers for ' all their crimes and trespass against the law . . . and then returned home in triumph over his enemies (who thought to have his life and estate) and was met by his friends, tenants and followers, the most of them on foot, the better part had gerrans, some had pannels for saddles (we call them back bughams) and the greater part of the riders without '."

Following a discussion of the etymology of the term " back bugham " Dr. Lucas goes on:

" We are therefore thrown back on the bare facts of the original text: that Montgomery at the turn of the seventeenth century knew that some, to him, unorthodox form of a saddle was called a ' pannel '. . . . As the word is, obviously, not of Gaelic origin, we must turn to British sources to discover that. We find it was a ' soft saddle ', a ' pad with a ridge before and behind for carrying calves ' and ' a pad fitted with ridges and used by millers for loading their sacks of corn and meal on a horse's back. .' And coal miners, too, their sacks of coal: the word and the article itself had a wide distribution extending from Scotland to Devon.

When James Loughran's second " pannel " for the Ulster Folk Museum became news he was requested by curators of English county Museums to make specimens for their own display. This interest amazed and puzzled James himself who, nevertheless, spent a busy and lucrative winter making " pannels " for them.

With the " pannel " made by James Loughran I always couple in my mind another truly unique piece of craftsmanship made by the late Patrick McCullagh of Curraghinalt, Rousky parish near Glenhull in County Tyrone. Known popularly as Padraic Phelimy Láidir—which means " strong "—he was seventy-eight when he died, and I first met him in our cottage in Glenhull in 1950. He was a native Gaelic speaker, a farmer as well as a craftsman—blacksmith, cooper, carpenter, harness-maker, shoe- and spade-maker of the traditional types, brush-maker—and famed poteen-maker. His memorable piece of craftsmanship, how- ever, is the rush woven saddle and ploughing harness he called " tuigh Mhuire " now housed in the National Museum Folk Life Section and in the Ulster Folk Museum at Cultra in County Down.

Rush-plaiting and weaving is one of the oldest crafts known throughout Europe, now almost vanished and the knowledge lost. Patrick McCullagh was, as far as is known, the only man in Ireland who could make the complete sets of harness out of rushes. So unique indeed was this beautiful piece of delicate craftsmanship that when The British Association for the Advancement of Science met in Dublin in 1957 McCullagh's harness was proudly exhibited by the Folk Life Section of The National Museum of Ireland.

Like James Loughran of Annaverna in Ravensdale, McCullagh kept the old knowledge and crafts alive—not only in the head, but in the hands as well.

LONG NIGHT IN THE SPIKE

This is a folktale which I first heard as a young teenager around a fireside in Dromintee in South Armagh. At the time I took it to be a narration of fact—until I heard another storyteller tell it also as fact! The real fact is that it is the type of tale storytellers told as personal experience. The version I give was, however, told by a man, a bachelor, whom we all knew had been, among other things, a tramp navvy in England and has stayed in English workhouses, then known as " Spikes ".

" Somewhere in England I have a son an' he's not a drops blood to me. There's not a word o' lie in what I'm goin' to tell yous. It's all down in black an' white in England wherever they keep these things written down: about me an' me son I mean.

" It was somewhere near the south of England. I was on a navvyin' job an' when it wound up I was footin' it on Shanks's mare. An' comin' on night I headed for the Spike in this town, a town something the size of Newry here. Talk about rain! The heavens opened in the evenin' an' it come down in lumps. Not a dry stitch on me when I got to the foot of the hill leadin' to the Spike on the edge of this town. It was around this time o' year too, at the fall of the leaf. Poor shelter. But wet as I was there come this unmerciful cloudburst an' I had to find what shelter I could under a tree.

" Not a sinner to be seen. I was wet; I was cold; I was wall-fallin' with hunger. An' then, in the light of the street lamp— all gas-lamps then—I seen this woman. In thon rain the light was little better than a moon behind mist. But I could see she was a tight butt of a woman with a bit of body about her: in a coat and a big hat. She was as wet as meself an' she stood in under the tree too.

" ' It's a rum ole night ', she says; an English woman. Around thirty or so, the same age as meself at the time. Then she says to me: ' Are you for the Spike ? '

" I said I was, and the way she asked I knew she was headin' there herself.

" Next she says: ' Ever been in this Spike before, chum ? '

" I said I never had, not tellin' a word o' lie, and she says: ' It's not a bad one for the married blokes. When they've got the missus with them that is '.

" That wasn't news to me either. Spikes is good or bad— accordin' to who runs them an' to their rules. Rules in Spikes ? Aw, bedad they have rules all right, as you'll soon hear.

" The rain eased up a bit ah' the two of us set off up the hill to the Spike. She walked foot for foot with me, right off the road an' up the avenue. Then she says:

' Tell you what, chum. What's wrong with you sayin' I'm your better half—your missus, you know. It'll mean better grub an' a better doss for the night for both of us. Watcha say ? '

" Well, it was six of one an' half a dozen of the other to me. I'd be on me way in the mornin' an' so would she. So I said: ' Fair enough '. She asked me me name an' I told her: Shan McAlavey.

" There was a porter to let you in. He was asleep when we got there an' had half a mind not to let us in at all. Many a long, weary hour after I wished he hadn't. But the English woman tongued him word for word an' he got out the book an' took down our names. The two of us trooped on into the body of the house. And we weren't our lone let me tell you. There was a good fire an' they gave us porridge to ate; the sort that'd run a mile on a deal board an' never leave a trace of the oatmeal. But we lapped it up an' damn glad to get it.

" I dried meself as best I could. Then she went her way to her quarters an' me to mine. I rolled into bed an' slept as snug as a bug in a rug till mornin'. Oh, a lovely bright sunny mornin' after a night of rain. Got up. Got a bite o' breakfast. Had a bit of a smoke. Stretched meself to get the life back into me bones, an' then I set off for out an' away.

" I only got as far as the door when this man stopped me; a sort of a workhouse master's-under-strapper, a big bruiser; the sort that looked as if he got his fill to ate, an' his time to take it.
' Goin' somewhere? ' says he.

" I said: ' Nowhere in particular '. I'd make up me mind as I went along.

' Come here, Jack ', says he, and caught hold of me like a polissman. Me name, as you know, is Shan, not Jack; but when you have your hand in the dog's mouth the easiest way you get it out the better. He pointed to the rules hangin' on the wall. An' sure I told him that I couldn't read—an' to put me foot further in it, I told him 'twas the wife was the scholar in our family.

" So he said he'd read the rules for me. An' he did. The husband had to stay an' work a month hard for every week his wife stayed in the Spike. (Rules of the house.) I began to smell a rat, but thought it better to act the greenhorn, the innocent fella that knows nothin'. An' says I to him:

" ' You're a decent man, an I can tell you come of clean an' decent people, an' isn't it you that has the learnin'. Tell her ', says I, ' to follow me. I'll walk easy '.

" Says this big bruiser: ' You're not walkin' anywhere, Jack. Not for a while anyhow. Your missus ain't walkin' either. What sort of a bloomin' man are you? Didn't you know? Your wife gave birth to a baby boy last night an' she'll be weeks here '.

" You coulda knocked me down with a feather. I felt as weak as water. I lost me breath. When I got it back I started in me own mind to call her all the oul'. . . . . All right, all right, I'll not say it before you good decent people. (Maybe she's dead now anyhow an' needs prayers instead.) But I says to meself: ' May the divil roast her, an' double-roast me for lettin' her trap me. Her lyin' up here an' livin' on the fat o' the land for three weeks or a month, an' me havin' to slave for her, workin' a month again every week she's here. But take it easy, McAlavey ', says I to meself; ' nothin's bad that couldn't be worse. You're not bet yet '.

" The workhouse master's-under-strapper was turnin' over the book, an' he says to me: ' No occupation down here, what are you? '

" Says I nice an' innocent: ' I'm a melodeon musicianer, sir. It's the only trade I was taught to follow '.

" He looked at me as much as to say, ' You're a liar '—an' he was right—an' he closed the book an' threw it down an' took me like a warder be the arm.

" ' Right, Jack ', says he. ' Melodeon musicianer '.

" He led me out of the Spike into a big yard alongside the avenue. There was a few fellows there breakin' stones for the roads. He led me to a heap of rocks, every one the size of a table. He pointed to a sledge-hammer with a head on it bigger than many a railway waggon I've seen. And then says he to me:

" ' There's the rock an' there's the sledge. Melodeon musicianer are you? Take whatever sort of music you like out of them rocks! '

" I failed away to scrapin's in them three weeks, for I was out there hail, rain, blow or snow, breakin' the rocks. An' not a sign of thon targer of a woman of mine makin' a shape to leave the Spike. But this mornin'—here she comes, an' this child in her arms, an' the pair of them dickied up to the ninety-nines. An' I could see I'd have to work extra to pay for the fancy rig-out for the baby an' her too. You wouldn't get the time o' day for nothin' in thon Spike. Over three months I'd have to stay sledgin' the stones. I got as mad as forty cats in a bag. But I says to meself: ' I won't gratify her to let on I know her at all '. An' I started to make the sledge ring on the rocks, thinkin' she'd pass by an' wouldn't see me. But she seen me all right. When she comes abreast of where I was what does the flamer do? She holds the baby the length of her two arms an' she says:

" ' Say toodle-oo to Daddy, son! ' To a babby that couldn't talk mind you. Oh, a flamer! ' Say toodle-oo to Daddy '.

" What did I do? Sure what could I do? I could be unmannerly an' say nothin', but that'd be far off the way I was reared. An' sure it never made sense to bite your tongue for spite when you've scalded yourself drinkin' soup. So I held up me sledge like a decent Daddy should an' I shook it at them an' says I: ' Toodle-oo, son. . . . Toodle-oo! ' "

THE WIDOW'S SON

IT is now illegal to slaughter pigs for sale as pork on the farm, so that accounts of the job and the personalities of butchers and helpers will soon be folklore.

Anecdotes abounded and you heard them at every pig-killing.

" What was pork going in Newry on Thursday? " the resigned father might ask the wayward son arriving home on the following Monday.

To which the son replied: " It was going up and down the street in the farmers' carts ". He had squandered the proceeds of the sale.

His " failing "

One South Armagh tale was of the owner of two pigs, an old woman, who lived with her hard-working son. Unfortunately he had " the good man's failing ", and there was the constant dread that he might re-enact the sorry result of the story of the resigned father and son. A jovial, active, good-natured fellow who " couldn't thole to be idle ".

The day to slaughter the pigs was approaching; and it was thought advisable that if a way could be devised to remove the tempted from temptation, it should be followed.

It was the time of year when the " country was making hay ". It was also the era when squads of local men, organized usually under a leader, went to the hiring fair in Kendal and other northern English towns to work " at the hay ".

" Big money "

They were hired for a month's work and were paid the full amount if the squad completed the job in over two weeks, which they often did.

Only the known hard workers were taken in a squad, men who could maintain the pace and the clammy heat of green hay being piled into the sheds. And so it was suggested to the old woman that she should allow someone to induce her son to " go to the hay ". Meanwhile, the pigs would be slaughtered and sold and all would be well.

The plan worked. Glad of the chance to earn wages then referred to as " big money ", the son set off for the Newry boat on the appointed day, one of a small squad. The mother, in fact, went with him in the ass and cart.

Farewells

There was some pre-voyage celebration, according to custom; tearful farewells were taken, with admonitions from the women to all of them to " watch yourselves an' not be actin' the kalthera when you get the bit o' money ".

The squad boarded the *Iveagh* in Newry, and while she cast off and sailed down the Canal towards Carlingford Lough and the Irish Sea route to Liverpool, the mother set off for home to the Slieve Gullion country in South Armagh.

It is a long drag of a hill out of Newry, and an ass and cart made slow progress and the mother had a neighbour woman with her. Hay harvest money was a boon to the economy of those days, and they speculated hopefully.

On went the slow cart over the hill at the top of Cloghogue, along the road by the bog known then as " The Rotten Rocks ", through the village of Meigh to skirt the foot of Slieve Gullion and the ridge of Garriba, finest example of a glacial tail to be seen anywhere. The evening was bright and people were working at the hay in the fields.

There was even someone working at the hay in the mother's bottom field, next to the bog. Both noticed him, but couldn't tell who he was.

" Only I know our fella's on the salt water for England I'd swear thon was him ", said the mother.

The *Iveagh* by then was beyond the Carlingford Bar. But at Fathom Locks the son, it seemed, had remembered the pigs, ready for slaughter the following day. So, as the vessel dropped in the water being lowered to sea-level he simply stepped ashore, walked up the hills and over the country of Clontigora and Killeen, and was at home and working at the hay when the ass cart arrived from Newry.

CHARLIE GETS HIS OWN BACK

CHARLIE had bought her in Dundalk Fair, and the night he brought her home the neighbours called, as was customary, to wish him luck of the mare.

When Old Ned came on his stick he made them hold up the hurricane lamp in the stable while he had someone pull on her tail. Next he went to her head, and with the lamp held close, felt her ears and lifted her eyelid.

He said nothing till he was back at the stable door: " You know the art she come from, I suppose? "

The silence was more chilling than the early spring frost outside the open door. Then Charlie whispered apprehensively, " It's not so bad as all that surely, Ned? "

Ned twisted around his stick, draping himself in half-lights that kept changing places with shadows. " You leave her somewhere then where she'll be easy to handle in the mornin'. She's dosed ".

And dosed or drugged (Ned could do it himself with herbs) she was " a plaster " as South Armagh vernacular put it. Next morning, it seemed, she could have kicked you at the fireside from the other end of a wee field and then come and bitten for good measure.

Noted Dealers

Charlie's brother-in-law, Micky, an uncle of mine, was then buying horses for an agent in England. He had sub-agents himself, and among them was one of a noted family of horse dealers in equally famous Crossmaglen.

Charlie didn't know the seller's name (as if that would have helped anyhow) but " by the talk " of the man he believed he was from the area of Crossmaglen. Micky had an idea.

A back-to-back trap, with the kicking mare behind on the long rein, left that evening with Charlie and Micky among the full load: the threat of combined action was the last hope in those days of retrieving the price of " a plaster " of a mare.

It was dark when they reached Crossmaglen, where a horse on the long rein has a significant plod of its own to a horse dealer. They had hardly stopped when a man came out, belligerent-like, till Micky called: " Is that you, Jack? "

Jack hailed him like a brother. " What brings youse here at this hour of night? " He peered this way and that through the shadow till he had seen the kicking mare. " Aw . . . So that's what it is! "

" Do you know her? " Charlie asked hopefully. " Howl on till I get an oul' top-coat ". When he rejoined them one man had transferred to the back to make room for him as pilot and he now carried an ash-plant.

" It's a lock of miles away in Monaghan ", he said, and the trap set off again.

Uncle's Verdict

As another uncle of mine, who had transferred to the back, said wryly: " It's not what you know but who you know, always was an' always will be . . . secula seculorum ".

Some time later the trap stopped quietly near a two-storied house which was in complete quiet and darkness.

Soon candlelight fluttered dimly in the windows, the front door opened and they swarmed in. The incoherent jumble of interrupting voices, fired by a courage that had replaced the previous doubts, ended when the man went to a jug on the dresser.

He took out notes and counted to them the price of the mare; the last pound was in silver and ten shillings short. He had given Charlie a luck-penny of five shillings and was now taking one of his own.

" Never you mind your luck-penny ", Jack cut in. " Douse down on that table the full price of the mare to this man here. Or do you see that ash-plant? I'll stretch the weight of it with interest across the broad of your back. Come on. We haven't all night ".

But no horse dealer was ever the sort to let his bone go with the dog, and he kept the luck-penny after all. In similar circumstances Jack would have done the same.

KATCHY THE " BOX "-PLAYER

EVERY fine Saturday morning four or five of us would race down the pad to his felted cabin. If two, or more, arrived simultaneously there was usually a mêlée as to who would lift the door off its hinges; if the bolt was on inside the door was shaken till wood in dry rot powdered out of an expanding hole like yellow meal out of a bursting bag.

" Katchy! It's all hours o' the day! "

The light would fall in ahead on the spittle-stained floor, crusted by clay carried in on boots till it was as humpy as a cobbler's rasp. The grate was always " black out ", cold as a November dawn, with charred cigar-end butts of whin grooving the cocoa-ash of bog-fir.

And we always found Katchy himself asleep in the settle-bed. We would stand over him, chuckling as his eyes twitched under the amber light. Black wire hair on his chest under the grey flannel shirt reminded one of horse-hair carelessly wrapped in cloth in a ragman's store. Hair grew on his head like a hay-stack which has been pulled into the design of a mushroom. His features were shy somehow, heavy, greasy-looking between the ham-seams running from eyes to chin; and he had firm, fat lips which seemed to have taken a set while lapping around the short stump of his clay pipe. He was about forty.

" Holy smoke! Wha' time o' day is it, boys? "

" Half-ten! It's a powerful day! "

" We're goin' for sticks ".

" Will I put on the scobbler? "

" *I'll* put it on! "

" Aye. Do, boys. Throw a grain o' tay on it ". Katchy would then wipe the grimace on his face, one lip would wet the other, and he would sit up, wriggling his shoulders.

We would light the fire from whins dumped in the corner above the settle-bed, cheering as the creamy-green booze floated up. Katchy would smile shyly. Water was poured so rashly into the scobbler—a soot-caulked tin—that it slopped over on to the floor, and it was pressed into the blaze among the smoke. Katchy would take his pipe from the earthen floor beside the settle-bed; several crackling whins were held to him, and we always hoped to see his hair and eye-lashes singe as he puffed. Like a rock figure coming to life, he would watch us while he smoked.

Someone would bound on to the form and take down the melodeon from the top of the rheumatic dresser.

" Aw, holy smoke, boys, there's a kay gone in it! Aisy, boys; which o' yous has a safety-pin? " He used safety-pins for improvised springs in " the box ", but usually stuck them in the top of the settle-bed, seldom delighting us with the operation of revealing the intestines of the melodeon. Instead, he would play a lively tune; and Katchy *could* play. In the middle of the tune he would stop.

" There's a cackler's pill in the drawer o' the dhresser, boys. Throw it on whin the tay's boilt ". His speech was throaty and

Horse harness which includes Bridle, Collar, Backband and Traces

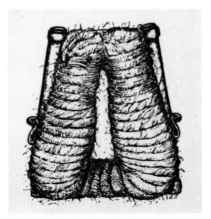

Ox Collar from Julianstown

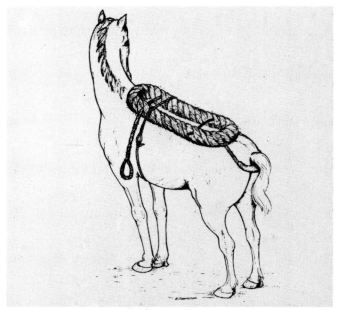

Back Sugan

Rush saddle from Curraghinalt

seemed to roll like smoke in his mouth before droning out, as from a cistern. " I hope t' God the boys didn't brek it last night. Look in the bleddy drawer an' see ". And, sometimes, we would find the egg broken in the drawer.

On wet Saturday mornings we did not give him breakfast in bed; for we could not go to the mountains for " sticks " or foliage-burned whins, *spadtha*, he called them, and we used to laugh. He would help us break and gather our loads, crashing the tinder sticks with his boots, and picking them up in armfuls, whereas we broke them one at a time. He showed us how to tighten and tie our loads, and would lift them on us; and our admiration was plain, if silent, as he lifted his own load from the ground, over his head and on to his shoulders. We used to boast that Katchy could carry "a donkey's load ".

Some fine Saturday mornings, however, we would lift off the door and find the settle-bed empty, and our spirits would turn as cold as the fire-grate. He would be away working in one of the houses. Sunshine had not the power of wine on such days; the scene of orange-flecked whin blossoms did not remind one, strangely, of a blackbird's or thrush's next. We would not sit on a warm rock, our chins on our knees, and plan to tramp—not walk—on the 17th of May to the big horse fair in Dundalk, which smoked six miles below us like bacon on a pan.

To counteract such depressing days, we invariably went to his cabin early in the evening and lit the fire. Katchy's was a famous *céili* house. Except on " courting nights ", or when there was a wake in the neighbourhood, boys, youths and men crowded into the kitchen.

The table was set in the middle of the floor for card-playing. Youths tossed halfpennies in the space vacated by the table, using a candle; sometimes a two-headed halfpenny came to light and the squabble started. A man held the space between the dresser and the door to conduct an original game of his own known as " pitch to the bowl ". He gave odds of four to one; and one had to pitch a penny into the bowl, and make it stay there to win, but the glossy sides usually let the penny slip out.

Katchy himself, when he was in humour, ran a " Put and Take " spindle on a half plate while sitting on the hob under the hole in the wall, where he could leave and find his pipe. One had usually to shout to make oneself heard.

"Hun tun! Hi, boys! Stump up to the bleddy kitty—the oil's runnin' out!" Though lamps and globes were too fragile for the atmosphere, a contraption known as a "phizoon" was used; it consisted of a twopenny ink bottle, oil, and a bit of tin wound round a rag for a burner or wick.

"Hi! Holy smoke! Do I have to spake again? The bleddy oil's runnin' out!" He would shout this above a squabble from the card-table, screechings in the corner from gamblers on one knee, and the commentary of the man running "four to one in the bowl".

"Stump up to the kitty, boys. One o' the gassuns'll run for oil". A card player would begin the kitty by tossing a penny on the table.

Katchy had spun the spindle, and the upturned side read: "Put four". He always reached for his pipe after losing. "Someone be to die in this corner since I was here last. I say, boys! Less o' the noise! Who's takin' up the kitty?"

When a squabble appeared like developing into a serious battle. Katchy tore down a roof-board and took out a small revolver, and order was restored. The people always said that "bad luck would shine on the house while a roof was on it".

Still, Katchy was a pacific man. One time a friend stayed with him. He had caught a rabbit, which he gave to Katchy to cook, while he went to bed. Katchy went out for a loaf, and a local playboy took out the rabbit and replaced it with a stone off the ditch. Katchy returned, and went to jab the rabbit with a fork; it snapped in two, one half doing a somesault over the hearth.

"Holy smoke! It's Mixie Arch's witch ye caught!" And wheeling round: "Or was Big Jack here?"

He took all their tricks and pranks in a resigned, cowering way. At dances in houses, too, no one could coax or drag him and the melodeon from the draughty shadows of the doorways, where he played while sitting on his hunkers.

On summer evenings dancers gathered at "the head of the road"; those were days when the sound of a motor lorry sent everyone scurrying like rabbits. On one hasty occasion Katchy had to toss his " box " over the ditch before running; and while jooking behind a hedge as the lorries went by he said: " Holy smoke, boys—yon brucken (broken) kay was playin' *The Soldier's Song* an' me lavin' it! "

They swear it is true that a man made two trips to his house one harvest to get him to tie corn. He made the third trip at dinner-time and found Katchy sitting in the settle-bed playing the " box ".

" Why, damn yer sowl, I thought yeh said you'd be down ".

" Aw, holy smoke, Micky—houl' on an' I'll be with yeh! I got on a bleddy tune there an' I couldn't get aff it ".

Someone set fire to the house after he left; the door, off its hinges, hung on the chain-lock. It was our parable: we were shown how bad luck follows the card-houses. Still, we could not understand why old women's tongues clattered about him.

The lads (" gasuns ", as he would say) broke up his settle-bed, his table and dresser, and burned it in the grate under the gaping sky for that primitive thrill of fire and tumbling smoke. Then they began to gouge the stones from the walls.

I last saw him outside an " Irish Hall " in Liverpool, with a melodeon under his oxter.

LOAN OF A SCYTHE

A WEE little over fifty years ago (not counting some of the time I went barefooted) I had the neck of the devil. I must have had: I even asked a neighbour in Balinamadda at Slieve Gullion for the loan of his scythe.

In those days—perhaps in these—a decent mower would sooner lend his good Sunday trousers to you to dam flax rather than see strange fingers handle his scythe. I didn't know that at the time.

For a scythe is part of a good mower's personality, more an expression than an extension of his arms and being in harvest.

He would take it to bed, instead of hanging it in a bush, if it weren't so dangerous, just as he might a cornaptious offspring, if he had one.

To Measure

A mower, understand, had to be measured for his scythe more elaborately than for a new suit.

I had heard that but didn't believe it. The year before I had mown part of the bog with my uncle's scythe.

The blade was worn to the design of an old pen-knife, and was due to break anyhow. Now we had not only the bog to cowp but a long garden of oats already ripening fast; and I had no scythe. Every neighbour had a scythe and Jack was amongst them.

Instinct tutored by the asides of hearth-stone talk must have sent me to Jack. No one, I recall old women saying, had ever heard his wrong word, even heard him talk above his breath, except the evening he had finished changing the window to where the door used to be and vice versa.

On the dresser the cat had got its head in a milk jug. Startled by the rattle of our boots and the fling of a cap it fled and leapt for the light above where the half-door used to be. Even then Jack was more annoyed by the laughter of one particular céilíer than by the crash of the new window pane outside.

Cross Dog

He would oblige you with the shirt off his back, too. Even when he couldn't he had a *rann* of an excuse that left you with entirely different thoughts and you forgot what you had asked him to do.

He was an amiable man who seemed to find the world or its people quietly amusing. Strangely, he kept a cross dog. Thinking of that dog and his *ranns* and his scythe, I wonder, now, if he weren't something of a sardonic philosopher who really knew how to handle temperament and to apportion obligement; for isn't it wiser now and then, unfortunately, to be able to regale with interesting excuse rather than oblige obediently too often?

I knew none of that when I went for his scythe and wouldn't have believed it if I had. His dog, as usual, made circles round my flailing stick, and Jack came out, making mock grabs for a stone till the beast twirled into its barrel, growled a few times, yawned, and then rested its greying nose on its paws, only rolling the white of its eyes now and then to make sure I wouldn't take off without pursuit.

Off to Mow

Jack had the wooden pipe in his mouth. Even when he talked he held it in his teeth where it made an intriguing tattoo but never slipped, though ash danced for ever out of the bowl.

I told him I was going to mow. I now realize he was a shrewd observer of life, at least among small angular fields; for he never talked of banal things like the weather, except by accident.

Always the focal point was positive, as on that evening, when he satirized the work a reaper had done and taken all day to do it. Next there was a new, red-leaded gate to comment upon, a tethered cow, the idiocy of a boy sent to peg stones into oats to chase hens.

" They'll catch the scythe-blade an' leave heads ", he said, and shot out quickly: " Of course a good rake— "

But I had seized my chance to mention the scythe, his scythe.

Expression imperturbed, voice seeming to noise a gentle chuckle deep down, he says: " Well, well, the scythe you want ". I said it was. He put his hands under the tail of his coat and clasped them.

Rann

" I had a mind to use a new blade the year—I saw a good blade; well, they looked good anyway, though you never can tell till you break them in. They're in that shop in Newry. Maybe you wouldn't know it, though. It's just up from the Canal in . . . in. . . . Oh, what's the name of that street now. . . . It doesn't matter anyhow ".

" It's a good house for hardware anyhow, always was. Course these places change hands. That field of Campbell's is stookin' well. . . . Anyway, what was I saying? "

I said I wanted the scythe and he half turned towards the bush.

" It's a fellow from Mullabawn has that hardware shop now. I think I know him. I mean his people come from Mullabawn; from that townland. . . . Oh, what's this they call it? "

He did it much better than I can remember it, and went on talking even though there was no scythe in the bush. He looked hard. Now, who would have taken the scythe?

The Scythe

He went over several possibles, and before I had known it he was talking of rakes. American rakes lighter than the Irish ones, but costly. He took me into the barn to show me the new one. There, in the couple, hung the scythe.

I pointed it out after his eyes seemed to have missed it. Well, well, so it was. He took it down. And then and then he measured me. Elbow to the point of the shed, my fingers fell short of the first hand-grip. Arm's length short of the next. My foot-swing to the blade-point was over an inch out.

He assured me it would murder me to mow with the thing, and confirmed it by a final measurement across my shoulders with the scythe upended as if for sharpening.

Lock of Days

He said I could have it in a lock of days if he were finished . . . but I doubt if I heard him. All the onomatopœic gigglings, laments and snappings from the quiet dusk airs of scythe-blades being sharpened, came to my mind with a voice no longer born of a whet-stone rasping steel.

Going away it was his dog hurtling over the wall that dispelled the mesmerism. I could run and leap then and, anyhow, the dog never went further than the bog pad. Going over the bog the mesmerism returned; and it stayed long after the day my Uncle Peter mowed the rushes and the garden of oats as well.

I WOULD NOT WEAR THAT MEXICAN SOMBRERO

THE young fellow mowing the overgrown lawn and wearing a big straw hat wasn't a very good mower.

But neither was I when I wore a Mexican sombrero as wide as a stook of oats and with a crown sheaf-high in all colours of the rainbow. I wore it one scorching hot day at the foot of Slieve Gullion in South Armagh.

My old school-master, having retired, went off for a trip to America, and when he returned I was asked to help in the mowing of his field of hay. But the mower didn't turn up and the scythe was left to me to handle alongside my old master.

I would have given my shirt to be miles away, for I was still young enough to feel somewhat under his thumb. I knew, too, he had written me off as perhaps the worst of those " scholars " who had disappointed him, even if he now felt he was partly to blame himself.

Whatever the real cause, I think he really gave me up on the day he told me I was " a born rebel from the toe-nails up, same as your father who threw the slate at Mr. Larkin and hit the school clock instead ". On that day my intention was to use an ink-well as a missile, for his tauntings goaded me.

Now I know he was a good master, one of the best, in fact. But I doubted if I could please him with my mowing. We used to dream those days of reaching a time when, as the vernacular put it, we would be " fit to cowp an Irish acre a day with a scythe ", even go one better and mow five Irish roods. I was not within a beagle's growl of that class.

I began to blame his old scythe; he said it was not his scythe. Next I complained that it wasn't " set " for me as a scythe should be set; he told me to go to a forge and get the smith to adjust the hand-grips and tilting of the blade. Only then did I realize, with even more embarrassment, that the master was deferring to me and not I to him.

I just mowed on and not one word of complaint did he utter when he tossed out my swarths and found the teeth of his rake trapped and tugged by the " horse-jumps " my crude skill had left underneath.

Suddenly he noticed that I was hatless. No hat . . . in this heat. Far too dangerous. I must come and rest. . . . At least then put on a hat.

I told him bluntly that I didn't own a hat, which was as true then as it is now; I wear a cap. He must have thought I was being stubborn and defiant again, I said to myself, as I watched him get up at once and go in the house. I mowed on.

When he came out it was the Mexican sombrero caught my eye like sudden lightning in fancy reflected colours. It didn't look quite decent; I was sure he was carrying an armful of female remnants such as women used to love to toss up in a sunlit examination on stalls in Newry market. When he told me what it was I couldn't believe it, a real sombrero. He told me where he had got it, too, in the cowboy country.

But when he asked me to put it on I reared. He appealed, remonstrated, called out family reinforcements, but I still refused to put the thing on my head. I could imagaine every hedge-hole and gap filled with faces of buckoes who would rejoice to see me inside that hat.

In the end I put it on to please him and felt I was in a tent of gaudy moss. Then I lifted it off, and said the brim was far too wide, the crown too high; I left it aside as if it were a coiled, sleeping snake and went back to my mowing.

Not a word was said and I saw him pick up the sombrero and go into the house. When he returned it was simply a hat; he had cut about a foot off the brim all round. A strange alarm over such butchery came over me. I looked at the shorn sombrero and then at the master.

What he saw in my face—or thought he saw—I don't know. He was turning the hat round in his hands. He knew I would still refuse to wear it, so he didn't ask me to try. He gave me a despairing glance, dropped the sombrero to the grass and sat in the shade.

I'd forgotten the sombrero till the day I saw the young man in the big straw hat trying to mow the lawn.

A VILLAGE BY CARLINGFORD LOUGH

THE man from Belfast spoke of nothing but Rostrevor. The man from above Rostrevor talked of the Cooley hills across the Lough; while the people of Rostrevor itself spoke of the latest beaten favourites, lamented the days of the Scots visitors and the lack of any attractions in the village which might entice others.

Perhaps they rightly feel that their aloof village needs no self-commendation. As everyone knows, it lies about two miles from the famous Point, tucked under a towering cone of the Mournes, and happily by-passed by the main coast road to Kilkeel. It might be a village with a secret; and maybe the aloof grandeur of the Mournes has cast some of the watching loveliness among the minds of its people. For it was May when I was there, with summer blushing in the rising blossom of youth. The showers fell as soft as an infant's kiss, and when the light broke at evening, a million mirrors tossed on Carlingford Lough, and the peak over the houses appeared in the sheen of newly garbed heather and the cloak of forestry.

And running out on the way to Kilkeel, the road skirts the shore, where the surf played at hobby-horses, before tunnelling the trees which grow down to the water—a promenade as real as Nature intended.

It was here I met the Belfastman and his book, young and garbed for holiday. Paradoxical as it may seem to many, there are few peoples more sociable than your Belfastman. He loves to talk. He has the true instinct of communal friendship. It's just a pity that, now and then, he puts it in a strait-jacket and ties a tin can to its tail.

The Lough was brilliant just then. The light had splintered on the waters again, and low clouds left their anchorage on the Cooley hills to sail for Mourne. (What a mystical depth is in the sound of Mourne, to suggest hidden valleys and abandoned light . . . to glow on the relics of an old culture.)

The Belfastman and I were sounding the nature of each other's outlook while our eyes roamed the cabins squatting on the far hills like gulls after a dip. A fisherman below baled water from his boat with a tin. Now and then a lorry whirled by the road above us. Then quiet—the capering waves, the crigging of the boatman's tin, a footstep and, undisturbed, bird song ringing among the trees as if through echoing halls aired by the sea breeze. The purest artist in creation, the bird sings to please no man's vanity, but to express its own delight.

He loved the patriarchal quiet of Rostrevor, did this young Belfastman. He loved its people and their homeliness. If ever he won a sweep he'd build a house and live here, he said—and wouldn't I? And when I said not, he was word lonely. It is no gentle majesty that flings itself from the steeple-thrust of the Mourne peaks; the spirit cannot rest in its grandeur. Here is a beauty who must not be embraced, only renewed, lest the spirit tire of chasing the thrill of a regal loneliness; and in its frustration toss thought and fancy through the ribbons of the setting suns entwined in heather, in gorse of rocky peaks, or plaited in the wood-girt waters of Carlingford Lough.

Se we didn't agree. But we did agree that Mr. de Valera's courageous re-statement of the morality of international rights and the realistic sovereignty of small nations, had echoed like a cheer in the dawn through every parish in the land. And was it so strange that we should talk of this, and forget that out among the glittering waters ran the edge of an anæsthetic with which the political surgeons—in a so-called temporary operation—had atrophied the limb of a nation . . . while wardsmen deluded themselves they could keep it permanent and healthy at the same time.

It was then I recalled what had been said by the man above Rostrevor, the man whose eyes were on the Cooley hills. The Belfastman was telling how he planned and saved for his holiday, but I interrupted him to ask what he thought of the hillside across the Lough, strewn with cockle-white houses.

He knew the scene and liked it, and liked its people too; but why they dwelt in those inaccessible ledges he couldn't reason, for in parts they looked like spools bound to the rocks with a white thread of road. He knew their forefathers had been driven to the heights, but why and how did the progeny stay on? Sometimes we all wonder over that mystical fact. But once they were people of broad acres, and ran before the terror like waifs of the night, their belongings piled on a cart, into the sanctuary of the heights. The range of their land-love narrowed now; but the more it narrowed, the more intense it became, and the intensity is a heritage. It is when we recognize that passion we understand the two-story house, sometimes in its semi-suburban garb of vulgarity, hoisted under a rock on top of a hill.

It was the man above Rostrevor who told of a time when the people from across the Lough came over in boats to hold their Pattern at Rostrevor, who crossed to the 'Point to entrain for Newry, talking in Irish all the way. For no later than forty-five or fifty years ago Omeath was almost entirely inhabited by native Irish speakers. And he remembered their efforts to learn English. One man he knew studied the English poets, and used to astound " the gentry " betimes by his recitation in a broken English of the verse of the English singers. And his wife would say: " Arra musha you. . . . Will you quit your rhymin' ".

But I liked best of all the memory of the Loughsiders crossing to make their Pattern. So did the Belfastman. It stirred with a deep significance that helped us to laugh at the mock frontier tossing on the waves under the evening sun.

BUS ALONG THE BORDER

BEFORE the car became ubiquitous there were times when our country bus became a céili-house on wheels; times, too, when it afforded the spice of thrill and adventure.

Our bus never crosses the Border, but it runs close; and the Customs authorities desire you to retain possession of your parcel or, if not accompanying same yourself, that you write thereon your name and address.

Naturally this request was not always complied with.

For though our bus never crosses the Border, there is such an enactment as " transportation to a place for illegal exportation ". Sometimes the suspicion (as our local Press records) is justified. Sometimes it is not. But Customs authorities never make fish of one and flesh of another. You're a suspect.

Like herrings in a barrel

At any rate, in our bus you certainly get your money's worth. On market days you may get crushed, admittedly, in a way that makes you envy herrings in a barrel or hens in a crate. Buckets may rap your shins, broom handles ram your eye or thrapple, while anything from the sock of a plough to a farmyard graip is liable to draw blood from anywhere.

But you find the countryman, and his wife, with his natural cautiousness unbuckled, but with his wits still hanging on to the straps, so to speak. Scattered among the crush are the folk who believe they possess the talent to make a bit on the Q.T. by slipping odds and ends past the eyes of the boys in buttons.

Somewhere, too, are the old folk who remember when market-making was a weekly ritual, when streels of carts came home together from town, two or three cart-fulls piled into one, with reins tied to the " thrams ", and cracking their fill. The bus to them is " Oul' times again, but on better wheels, an' with a livelier beast between the shafts ".

Raggin' the bachelors

I've yet to hear of someone having made a match in a country bus, but it's quite feasible. Given time, anything may happen—unless some new and exciting commodity turns up on the smuggling fare. Smuggling has its dull phases, like any other branch of trade.

Even with prices what they are, the crack on the home journey is better than that on the outward-bound. And get a company of rural folk together in good humour and they always start to rag the bachelors. Someone is sure " to get on to him ", and suggest a likely wife.

" Aw, now ", says an old voice, " lookit the help she'd be to you in the land ".

" I could cry ", chortles the bachelor, derisively, " for all any woman does in the fields. For all she does she'd be better in the house; an' she'll find plenty to do there if she'll do it ".

After a silence someone suggests meekly that maybe he's " lookin' money with her ". " Arra, what money do you want ? "

he raps back. " If yeh get what does yeh an' a bite to ate—what more do you want? "

The men in uniform

That may be a philosophy of fatalism; and an admixture of both seems to settle on the passengers as the bus approaches a certain spot where a man in uniform steps out and holds up his hand. Instantly there is a shuffling of parcels.

If a parcel drops at your boot you kick it further on, just as, in school, you used kick on the incriminating spool-gun which fired matches at the master. For no amount or degree of wit has been known to bamboozle the gentlemen who are determined to have your parcels if they feel you shouldn't have them yourself.

Standing passengers get out. Old women foother in their baskets like hatching-hens turning their eggs under them on a nest. There's a wee bit o' this, a wee bit o' that, an' maybe a grain o' mustard.

" They're fond of mustard in your house? " says the man in uniform.

Who owns all this flour?

" Well, divil the bit more nor another then. But sure, when'll I be out in town again, God knows? An' if yeh send one of our ones, they forget it. An' the van comin' round never has it either ".

He moves on. Then: " Who owns this half-hundred of flour? " No reply for a while till " I do " trickles from the front.

" And what sort of stomachs "—he has turned the sack over— " have they in *your* house? "

" If you had the fillin' of them for a week you'd wonder yourself ", says the voice. Of course, if you feel you're caught you might as well be as witty as you can: it never comes up in court.

" They're in for a massed operation then ", he says. For sticking out of the bottom of the flour sack are the points of nails. It is now " Name and address and outside, please " and, likely enough, a passenger less.

There goes your parcel

" And who owns this? " A parcel off the rack. No one answers. You're afraid even to wink. He takes it with him, and there ends another hope.

He grilled me over a few iron objects out of Mourne, and destined for a museum. Wrapped in old canvas, they lay beside me on the floor. He eyed them and then eyed me with a look ten times as long as the proverbial arm of the law.

" Irons ", I said hastily.

" Show me the irons ", said he, too lazily to sound pleasant.

I did—triumphantly waiting for his disappointed grimace. They were rusted irons, old sheep brands, in fact. He turned them over, and handed them back as he moved on. " Irons is right, boy ", says he. " An' oul' irons at that ".

And the whole bus chuckled. I couldn't feel worse if I had a bag of rags.

BANTER IN THE BAR

I SAT alone, smoking. Through the window of the lounge bar I could look across Carlingford Lough and see, like a white hen on an evening roost, a skelping of snow on the far hills.

Then they bustled in. The stout man took a hard chair. The other whirled into the armchair and shook himself down comfortably.

They had clearly just finished work, and almost at once they began to talk as if resuming a discussion that had been so interrupted elsewhere that they had withdrawn before the topics should cool.

" The country's done. . . . Dead. . . . Dyin' at the root. . .". The tall man scooped me into the circle with that last declaration while the stout man turned and confirmed my initiation.

He had an ebullient feeling for life. The taller man had the straight face of a wit; the expression of a man who had long ago codified his philosophy and desired merely to salt it occasionally with an uncertain satire.

Green Desert

" In less than fifty years from now ", he said, " this whole countryside outside the town—every town—will be a desert an' politics and religion have nothing to do with it. A green desert of grass and bushes. I suppose they'll import wolves or something for the visitors to come an' shoot ".

" Now how could it be a desert? " the other chided. " What about the water?—you can't have water in a desert ". His laughter was magnificent.

" What water? " The tall man seemed taken aback.

" Imagine an Irishman askin' what water? " His laughter spilled gloriously like the froth of the drinks he was distributing, one being for me. " Isn't there always too much water? An' what about the bogs? "

" Import crocodiles an' let them shoot them . . . or better still ". He drank hurriedly. " Advertise Wild Irishmen an' let them come an' shoot us. That'd be better than the idea of your man that bought Killarney ".

The stout man then told of a man he knew, " a true blue too ", who was as mad as a bag of cats over the sale of Killarney, as mad as if it had been Scarva that had been sold as a holiday camp for American millionaires. And then he added:

" But jokin' apart, the countryside's done ".

" An' politics an' religion have nothing to do with it ", reaffirmed the tall one. He had been settling into the chair till his crossed knee was higher than his cap.

Rural ills

" Anyone that lives in the country that could live in the town these days must have a bad cut in his head he doesn't know about. Take outside this town: four miles to post a letter, no phone, milk every other day—an' it's two days old already—no water—no nothin'. No wonder people are sellin' out an' coming into the town ".

" Do you know what'll happen . . .? " the other began. But the tall man stopped his prediction by announcing his own remedy for rural ills.

" I know what should happen. All the country people should rise like crows before a day of high wind an' light in a lump in the town an' pick its bones dry. Every town ".

" Then somethin' would happen ".

" It's what would need to happen ".

They drank together as if it were a toast.

Almost at once they were on to another topic: their economy of introduction made me envious. This time the stout one led with gusto about publicans and pubs. He enthused about a bar that " smelled and looked like a bar with a barman who could talk: I like a man to use a bit of his own loaf an' not mine all the time ".

Wry face

With levity, as I discovered, I mentioned snugs.

The stout man's hands went up like a barrier and he pulled a wry face. " That's going too far ".

At the same time the tall one finished his drink and in what seemed the same movement of recoil, was on his feet.

" Time for the tay ", he said. And when I mentioned a drink: " You're hardly leavin' the country. See you some other time ".

I was alone again. No longer could I see the skelping of snow on the hills across the Lough; its presence indeed was no longer real. For the echo-thoughts of the personalities of two men seemed to bounce around me like balloons of lingering smoke; while two empty glasses, with slithering wrinkles of froth beginning to settle, made faces that grinned at me wryly, fixedly . . . idols thrown up by an indeterminate agreeable clamour.

A WALK NEAR THE MOURNES

THE last shower out of the nor'-west brought snow with the rain. It splashed on the window-panes to leave speckled stains like wet elongated thumb-prints which lingered before melting, or until swobbed away by the tadpole wrigglings of the rain.

When it cleared I left Clontifleece to walk down to Warren-point, about three miles away.

The " duskus " (as we'd say in South Armagh) was settling in calm and quiet on the fields: calm and quiet, too, the high-flung clouds hardly seemed to move, exchausted and broken though still grey and untouched by any sign of evening light.

Along the holms and shrub towards the Moygannon river all was still, except for one interlude, when a startled blackbird spilled an erratic flow of notes that sounded like marbles bouncing down the stairways of the thickening dusk.

Menacing

" The bird that sings too soon ", said the Ravensdale story-teller, James Loughran, later that day when I mentioned it, " will live to rue it. She'll get storm to her tail ". He can quote a folk saying on almost any incident or event in the turns of life in man, bird, or beast.

I wondered what he would have said about the cloud on the menacing wall of the Mourne range over Rostrevor; a sprawling discarded cloud, tattered by gusts which had swept up the storm in that last shower.

I looked at the big field beyond the Moygannon road. The first ploughing had begun, and two rigs of furrows swept up into the dusk, disappeared in a high fold, and reappeared further on, as if totally out of alignment with the furrows at the bottom.

It reminded me of the tale of a Slieve Gullion ploughman who came on a cache of an old schoolmaster's pupil-fetched whiskey near Dromintee Church, and of how the ploughman's " scrapes " or furrows were in a " twist and thrah " by the time the master went in hopes of gratifying a thirst.

Just then the stubble field filled with imagery, as if trying to bring to reality a yearning for the dream-memories of harvest.

The western sky had cleared into a pale, icy blue that might have been an artist's smock as he mixed the wonder colours in that butt of sky beyond the hills of Fathom and Slieve Gullion in South Armagh.

The dreeping glow spread a secret life over all the landscape. The very road on which I stood seemed to change and display new personality in the gloss of burnished pools, especially at the bends. Around one bend an ageing tree, winter padded, it might have been with ivy, could have been an old lady from the days when they wore garments with lace and bonnets showing the glint of black beading.

Magnificent

" Coarse weather, Mickel ", said a cyclist as he walked his bike past. I made a reply and he added, without stopping: " An' there's a sky full o' frost ".

Through a screen of young ash shoots as bare as twisted, wrought-iron bars, I saw the western sky. The sun had gone before that last shower had ended, but the colours were now magnificent.

The artist might have been daubing the upended cauldron of some new form of transparent bronze, just out of the mould, and cooling off in a merging of tints and running colours from reds and scarlets to an inflamed murky brown.

Disturbed

Against it I could see the outline of Slieve Gullion, blubbering flecks of cloud. This wonder mood indeed might have been re-enacting a scene from ancient days when the Cailleach Biorra's lake on Slieve Gullion was an active volcano giving off smoke and steam.

Near roadside houses shadows became disturbed; buckets rattled and one heard rubber boots moving through slush as the foddering was done. A single star shone over Knockbarra to match a window-light down the Moygannon road. Other lights now shone from Omeath across the lough, as if from a dark room with a wide, gaping door.

Then I noticed the new moon, still pale, although the light in the west was rapidly cooling.

By the time I was at Clonallon the cloud had begun to move like clusters of shawled women relieved of some vigil. Maybe that's why the moon brought an image of the uplifted prows of a curragh, silvered with the scale of fish, making for home and safety through the exhausted roll of the swells of the sea.

MAKING HAY IN SHANE'S GROUND

IT was an outlying farm consisting of one humpy field which
stretched from the bog to the county road: Shane's Ground
they called it.

When I passed it the other evening a tumbling rake was
gathering hay into rows, as neatly as a razor swipes suds off a jaw.

When I came back a tractor was drawing into a wide, uncouth
gap. The trailer was loaded with forks and hand rakes and
capering young men who, like troops into a mock affray, leaped
off before the yoke stopped. They would, I reckoned, have the
piece up before the dusk had thickened.

It used to take Mickil and I a day and a half to gather it—
providing no undue distraction came along the road while we
were working there.

Light-hearted Workers

How Mickil would have welcomed the sight of the new gear
and the squad of light-hearted workers. Then I wondered would
he? He was quick to abandon the scythe when he could hire a
neighbour with a new reaper " workin' on the country " for
wages. He was first to " yawk in a thrashin' mill " to thrash his
seed hay, while everyone else thrashed it with flails.

He went back to the flail in after years, back to the scythe now
and then. Still, the flail has now gone to a long rest in the couples
of the barns and everyone " yawks in " a mill. A strange man
with strange humours was Mickil.

Year in and year out we seemed to be making hay in Shane's
Ground. He kept hay growing in it until the ragweeds must
have outnumbered the *cushogs* of grass. He had a reason: " Ah,
it's the divil's tramp for a man of my time o' day milkin' cows in
Shane's Ground. It's half Purgatory luggin' cans of milk night
an' mornin' ". He kept cutting Shane's Ground until at last he
observed wryly that " you would need a pair of specs, a wobblin'
brush and scissors an' comb to cut, for it would jook any blade ".

He swore at the choking down of weed blossoms and with a
sudden twist of sour humour said: " Dammeskin, but if two tight

fellahs got a bit thick they could carry it all home in two burdens
on their backs ".

A Proclamation

For all that, the cutting of Shane's Ground was a sort of
proclamation that hay-time had arrived. Men asked one another
if they had any hay cut, and then both agreed that " it was a wee
tot early ". Then they were in swithers whether to begin the first
spraying of the priddies or to " cowp a field " of meadow hay;
but they had their indecision settled late one evening by the
rattle of a reaper. Instinctively everyone knew where it came
from.

The pensive mood of pause in summer work was disturbed
by that sound as of a frantic grasshopper drunk on dew for the
first time. A new and hectic season had clattered in. And, as if
to confirm it, Mickil was usually seen trundling through the late
evening light, a fork and rake on his shoulder. He had been
called by that sound from a chair by the fire.

More Rain, More Rest

" It'll rain . . . it'll rain ", they'd say as he passed. " There'll
be thunder and lightnin' an' heavy showers ". This was a
facetious allusion to a reprimand from " The Man Above ",
because of the poetical way Mickil was cursing the man who had
decided to cut Shane's Ground for him.

Mickil took up their words in his own way: " Sure, the more
rain, the more rest. The good weather's not always the best ".

He had a standing order with men who owned machines to
cut Shane's Ground whenever they liked. Men with new
machines and horses new to reapers tested gear and teams in
Shane's Ground. So that sometimes it seemed to have been
bitten off here and there by a sow-pig carrying mouthfuls of grass
to make her bed for her farrowing.

Sometimes it was cut for a week before being gathered, if rain
delayed the work. After that it would be easier to pull burdock
heads from a child's hair than to rake the skift of hay from the
rising under-grasses.

Cry of a corncrake

The evening Shane's Ground was cut I would wait. Sure enough, I would hear him: " Is he in bed or asleep or away on his ramble? " He would begin to swear at the man who had cut Shane's Ground so early, and tick off a list of jobs which he meant to do first. He would light his pipe and decline to come inside.

Like the scringy hinges of dusk caught in the late wind, the rasping cry of a corncrake would come. " Hurra, bad luck to her. Listen. She hasn't her fill of rain yet ". He would move off. " If the morra's good I'll have to put it up, I suppose ". I needed no other intimation that he expected me to help.

Ducks in a pond

And I did, and liked to. He was always then a new man, with a mood as happy as ducks in a puddle. There were grey days and good days; but we always went with free hearts, well equipped for our pastoral expedition.

We had forks and hand-rakes, a scythe and a sharpening stone (the scythe to mow noticeable bits the reaper had ridden over, and to cut grass for the tops of the cocks). We had buttermilk in a three-quart can, and provisions for the day in a wicker basket. We also had our dinner of new priddies which some neighbour would have to boil for us. We had butter and greens, very essential ingredients for making " champ ". One's first taste of the new priddies should be as " champ ".

Mickil would stop when he met a neighbour and whisper with mock secretiveness: " They're late an' lazy hasn't *some* hay cowped ". And he would walk on, chortling. Sometimes a neighbour would forestall him: " If yous don't come back, sure yous'll write ".

Lining turned out

He would hide the scythe and stone, put the can in the shady side of a bush, and carefully put his coat over it. He would wait whimsically until I flung mine down. " The Irishman all over. One time I was at the hay harvest in England, an' I asked the boss for a job. ' Right, Paddy ', says he. ' Throw off your coat.

There's five of your blokes across the hill '. An' d'yeh know how
he knew? Every Irishman's coat was flung down with the linin'
turned out ".

He would take up a rake, and curse at its few broken teeth.
Then he would laugh: " ' Aye, Paddy. Can tha make 'ay? '
' No, but I can shake it up to the hay-maker ' ".

Making hay in Shane's Ground always began like that.

THE TINKERS THAT NEARLY TIED HAY

*When a tinker-woman, chewing a head of oats, passed me a while ago
on a road in the Glens of Antrim, I remembered two other tinker-women
in association with two other harvests in two other counties, Tyrone and
Armagh.*

IN the Tyrone incident the people had been heart-scalded with
tinkers. For a week they wove canopies of blessing in brogues
that rolled over half-doors and folk fears with the lament of
western breakers, smashing all in a spray of invective with the
rocky edge of their tongue when the litany of appeal failed. Old
country women are still notoriously susceptible to the sequel of
bad luck supposed to follow the " potfuls of prayers that tinker-
women pray " when their technique gets hot.

This damsel's mettle got hot, too, but it happened to be
dinner-time. (What desperation drove her to make a blunder
like that?) So the man of the house rose from the table and took
over from his mother. They had a few parries, and then he says:
" There's plenty of harvesters wanted—I want harvesters. You're
fit and able—why don't you work? "

" I'll work me fill in death ", she says. Through the window
I saw her go, insolently, triumphantly, hitching her shawl on the
one shoulder like a bandolier.

The South Armagh incident had a different and a somewhat
more colourful development. But then it was a different type of
character who went to the door. Nor was it the kitchen door

either. We were, in fact, in the boiling-house across the street doing a job to the driving-seat of a reaper with the fan-bellows. When the tinkers arrived—all five of them, three men and two women as we learned later—the support of the driving-seat was in the fire on the hearth and I was piling a white forge-heat around it with the fan-bellows. The fans roared and clattered like a threshing mill and we heard nothing except a faint grind of wheels which might have meant anything.

He was on his knees at the time, alternatively using the tail of his coat and his cap to handle the hot iron. He was grimacing into the heat and seemed to be brooding deep decision. Like myself, he hadn't had time to shave since the harvest began. It was half-two in the day; but even so—disproving Wilde's wry quip about the felicitous effects of a good dinner—he had moods as unpredictable as harvest weather itself. Wilde, anyhow, never had to tie; nor did he know how tinkers can pester people, pilfering this and begging that, from eggs, boots, to trap wheels— in this instance the trap itself mouldering in a shed down the street.

The hullabaloo happened so suddenly that I'm still not clear on the exact cause. I swear it was the hen set him off; the hen laying in an onion-box fastened to the wall where the dog couldn't get at the eggs. Because normally he was the sort who delighted to match his invective with a tinker, badgering her curses back down her teeth with a counter-blast of rhetorical epithet mulled on some barrack square.

Anyhow, he signed to stop blowing and this time grabbed the cap off his head as he got to his feet. Near the threshold was a half-hundred weight deputizing as an anvil, while the pigs' pot we had lifted off stood steaming midways between.

And then we heard his mother buckling into the tinker like a day's work. And then, too, the hen began to cackle and flew to the edge of the box and we heard nothing but din. He swore at the hen and waved his cap. She flew on top of an old dresser. Next he made a dive for the iron in such a way that I leaned back hastily on my stool.

I fell among calves' buckets, an old pot, and a few basins which toppled off bags of meal. Possibly it was this clatter which really startled the hen. They both, anyhow, made for the door at once, the hen flying across his path with a screech. Instinctively he put up his hands.

I smelt something burning—feathers or human hair I never knew—and heard a single oath. He had, on the way, crigged his shin against the pot. Then, with a growl, the iron smoking like a rifle—and held like one—he charged out the door after the hen.

Possibly he tripped over the half-hundred weight and only stumbled into the woman. I heard a wild tinker yell. Then, like muffled thunder, those wheels ground again and a pony galloped as her compatriots abandoned her to the—stake. For when I got to the door the hen was entangled in some netting-wire and his mother was releasing it while, at his feet, the tinker-woman was on her knees, the eyes in her tanned face as stark as in a kipper. Over her head he waved the driving-seat which left trajectories of smoke like a stunting plane.

" I'll brand you like an army blanket ", he was saying, making mock lunges and growling through his teeth. " I'll put you from plunderin' on ould country women in this country ". He pulled wild faces, and she kept yelling.

His mother interceded and the tinker-woman said: " Ma'am, but it's me pities you with such a cross-natured man ". His mother ordered her to go. I looked at him.

For a moment he glared. Then he chuckled and let the iron clang beside his boot. He looked philosophic and wise and stroked his bearded jaw. Then he said: " No. I have a better plan. I'll stretch your hide afore night. Can you tie hay? " he bawled, and without waiting for an answer: " If you can't you will. From now till night me lassie. . . .". But his mother hooshed her off as she would a hen.

She went, with only a solitary backward glance. He was grinning with silent laughter. " It was me full intention to stick her between Tam an' you in thon thistles. That mightn't work either: Tam might make her tell stories ".

And we turned back to resume our job on the driving-seat. Another tinker triumph!

SPRING COMES TO THE GLENS OF ANTRIM

IN Layde, the headland north of Cushendall, the morning sun often came in either fantasy or myth. It would break like a bud bursting from the sea, or like a character bent on mischief emerging from a folk-tale, rising from beyond the knuckled points of Garron. The waters would bleed and cloud would transform instantly, then scorch and scatter like sheep aware of sudden light.

At the same time the Glens glowed freshly, blushing in green wonder. Almost as suddenly the magic was over. The ogre from the tale had had his moment and was benevolently transfigured; cloud would reappear in burnished mauve and cool rapidly.

But it wasn't like that the morning spring came. On that morning everything had disappeared under fog and the world was swaddled in a tense stillness. No sound came from Red Bay lying between us and the cliffs of Garron and Ardclinis.

Less than half a mile below at Obb, a natural harbour linked in tradition with Dane and monk, stood the walls of the old monastery of Layde; but I could see nothing. Indeed, I could barely see the tower-like chimney-stack of the ruins of a castle twenty yards from our door—an appropriate monument some might say, to have beside the abode of a fellow primarily afoot for folklore.

Almost in mime, jackdaws were finishing a nest in the top flue of the chimney. It is all that remains of a bastion of the MacNeills; its story is as shattered as its walls.

Cheekily the jackdaws strutted like bewitched sentries. Weren't the Children of Lir on the Sea of Moyle out there? On a ledge further down, from a mat of grass, a single bleached ragweed shivered.

Below at ground level in " The Brandy Hole "—nicknamed from days when wines and tobacco were hidden there by smugglers or lodged by revenue men—a black hen scraped the midden in what had been the main apartment.

As I stood by the castle a consciousness of sound stirred. The fog persisted; but from every burn tinkling its way to the sea, bird song seemed to follow the roll and diminishing drop of the streams, each now like an echo of the other.

I went towards the road down the lane of bumpy sandstone rock. My neighbour and his friend with a pony cart were coming up.

The cart turned up the loanan and I listened—half with memory—waiting till the raucous chortle of the wheel-shoeings softened into an ironic chuckling once they reached the rutted grass near the manure heap.

Flowers flash

Then I came back. On the bank above the well a dandelion showed a face as bold and as flushed as a trapped schoolboy caught in the act.

There, too, was a daisy, prim and demure—but a rooted divil underneath—all eye and wonder, both the daisy and I.

Daffodil yellow flamed towards the dainty droop of clustered pink from French currant blossoms so common here. All must have been there the day before but I hadn't noticed.

On that morning in the fog they seemed to caper almost in one concerted motion, organized as secretly as the rise of sap, and every stray sound had meaning and purpose, like the mild bedlam of an orchestra tuning for the first overture in a studio.

Oisín

Later I left for the head of Glenaan. The sun was still hidden, but light had seeped on to the sea; in mirror-flashings it danced on Red Bay as dust specs dazzle in a sunbeam in a darkened room.

Four teams were ploughing the braes in Glenaan: four teams of white horses. It was up Glenaan, says the local version of the saga, that Oisín rode on his white steed.

He stretches an arrogant, if often allegorical, foot to help some men roll a mighty boulder aside but the girth breaks, he touches earth and finds mortality and the prosaic around him.

I mentioned the tale to a young Glenaan ploughman. He had his own prosaic explanation for the four teams of white horses, as I knew he must; but his account was the folklore of livelihood, nevertheless.

Halo of gulls

When I returned to Layde that evening the fog had gone. One scroll only was tucked behind Carnaneale which, like an indicator on a horizontal dial over Glenariffe, points a folk finger to the mid-day sun.

By then the sun itself had gone and Red Bay was as still and mysterious as a well; it even reflected to the very centre of the waters the blurred image of the Ardclinis and Garron cliffs, scored as if by strokes from a fabulous pick.

Fields were dull with evening, with manure and upturned earth. I watched a ploughman, haloed by gulls, turn his last furrows patiently . . . turning history and life, even time itself . . . while a last ray strolled the length of Glenariffe where the braes look as if they had just slid from the clutch of basalt rock. At Foriffe and Kilmore, hidden behind Lurig, they wave-leap back to buttress the cliffs.

Maidens wink

Early night was gathering about me and the abandoned castle of Layde. The Maidens off Larne winked thrice, coquettishly, and the lime-kiln up Ballyeamon doffed a late plume of smoke.

A window light opened an eye from Ardclinis. From Garron, under the Divil's Bite at a turn in the famous coast road, headlamps burst with a glare as if from the sea itself.

Below me lay Cushendall. On the right Lurig drowsed, mystic and flat-headed like Fionn's fabulous hound, limestone jowls trapping the after-glows.

Then the lights were on in Cushendall, white and green or a deep blue; and they jewelled a collar which might have slipped from the hound of Fionn that was Lurig with his rocky paws in the sea that spring evening on the Glens.

TELEVISION IN A GLEN OF ANTRIM

I STRODE down the kitchen from a Glens of Antrim fireside—
and sat at the dresser in Lime Grove, London. In Lime Grove
I had a crack among a few characters with the Curfew Tower in
Cushendall behind us.

Not a Glensman outside the show was any the wiser, and
neither would I had I been in their place. Because in Television
the extreme and the disjointed can be smoothly shuttled till the
twain does meet; in one stride the film shot and the actual live
broadcast can meet without scarcely a broken breath.

What a medium for propaganda! How it could outpace the
film as we understand it when projected in comparative innocence
in a cinema. I suppose we have been warned.

But these may be indicative impressions by a folk-wise fellow
who hasn't apparently ever been excited. Let me add that it was
a single, solitary appearance—so far. Yet it didn't stop people
asking silly questions: was I nervous (a folklorist nervous, mind
you!), was I really there and—God forgive them—how did you
break in?

I didn't: I was lured in. The TV unit came to the Glens
looking for two things only, neither of which included me. One
was a photogenic fairy thorn, the other a traditional fireside with
(blandly) electric light laid on. I give credit to that change of
popular attitude which thought the admixture feasible in an
Ulster glen. And it was.

Pork market

Going along to verify the matter we talked of television.
I had seen it but twice and knew in my heart it was here for keeps.
Yet I denounced it in favour of sound broadcasting: radio preserv-
ing the imaginative stimulus as the old storyteller did and all
that, helping—not making—the mental picture and pattern
for you.

I did pontificate that the mind has a habit of adapting itself
to innovation certainly: and it was then I think the producer
decided to make an apostate of me and wheedle me along by
hook—or bike. In the end I actually rode the old bike down

Lime Grove past the Curfew Tower of Cushendall more real than itself in a slide-flash on a canvas screen at the back of the studio.

The studio itself was a revelation. I had known make-believe on radio; but this was astonishment. Going to a set is like walking through part of Smithfield market where second-hands are piled, as the studio props were piled: gear of all kinds. These are the props of illusion which, on a screen, present realities from all over the world.

To me the studio was disappointingly cramped. Cables trailed here and there and ended in a kind of snake-pit behind the set. Groups of people stood around chatting, and I thought of dealers putting their heads together before a pork market opens.

Cross dog

You hear the voice of your producer and after a while locate him behind a glass panel as high as if he were on the bridge and you on the deck of a liner. Everyone is very nice and helpful, and almost everyone tells you to " forget the cameras ".

You can't forget the cameras, however, but treat them as you would a cross dog. It's no use pretending you don't know they are there, but let on you're cool and collected—ignoring the bark, expecting the bite.

After several false starts rehearsals began. There was another when they wheeled on the bike I was to ride and I'm still convinced that some private museum had an empty stand during those few days. In radio rehearsal you merely say the same thing, differently: in television you perform as well. I had anticipated this and had fished out a prop-box like a milking-stool to take the weight off the waiting feet. But it had to recur so often that in the end I was ready to put the ould bike round someone's neck.

In the show I was supposed to have ridden off . . . out the Cushendun Road. Actually, I legged it. The space may have appeared as wide as a street but it was less than two yards, with a further two yards off-set ending against the wall.

A fugitive

There was no make-up—apart from an apologetic pat of face powder to tone down glitter where my hair used to grow. An old

car on the set was made-up certainly, with mud and bits of string:
I had drawn the line just there. This was an English idea of an
Irish joke and it amused someone—whatever about the viewers.
What amused me was their amusement at what they thought
should be amusing.

It all had one reaction I hadn't anticipated: though if your
philosophic outlook is aligned a certain way this is the best part
of all. Odd people in the oddest moments recognize you. " Isn't
he very like the fellow was on television last night ", says the
woman on the boat coming home.

She asks, and you forget that when you open your mouth to
prevaricate—it is the fellow. At Ballycastle on my way to Rathlin
a stranger asks the same and helps to carry some of my gear to
Jimmy McCurdy's boat at the pier. I felt like a fugitive.

Oddest of all was the incident in the lift of the hotel in London.
I got talking to a middle-aged woman with an over-polished
accent—though she said she was from Sligo. I confirmed I
was Irish.

" There was an Irish show on television last night ". She was
looking straight at me. " Very good in parts. The scenery of
Antrim was grand. But I didn't like the actors ". Heaven
forgive me I asked her why. " Mostly mis-cast. Spoke with too
much of a brogue in the kitchen scene. But the scenery was
grand ".

Meself and me Glens neighbours in that kitchen scene thought
the scenery was grand too.

ONE FAIR DAY IN CUSHENDALL

" FAIR DAY! " exclaimed the Glensman. His arms waves a
circle around the cross-roads and swept dismissively up the
roof-steep ascent of High Street. " On that ground ", said he,
" for the last few fairs here in Cushendall an' you wouldn't have
seen as much as a goat ".

When I got home I looked up my Glens of Antrim diaries—
the adjunct to our folklore collections. Here is part of my account
of a Fair Day in Cushendall in May, 1953:

This is still one of the important fairs of the year here, held on the 14th May this year. It is a church holiday, too, for most; and people returning from Mass—men and women, young and old—clog and cluster along the streets. The centre is at the cross-roads around Turnley's Curfew Tower.

The old Fair Hill beyond the summit of High Street has been abandoned, of course; and beasts for sale are stood on the streets. Already an angry woman in a doorway is wielding a sweeping-brush to belt a bullock from her threshold which is stained with dung.

The cattle steam and smell. There is that familiar Fair Day sense of a thousand secretive whisperings, rioting now and then into a shout at a beast. Friends are hailed and greeted cautiously; for the risen voice implies money or a deal, to be noted for discussion later in pub and at fireside.

I reckon there can't be more than ninety or a hundred head for sale, and only two horses. I think of the accounts I've written about the famous Cushendall pony, the pure breed now extinct: the owner of the last stallion, they tell, rode his horse to Bally-castle Lammas Fair, got his bundle of fish off the Islay men, and then rode the horse up the steps into a dance hall, circled the floor, and rode out and home to Cushendall. Among a group looking up the hill at the two horses I see the man reputed to have owned the last of the true breed of those ponies, famed for stamina and grit.

The group moves away . . . except that Glensman. He seems lost in a daze of incredulous realization. The end of the horse itself? Or is he recalling the tale he told me of the Glensman who rode the stallion pony up the steps into the dance-room at the Lammas Fair in Ballycastle? More than likely he is assessing the price—including a luck-penny.

A man says about one of the horses: " She's the best mare in our country ".

" If she is, the rest must be a poor lot ".

Men stand in the familiar, almost conspiratorial knots. They move almost in slow motion and sometimes talk over their shoulders. A dealer circles a calf as if it were a land-mine primed to explode at a touch. Suddenly he catches the calf by the throat and makes it cough and then steps back, studying it intently.

Men on business in the fair wear the Sunday navy-blue jackets and blue overalls. One trots a horse along Shore Street, and as if by concert, men line the pavements and lean and watch, but say nothing. The horse is trotted back, and one bystander yelps at it: but he is a dealer. Like dealers everywhere he wears the bleached dust coat " straight up and down like a yard of pump water ". He carries a long cane.

A Glensman I know, arms folded, his hat tipped over his eyes, whispers me to a halt. He nods at a bedraggled white cow in charge of a young fellow who is refusing the offer of an older man.

" What's the cut—can I be of any help? Split the cut ". (In other Fairs they talk of "splitting the difference" between the seller's price and the buyer's offer.) I mention this to the Glensman; he whispers:

" Watch this manœuvre well. Watch close now. The father lettin' on to buy off the son to draw the crowd an' set the price right . . . watch. They're from one side of Ballymena ".

I noted the outcome of the mock deal: of a bell-ringer announcing an auction: of events and people and personalities met in the fair. And I noted that " the sun shone; the afternoon was warm. The hills, as close as fingers and thumb, are gloved in satin-green. But already the pubs are full of laughter and good cheer. This May Fair in Cushendall will soon be over for another year ".

Or for ever? It was.

WILD STRAWBERRIES IN GLENARIFFE

IT was Glensman Professor Séamas Delargy back on holiday who persuaded me to climb to Carnaneill with him. From our house in Layde above Cushendall the peak of Carnaneill showed like an indicator on the wavy dial of the mountain itself.

" Twelve o'clock Hill " was the name the folk mind had tagged on to it, dating back to the days when people reckoned the

time of day by such ready natural circumstance as a hillock underneath the mid-day sun, or a shadow on a door, rather than by
any consulting of watch or clock—if they had them.

That day it was a stirring sight to look down on ripening fields
and see the countryside as if urgent and posied, eagerly awaiting
some mystic cue as it were, before the harvest.

A lesser hill than Carnaneill would have satisfied, but I had to
go and I'll never regret it.   Cloud chased sun and the soft airs were
welcome as we made our way up because once beyond the rough
ground and the bank of the old railway, the mountain slope
became as steep as a roof of old scraghs.   To rest and glance back
was wonderful.

On the level floor of Glenariffe the fields seemed to sway in
the sunlit wind, and the effect was like the sea washing the strand
at Waterfoot.   One thought of the eternal sound of the surf and
the whispering melody of an evening breeze among the hard
heads of grain; in imagination the sounds interchanged and almost
echoed as one.

It was at that moment that my companion asked if I liked
strawberries.   I suppose I laughed, but I had no retort; my mouth
was too dry, anyhow.   And then I saw him pluck from the grasses
and go on plucking.   Around me, too, the earth offered refresh-
ment as readily as those white houses below; dainty strawberries,
not in profusion, but still strawberries and tart and luscious.
Out of the hearts of our hands we ate them in silence while
shifting lights and shadow swept across the land below.

Part of the way up we had the company of dun-fleeced sheep
fresh from the dipping trough at the foot of the hill.   We could
still see the two men working there, helped by an alert collie.
Knowing our interest in folklore one of the men told us a version
of the Glens fairyman they call a *gruagach*—the wee hairy man who
does good turns for people till they make the understandable
mistake of trying to repay him in kind for his services.

We had tossed flecks of humorous and allegorical explanation
back and forth till the man holding a leppin' young ram had his
say.   " If any *gruagach* ", he began, holding the sheep with one
hand and smearing it with red dye on the shoulder with the other,
" hada made a shape to take this job off me in a thronged time

O

like this, I'd a known how to keep my mouth shut an' me hands
to meself ".

From high on the hill we could see just how " thronged " was
that August day. Some people were still saving hay and others
were pulling flax or steeping it in the dams. The breeze sweeping
up the slope didn't let us miss the stench either.

A thronged time surely in the Glens—not to mention homing
visitors and their insatiable appetites for soda farls off the griddle
and home-made butter, dreamed of for the past twelve months
at least.

Further up the hillside the strawberries gave out, but there
were compensations in the scene below and around us. Sunrays
filtered through crags and knuckles of hill as if actually making
a delicate green spray. It was almost bewitching to watch the
rays become aerial brooms which swept shadow and reality before
them over the corn fields up the glen.

When we got down that evening—after a delay in the straw-
berry beds—the woman of the house was churning " a wee drop
for ourselves " as she put it. But I knew, and my companion
knew, it was a special treat for himself, for the farls were on the
griddle on their edges and the fire was in *greesha*, just to keep them
hot and right for him.

THE MOWER AND THE CARTERS

HE was, admittedly, both a wit and a humorist: that is, he
had a mind which could let instinct dart a retort off the last
word of an adversary as if using it like a stepping stone, or he
could restrain that impulse and let his mind plan a slow effect,
as with the carters. For while wit must drive humour can dander.

There was no dandering over his harvest, of course. He was
a small South Armagh farmer and a pahvee as well. A pahvee is
a pedlar of cloth which you buy and realize you don't want only
when the pahvee has been gone half an hour: wit and humour—
and blarney—help to bring off sales. So they say.

My man wanted to get his harvest finished so that he could fit in a spot of pahveeing before the winter. He had to mow with a scythe, while I lifted and tied the sheaves; help was scarce, but wages in those days stayed at a fixed half-crown nevertheless. Possibly I learned something I haven't yet digested for these men had developed the innate rustic philosophy to a point when satire and a civilized sarcasm changed places without your knowing it.

He was a fair mower but it took us a full two weeks to mow an acre of oats. The weather was primarily to blame, because each morning the rain seemed to show a malice of its own and kept off until we were in the field. A mower those days stripped to the shirt, slipped off the galluses (braces nowadays) and let them trail, wore a hat which appeared only once a year, and often carried a heavy sharpening stone, baby-kangaroo-like, in his hip pocket.

The field we were mowing was along the main road between Dromintee and Newry; it wasn't his own field either, but dear conacre for which, irrespective of the state of harvest, he would pay big money come November.

At that time men from Forkhill and Carrickasticken, facing the warm wide acres of Louth, used to haul potatoes in stiff farm carts to Newry and were known to us as " the priddy carts ". And they would pass our field of conacre corn just after we had arrived and were standing there in the rain.

The bantering was half traditional and, on reflection, psychologically sound, despite its façade of apparent indifference.

" Away home to your bed, you old dote an' have a grain o' wit "—" wit " in rural parlance means " sense ", of course. " The Cailleach's in your oats, man; get a sail on your scythe an' let her be ". Or: " If you've no coat I'll throw in an ould one for you the morra ". They even told us to be careful that the new scythe blade didn't catch a chill. The rain was their ally, and I was young enough then to think that the rain would have to give over before my man could uphold the honour on our part of the parish, and his own reputation as a wit, with a really top-class retort. But he never made them an answer.

There had to be a final morning. We had a few swarths mown and tied in sheaves when the rains fell once more. The mower

swore at the skies and made a grim face. We put on our coats
and went to the hedge for shelter, and in a while heard the sound
of the priddy-carts' iron shoeings which in those days made a
rolling thunder distinctive enough even for the household dog to
detect them when two miles away, and we knew those carts.

I felt he would tell me to press closer into the hedge where we
couldn't be seen—but then our few rows of tied sheaves were wet
evidence of our presence somewhere. He must have seen the
point at the same time. For he threw off hat, coat and vest and
ran out into the rain telling me to follow. I was sure he was mad.
He certainly seemed mad the way he was moving in the downpour
just as the carts came into view.

Better than all—he was singing as well.

Once they sighted him you could sense their chests swelling
to gather breath for the bantering; but before they could speak he
beat them to it. First he swung the scythe above his head and
shook it at the heavens and the pelting rain. Then he cried:

" Man above! You're gunked this time! It's dung I want.
Not straw! " And he went on mowing and singing as he mowed.

The men on the carts went by without a single word. But once
they had gone out of sight he dumped the scythe and ran for his
coat. We got home as fast as we could; and he went straight to
bed, chuckling to himself all the way up the stairs, except when
he called for a dry change.

RATHLIN ISLANDER SWORE ME TO SECRECY

*My first storyteller on Rathlin was an old woman: and her greeting
almost startled me. " I'm always glad to meet someone from Ireland ",
she says. I append a folk-tale of hers.*

TALES of the supernatural on Rathlin Island, off the Antrim
coast, include those about *The Saack Bann:* this was a
ghostly white ball or sack of wool which was said to roll on the
road. Mermaid stories are told all down the Antrim coast as
far as the Glens as well as on Rathlin: even the story of the man
who married the mermaid, and how, in the end, she had to go,

unwillingly, back to the sea, leaving a family behind her. In Scots folklore the seal sometimes takes the place of the mermaid.

Mermaids—and mermen—were said to wear a belt of fine weed or human hair. If you captured such a belt you would never, so the story claims, " be lost on salt water ".

I heard legends about Cuchullain, St. Columba, monks and monasteries; about Norsemen and their assaults on the island. Bruce and his famous spider are still remembered. In the historic lore there are many accounts of the massacres by Scots and English. One man told me why I must keep his story of the Campbell massacre a secret; because, he said, he knew *why* the Campbells had so wantonly slaughtered the islanders.

I've had to swear secrecy over the telling of some charms, even sterility rites supposed to result in a childless marriage. Some of these " charms " call for the use of human hair, others for parts of a fish, knitting needles, or fire. Best known, perhaps, is that called " The tying of the knots ".

If a girl were jilted she went to the marriage ceremony and " tied the knots " on her successful rival. When the bride was asked, " Do you take this man to be your lawful husband? " the jilted one secretly answered, " I do not "—and tied a knot on a cord of handkerchief! She did this three times in secret reply to the three main questions in the marriage ceremony.

It may sound amusing to us to-day, but the " charm " was said to fall on the husband: I've been told of girls who were killed because of this belief. I can't even hint how the practising of such a " charm " was discovered: but when it was discovered the girl was compelled—often at knife yoint—to undo each knot and to untie her words. (A similar belief was told in South Armagh).

The thrice-knotted cord was said to be used in beliefs and charms for " raising the wind ". Around Portglenone I heard how a storm was created in Lough Neagh with three ordinary bowls! I like best the Rathlin account of the three men who crossed to a Scots isle: there is, of course, much tradition about trade with the isles. However, when the men went to leave they were either blown back by a gale, or becalmed.

In the end they were told they'd better see an old woman and, as it's put: " Pay her a trifle and she'll let yous go home to

Raachery " (Rathlin)—the implication being that she was controlling the weather! They do so and are given a cord with three knots. They loosen the first and a gentle breeze takes them out. They loosen the second knot and the breeze stiffens. They'd been warned not to undo the third, but entering the Bay for home they decide to try—and a gale blows them back to where they'd started!

I collected many charms and taboos about boats and fishing. No old fisherman on Rathlin would allow his boat to be turned other than with the sun.

Lastly, I must mention " Green Island "—Fairyland—or " Tír na nÓg " as some call it. This is an island supposed to appear every seven years between Rathlin and Sheep Island. On Rathlin and in Ballintoy tales are told of people seen at work there; of servants being hired in Ballycastle Hiring Fair by the mysterious folk from Tír na nÓg.

Rathlin is an island washed by successive waves of Anglo-Scots myth and legend and historic story: but now the last drops, some still in Gaelic, are slipping away forever. " The island's done ", old folk have said to me, remembering days of larger population: yet tractors outnumber the horse on Rathlin. I always remember one night when someone recalled a tradition which says that only two men in the end will be left on Rathlin. And an old islander retorted:

" That couldn't be true. How would two men handle a boat? "

The younger men laughed and talked of helicopters; but the old man's remark nevertheless came straight from a temperament that is behind all Rathlin life and folklore, like the following tale:

THE RAGHERY MERMAID

Taken down in August 1954 from Rosie McCurdy, aged eighty-three in 1954, Ballinanard, Rathlin:

" I heard Donal n'Ruagha tell of the Rackery mermaid. He would know; for it was to a house in The Upper End she come, to a house in North Claggan. He never named the man who took her—Oh, glory be to Moses I heard him tell that surely. This man seen her at the rocks, and she had her cloak off her, what sort it was I don't mind. But he got the cloak and took it and took her home, and he hid the cloak in the scraghs of the thatch and she didn't know where it was. Donal wouldn't say his name; but he said she was happy, very happy, in North Claggan, and never wanted to go back to the sea or ever spoke of it at all. She had a family to the man, and was married—whether she was married now I'm not sure, but he was living with her and they had this family sure enough, she had, the mermaid. Till one wild day come and the wind was that bad it was lifting the thatch, and she was out doing something. Her man was there too, trying to hold down the thatch, and this squall lifted the thatch where he hid the cloak. And before he could stop her, or reach her, she lifted this ladder and put it to the roof and was up and got the cloak and away. He followed her but he couldn't reach her and she got away in the sea and never was seen no more. The children lived and he reared them. They said you would never know the difference between them and other children only they had very flat feet ".

' SCHOLARS ' IN A BARN

" NOW, you're a scholar ". Because the rain had come during the dinner hour we had retired to the barn to enable herself to clear the things up while we smoked. We were seated on bottles or bundles (bothans really), of old straw. I was happy enough until he started it.

Outside, we saw the rain through the open door dance on a puddle like ephemeral elves.

The others did not find any solace in that thought; instead, they muttered habitual epithets at the halt in the labour.

" Now, you're a scholar ", he began, and held another match to his pipe when he saw me wince involuntarily. I was the cynosure of a dozen eyes, for the dog seemed to sense the rather malicious joy which betrayed itself in the eyes and voice of the old man.

" Well, I met the scholars ", I murmured defensively.

" Now ", he began jubilantly, spitting over his boot and then rolling over to recline on his elbow, with that pipe jutting out from his jaw. " Now, a girl married a man——"

" Them was the days ", someone interrupts with an ironic chuckle.

" Hould your tongue. A girl married a man; an' when they got married, he was three times as ould as her——"

" Ireland again ", I interrupt deliberately, still on a prevaricating defensive.

" Aw—hould your tongue, can't yeh? " I have him irritated. But the rain has lost its beauty for me now. " Ye'll need your considerin' cap for this me bucko. He was three times as ould as her when he married her, an' when they were fifteen years married he was only twice as ould as her. Now, how was that eh? " Again he spits, the expectoration epitomizing the expected triumph of the old over the new.

" You mentioned that one before ", I castigate.

" Three times as ould? . . . then after fifteen years only twice as ould? " They're all puzzled now, thinking while I try to simulate a look of secret knowledge. Mutterings and echoing pauses; the clack of spittle on the cement floor, and then:

" You're talkin' through your hat, man ".

" He's not, then ", I emit, while I hope to Heaven he can explain his poser in simple terms.

Well, he has his calloused hand extended, the fingers apart, and he ticks off each point as he advances by tapping each respective finger. The pipe still juts from his jaw.

" Yeh see, she was fifteen herself when she got married an' he was forty-five. Well! Wasn't he three times as oul' as her. Now—after fifteen years she was thirty, an' wasn't he——"

" 'Pon me sowl, that's a good one! "

" Is the rain quit? "

" It won't the day. Now here's another. There went two men down the road, two women an' two childher. Yeh never heerd this one, skipper ". But the rain is almost off. A new interest has also fevered the others, and I don't care for that gleam in his eye. I get up.

" Come on, boys. Make a start—just the same as if it is mornin' ".

He is vexed. " Are you the gaffer, eh? " he throws at me.

I chuckle a reply. He forgot that he once stuck me with that poser, before an audience as usual, and my stock slid to rock-bottom on the Exchange where ' scholars ' reign. You want to hear it? Well, the two men were the women's two husbands, the women's two fathers, the children's fathers, and the children's grandfathers. Oh, yes, it is possible.

The two men, no relations whatever, had married; their respective wives dying and leaving each a girl. At the marriage-able age each girl married the other girl's father, each union again producing a child each. Now—

But he could tell it better than I. Figure it our for yourself.

THE COBBLER WAS A REBEL

THE report on the cobbler had little to say. It didn't mention his occupation, although that didn't matter. It didn't mention his age. It didn't mention how fitting it was that a band, for the first time in the history of the parish, should attend his funeral. The report simply said, as most of them do, that he had been buried to the strains of an Irish lament, with " The Last Post ", in Dromintee in South Armagh, and that he had been a member of that Company in the Fourth Northern Division of the I.R.A.

Not a word or whisper about his connections with the I.R.B. and the Fenian Brotherhood which preceded it. For this cobbler was nearer eighty than seventy and had been a rebel all his life. When the first company of Volunteers was founded, under cover of a dance in the local school, he was there. Someone knew. Someone sent for him and he didn't need a second bidding. The sons of the Volunteers who joined after him that night played in the band at his funeral. His name was Eddie Casey.

Two weeks before he died, I was back in South Armagh and dropped in on him on The Old Road. It was after twelve, and his light surprised me. He rarely sat up so late, although his house was always a thronged céili-house. I went in. He was sitting hunched at his fireside, and the white head, cropped close with a sprout of fringe, turned to look.

The pile of boots in the corner was smaller than usual. A new bend of leather (on which we often sat when seating was thronged) stood tied beside the remainder of the old one. But the iron last on the block of wood was somehow like a stumpy, stripped tree amid the fallen leaves of leather clippings. He used to clear them away each night, I remembered. The delph on the dresser he cherished so well were furred with dust; and the shadows it held were no deeper than the shadows in his eyes. He had been ill. And he seemed lonely that night.

He used grow lonely some nights he once told me, and would think of the comradeship of Volunteer days, or would take down the flute and play. But the flute was silent that night, too, hanging under a shaking of dust above the boot-laces and whangs, wax-ends, heel-shods and toe-plates.

Here, as he soled, pieced or stitched our twisted brogues (so badly worn no other cobbler would even hole them with an awl), he talked and told us stories of the Fenians and the Volunteers, of football teams and flute bands.

He was no braggart, boaster or bigot, just quietly maddeningly consistent in argument, allegiance and everything else. He never saw planks when straws flew in the winds of the transient hysterias of one kind and another; and I never remember him saying he hated anyone. But he loathed jazz, humbug and the new self-centredness and snobbery. He used to pontificate a little and be sentimental towards the Volunteers, and he was " just football crazy and we're all half-mad ".

He was always coaxing us to form either a band or a team. While mending our boots he taught us how to play a flute, or the kettle-drum he kept in the room, or would jump up from a job when the notion took him and thump a tea chest as he would a big drum. He knew the background of every mother's son in the parish (and Ireland as well, by implication); but when a logical assessment of argument and conclusion pointed to an inevitable, unprepossessing fact, he never uttered it: he would wheel on his stool, ram his pipe in his vest pocket, and loudly hum " Down the Glen " as he beat time with the hammer on a piece of leather on the heel of the last.

Some called him a cod, as some always must when confronted by this type of character; but he never cared who misunderstood him.

" Curse Ireland for a change ", he once said, " for England's cursed long ago ".

Just the same, when we used " draw him out " and the rafters rang with our concerted denunciation of some ideal, he would take the awl and clear us from the house.

I wasn't there when the band played the Irish lament for him, but I could get the scene perfectly. Down the hill from the church lay the blackened, bullet-gouged ruins of McGuill's where his company had been in action. In the graveyard at the corner stood the wind-warped larch. More than ever they would resemble old, defiant men who, like himself, had strayed into a symbolism of man, place and purpose.

In free, legendary winds from our Gap of the North they used lament and roar by turn. They used urge one interpret, it often seemed to me, the story that stared from dead gables in the heather; that throbbed for expression in the stony veins of ditches around palms and fingers of little fields; the story crying challenge from the breasts of mountainside bared by cultivation—challenge and triumph.

The pipes that day lamented more than the rebel cobbler. The bugle call echoed tribute to more than he. He would have been first to say so, and his creed already had. But I wonder, in his loneliest moods when flute and memory failed him, did he ever dream of such a tribute as his comrades, and their sons, gave him.

To football field and band parade, through hell and hot water—in a significant devotion—the young always followed him and they were there at the end.

OLD COWS SOLD WELL IN NEWTOWN

THE two men in this tale were my grandfather, John Campbell of Balnamadda (which means " Dogs' Town ", by the way) and his son, my uncle Peter. They were both country carpenters in the days when their wages were half a crown a day. My grandfather also had a small farm—eight or nine acres, a lot of it bog. And they had this cow to sell. Times must have been particularly stiff and money tight, when they decided to drive the cow to Newtownhamilton Fair, a town right on the north-eastern rim of the ring of hills around Slieve Gullion, Newtown as we know it: decent people with a lively wit, but one helluva cold spot on a winter's day. There was snow in drifts on the road the day they set out with the cow, and the sky threatened more.

" A day ", as my Uncle Peter used say, " with the real *kahr* of winter about it ". *Kahr* means grimace. When we'd get him to tell this tale he always added: " I wouldn't do it again for a fieldful of oul' cows, an' every horn on them stuffed with diamonds ".

She was an old cow in poor condition. " You could hang your coat ", Peter would tell, " on any of her hip bones ". Peter was tall and lanky; my grandfather was a small man, and wore a beard and whiskers, with a hard hat up above. They got to Newtown, where trade was bad, and snow showers skelped them all day. In the heel of a bitter evening they sold for a lot less than they'd been asking, and darkness was on them as they hurried away—" with the curse of Newtown on them ", meaning they didn't wait to take bite or sup or a drink there. They were making to a certain pub in Mullabawn, half-ways between Newtown and Dromintee. On the way more snow fell. They must have been glad to reach the threshold of that pub and get inside and close the door behind them.

The publican was a big man, " as strong as two or three ", and a great friend of my grandfather's, who often worked for him at his trade. His name was O'Hanlon. But the first word the publican said was: " Get out! " To my grandfather, and meant it too. Peter said the old man stood there—the beard and whiskers frozen stiff and packed with snow and all he could see were two eyes shining away in on the snow-man's face. " Get out—or do I have to throw you out? " says the publican. They didn't move.

Then, Peter said, the publican just " left his hand on the counter and was over like a greyhound ", caught a hold of the old man, opened the door, and pitched him outside. He closed the door and went behind the bar and set up a drink for Peter, who stood flabbergasted: he'd been sure the publican had been joking. So he says, when he got his senses back:

" When you threw me father out you better throw me out after him ".

" Who? " cried the publican. " Your father? That's not John Campbell of Balinamadda I threw out of my house— aw, no . . .". Over the counter he leapt again and came in— many a time Peter described it—" with the oul' fella in his hands as if he was a child, and him pawin' the snow off the whiskers and beard on his face ".

" To think ", he kept saying, " that I threw John Campbell outa my house. . . . An' on this night of all nights. . .".

It was a case of mistaken identity of course: the snow with two perished customers unable to talk. It seems that on some night earlier " a gistra ", as Peter put it, " a contrary wee gistra of a man was risin' bother in the bar an' he ordered him never to set foot in it again. He thought it was the gistra back again, with the snow on him ".

Well, after that they got something to revive them at the publican's kitchen fire. A meal was set down. He kept apologizing all the time. And when they got up to go he bid them stay, and ordered someone to take a horse and trap and leave the two travellers at home. " Not one foot ", says he, " will they leave on the county road from this door till their own street ".

And neither they did.

EVENING INTERLUDE IN A SOUTH ARMAGH PUB

THE vociferous tongue may sometimes conceal the vacuous mind but, psychologically, it can also unwittingly mask a secret unease.

Entering the bar I sensed this undercurrent like a communal concern tongue-tied by taboo. The boisterous banter sounded too self-conscious, even though the evening was the aftermath of a local wedding and a time for boozy recollection or commiseration, for satirical and even sarcastic retort. They also had the additional excuse for such oblique and domesticated clan-clash in the presence of an " outsider " from Monaghan. A total stranger here would be thoroughly alarmed at the bellicose-sounding riposte; but every one of the men along the bar knew how to give and take a joke in a style of repartee honed on a tradition in which wit must leap and clobber, in which humour, though given time to dander, must at least stomp.

" Oiney, Mick, Kevin, John, Peadar, Joe. . .". I named them as I walked past down the bar to stand alone.

It is not an old pub but replaces a famous tavern burned down in 1922 following an ambush between local IRA and Ulster Specials. One of the men along the bar had taken part in that engagement on the Republican side. The others, apart from the Monaghan man, had been school-mates of mine: and better than in any mirror each reflected the onslaughts of time upon one's own figure and countenance, upon hair in fleece-white cap or badger-grey or, as in my own case, the " rat's pad round the ears " tonsuring the bald pate.

The evening was splendid. One spacious window facing north-east was filled with a living mural of bog shrubs in lichen blue-green haze, and rising beyond the bog a hillside of fields and cluster of white-washed houses we know as a *Bahwin*, our phonetic rendering of the Gaelic word, *bábhún*, or bawn, which in centuries past kept out the two and the four-legged marauders such as wolves. Dominating the scene was Slieve Gullion, domed and mysterious as ever, with the spiralling scamper of erratic fields skirting the new forest before losing themselves amid high rock and heather. Only one house, a new one, survives up there now, a single blaze of electric isolation in the mountain night.

Beyond the hip of the mountain lay Mullabawn of song and story, and Ballykeel, home of our last scribe, Art Bennett, who once said that history and tradition hid under every stone in South Armagh, a conviction which in later decades Eoin MacNeill reaffirmed to remove any suspicion of parochial chauvinism.

Directly west of the bar lay the terraced village of Forkhill where the eighteenth-century poet, Peadar Ó Doirnín, had been found dead in his school. The village lay out of sight in a hollow of its own hills straddling a river and the Old Bridge where men had been publicly hanged.

Somewhere a British Army helicopter made sound like the now extinct threshing mill soughing out of season. In and out of the talk and helicopter noise the Old IRA man was saying:

" The botched job is always the botched job. You're better to punish with it at the start or you'll be patchin' all your life ".

A folk saying can apply to a host of exigencies, but I knew he was referring to Partition. Barely visible beyond the gap at Forkhill lay the Border and " The State ". One should apologize for using that term; but in areas as tradition-minded as our own the folk mind still coins labels stark, sly and satirical—but enduring; the colloquial adhesive from recesses of this outlook continues to defy eradication whether applied to person, place or event, despite the vicissitudes of decades or the scrubbing and re-writing of political constitutions.

In a diffusion of evening light the bog road to Forkhill showed up in a blinding bronze. Cars flicked to and fro. All of us could remember the ass and cart on that road: imagination brought earlier transports into reverie. For the road incorporates an intersection of two ancient highways, one which led from Tara through the Gap of the North, to Armagh City; the other an ecclesiastical route which connected through monastery and " shankil " Connacht with Carlingford Lough. Along the former the defeated Hugh O'Neill retreated from The Gap before Lord Mountjoy in 1600 and the Plantation of Ulster was assured; along the other, rapparee poets like Séamus Mór MacMurphy and Ó Doirnín rode; later came the Forkhill patriot, Locke, in 1798, eluding his pursuers until caught and slain near Dromara in County Down. Along it too, until the early years of this century, the Connacht migrants walked. In male groups only, clad in homespuns and the traditional black broad-brimmed hat, they slept out along the way until boarding ship at Fathom on Carlingford Lough to cross to the harvest fields of England. They spoke in Gaelic and were sometimes flummoxed to find in " The Black

North " natives who answered likewise when they supplied them with food.

Into such reverie on the hill out of Forkhill living dots appeared, walking close to the road margins or *sheughs* as we say. We had been hearing that the Paratroop Regiment was to return to our district and to Newry. No one else seemed to have noticed those dots, but the helicopter was joined by another and the thunder drowned all talk as they swept over the bar. Then out of the quiet of their passing a voice emerged vociferously in adamant statement which might have been insisting for the past five minutes:

" You'll take a half-one or you'll take nothin' ".

" I'll take no half-one. I took enough half-ones yesterday to pickle a dead hand ".

" Now, begod, he's trespassin' in your line of country, Murphy! "

Folklore: the dead hand of sorcery and witchcraft, reputedly possessing the power of the *Noinden Ulad* in which the men of Ulster had been cast into a nine days' sleep so that Cuchullain had to defend the South Armagh passes around us in single combat against the western warriors of Queen Maeve.

The specks in formation on the bog road were closer now and had been noticed. The helicopters continued in a criss-cross sweep of engine thunder. (They sometimes flew so low that the rotary blades sucked covers off prams and washing off hedges, and outraged young mothers and old women shook indignant fists at the skies.)

Someone addressing the Monaghan man became audible:

". . . so how the hell did you get to this part of the country anyway . . . if it's no harm to ask? "

" God's curse the bit ". He had been a hired servant boy and told his tale of hiring fairs in Carrickmacross and Dundalk. Two of the others joined in, all exulting in bygone hardships and labour; they had themselves " stood on the hiring ground in Newry ". One had since done a spell at our indigenous pahvee-cloth peddling and remarked that he had " sold well in a house he had been hired in. Cleaned them out! "

" They owed it to you. They had us all workin' for buttons. Isn't that what half the trouble in the whole country's about, North an' South? "

A man moved from the group to whisper:

" They'll mount a road block at Cloughinnea Cross or here. Wait an' see. We'll surely have them in. Did you hear they lifted two of the young fellows at a road block the other night? "

I had: that knowledge of course accounted for the sense of unease and concern behind all the bantering.

The helicopters thundered past once more and drowned the talk. When words became coherent again the Monaghan man was saying:

" Land? Where's the land? A snipe would break he's neck on it here afore he'd break his fast ".

In case I had not heard the phrase I noted it on my newspaper for inclusion in the Glossary of Anglo-Irish Idioms and Expressions I compile as part of my job.

" Ah, sure ", the banterer drawled mockingly, " God had so much land left over here He had to pile it up in heaps. An' sure God's good ".

" I'll grant you that; He always provides compensation; if a cow beast here finds the grazin' poor at least she has a choice of good views ".

We all roared appreciation. And then someone asked him (he has, by the way, lived in our area for the past thirty years at least) what made him stay among us in the first place.

" What the hell but security ". This is guttural modulation of sarcastic mock sincerity, as if now bored. " Aren't yous the best secured people in all Ireland—above an' on ground level ".

His final words and the guffaws following were drowned by the helicopter flying so low in a thunderous swoop that the glasses on the bar made shivering reverberations. The British Army patrol was in sight now. And then two young men burst into the bar.

" Aw, no? Aw, hell! "

" Why didn't yous write or send a rusty pound or somethin' !"

They were the local men " lifted " at the road block two nights previously. Drinks were called for. Amid the loud talk someone asked " was it bad? " The smaller of the two replied indifferently.

" Ah, no worse nor the last time. Just a little maybe ".

" He told them ", cut in his companion, " that if they don't keep thon cell in The Brook in better shape as he left it he's bluddywell not goin' back! "

The inevitable awkward silence fell. After being picked up at the road block no one knew what had happened to them, or could find out where they were being held, a tactic compounding both the cynical and callous tentacles of a psychological anxiety process which deliberately involves more than the person held in custody; the delayed return of the offspring can make interludes of unease turn morbid somersaults.

Everyone remained subdued, as if it were, somehow, irreverent to laugh; as if each man within himself felt he should, all along, have been thinking of other and grimmer events—Long Kesh and its H-Block and young men like these two held in cages with only a blanket to cover their nakedness, degrading the jailer more than the jailed as psychological analyses of such situations keep underscoring as a warning to democracy. One remembered the Englishmen, clerical and lay, who recently warned against adopting the penal tactics of a former enemy on whom a world war had to be waged to eradicate those very practices. For my part, I recalled the tradition of the Forkhill Yeoman who refused to scourge the young 1798 suspect in Mullabawn along " The Whipping Lane " and was instantly divested of his uniform and clothing, so that he had to walk the river back to Forkhill until a woman near the village gave him a blanket to enable him to get home in decency.

The British Army patrol was now coming abreast of the bar. They were not the Paras. They looked young enough, indifferent, weary. A few glanced at the long bar windows as they passed. It was a good evening to relish a drink. But all bars for drinking purposes are banned to them. They turned east up the hill towards the chapel. They would then head either south to Glen Dhu and another section of the Border, or south-east towards Moyra Castle and the Gap of the North, where the same Border confronted them across the railway line in rocky terrain.

Out of my reveries I heard the Monaghan man tell a folk-story about a black ass. Some of my own companions capped it with another. Then they got back to the Hiring Fair and the fleas in the beds on the lofts where they slept as servant boys.

" Fleas! " cried the Monaghan man. " I was hired in a place in Cooley where there was fleas that could tread hens ".

Inevitably the Old IRA man had to remember the jingle:
" There was big bugs as big as mugs
That sat on the pillows and cocked their lugs
In the lodging-house in Rossio ".

The helicopters appeared to have gone. The bog road was strangely empty of traffic. A scene of quiet and peace. But the under-current of unease remained despite a resumption of the boisterous talk and langled laughter, as if the ghosts of history were stalking again in a living repeat of old scenes.

A well-dressed youngish man then came in with a traveller's receipt book in his hand. Some of those in the bar knew him and they chatted. In a pause a little later he announced casually that the first contingent of the Paras had arrived in Newry. In my reveries he might have said the Yoes or the Ancient Britons.

A CAVAN WELCOME FOR THE MAN FROM THE FEWS

HIS name was Jemmy Flynn and he was almost ninety years at the time I first met him.

With colleague Leo Corduff, who had his car, we went to the homely pub in Glangevlin. On the way I told Leo what I had learned about Jemmy Flynn: that he was good crack, that he had folklore as well as recitations and ballads. In the pub were storytellers already known to me, Michael Dominic (Magovern of course) and his friend, old Barney Magovern, who was on crutches. (A phrase tells you: " Kick a rush bush in Glangevlin and a Magovern runs out ".)

In the bar also was a young fellow, a very shy teenager, who listened to us chat and talk over a drink. I had done some broadcast or other and had published an article in a daily news-paper—perhaps the one I include earlier and called " South Armagh's Outlaw Poet ". There was, inevitably, reference from the printed story to " The Fews of South Armagh ". The shy teenager stood listening, not saying a word, looking as if he didn't know what to make of these two talkative strangers.

(" The Fews ", in fact, extended beyond Forkhill to Moyra Castle, where the woods really ended. Mountjoy's secretary, Fynes Moryson, in his journal, recounts how the woods were cut down following the retreat of Hugh O'Neill in 1600.)

We were given directions as to how to find Jemmy Flynn's house, and only then did I notice that the teenager had quietly slipped away.

We set off to find the old man's house. We watched for the almost hidden entrance to the lane, or loanan, to his house midways between the Glangevlin pub and Dowra, which sits astride the Shannon. And, of course, shot past, re-traced, and picked up the landmarks we'd been told to watch out for. Jemmy's house, we'd been told, was the last and well into the mountains.

We found the lane and drove up and on. There were a few gates to open. The lane surface showed tractor tracks. Then the afforestation began; amid the new trees we noted several ruined or " waste houses "; one of these I knew had been a small country shop. Not a sign of any inhabited dwelling, not a sign of chimney smoke. Again we feared we were on the wrong lane because the surface was rougher now and coated with loose broken stone which bore no track of anything. And then, suddenly it seemed, we saw the house, neat and white, below us. There was a very steep and longish run down into the street, or yard, where a clatter of dogs had assembled and were already moving around. Leo feared that were he to drive down he might have difficulty driving back up that steep incline of loose stones. I wondered were we to walk how we would survive the attack of the clatter of circling dogs.

Leo decided to drive in and chance the return. When we arrived and stopped and got out, apprehensively, the dogs surrounded us with tails a-wagging as if we were old neighbours.

And there was a man standing on the threshold watching us. This was Jemmy Flynn.

He had an agreeable expression and fresh countenance for a man then approaching ninety years, and he was bare-headed. He carried no stick and was in his shirt sleeves. We made some call of greeting, no doubt self-consciously, for the man hadn't moved. There was something odd about him I realized: not a big man, an upright stance, but still full-bodied; and then I saw why I had the impression of something strange about his stance: he had his left hand behind his back.

We walked up to him. He remained on the threshold, looking at us steadily. No sense of a smile of greeting though still an agreeable air in the countenance. He didn't answer. We spoke again as we halted before him on the threshold, hoping he would invite us inside where we intended to stay, maybe, for a few hours if he could endure our talk and querying for so long. But he said nothing. I can recall the odd impression I felt to this day: I had never had such an experience which was, in fact, beginning to embarrass me. Leo stood beside me and must have felt the same.

And then he spoke, casually, almost under his breath, an inflection in his voice such as a prankster might use. He asked:

" Which of you is the man from The Fews ? "

The Fews? Here in a remote mountain fastness of County Cavan? To even have heard of The Fews of South Armagh? I was really taken aback. I said I supposed I was the man from The Fews.

He didn't ask my name, or Leo's, who stood beside me. I felt he would now shake hands, but from behind his back he brought the left hand into view; it held a dark-green bottle with square shoulders. He removed the cork and handed the bottle to me. I took it tardily, even unwillingly. At once I thought: poteen.

" A mouthful ", Jemmy Flynn said.

I had had some curious and alarming experiences already from drinking poteen here and there throughout Ulster, and hesitated. He pushed the bottle firmly. Well, we were out to collect folklore and to humour and facilitate old people in order to get it. I would take a mouthful and raised the bottle to my lips.

It was whiskey, and good whiskey at that.

I took a mouthful and handed back the bottle. He took it and then handed it to Leo; I noted some apprehension on his face too. He raised the bottle and drank. Still without saying a further word the old man took back the bottle and corked it. And then out came the steady hand to me. He said:
" You're welcome, man from The Fews ".
And to Leo:
" And you, too, the man from Mayo. Come on in and welcome, and a thousand welcomes ".
We followed him into the kitchen.

I don't recall noticing the teenager present, but as I learned later he was the old man's grandson: he must have rushed home ahead of us and warned his grandfather of the imminent arrival of two talkative fellows, and retailed the conversation he had heard in the bar about " The Fews " and " County Mayo ".

When we left in late afternoon we had several tapes of his folklore and a ballad or two to bring for transcription and then to the archives. We promised to call any time we were in the area. I was in Glangevlin (" Glan " in the local parlance) on my own later and learned that the old man was in hospital and very ill; at his age no one could hold out much hope. But everyone reckoned without the stamina of that stout heart and attitude to life and living he cherished like a philosophy—as indeed it was; serious without being solemn, a nice quiet turn of humour and a constitution seemingly impervious to the ageing years; he recovered eventually and was back in his isolated home with the forest around him and the mountain to his back.

When we called some time later the archivist of the Department of Irish Folklore, Séamas Ó Catháin, was with us. The illness didn't seem, as we used to say, " to have taken a fidge " out of old Jemmy Flynn. He talked long and fluently to us, even when we protested that he would tire himself. Not a bit.

Then we all rose to go and they shook Jemmy's hand. It was my turn. But instead of shaking my hand he grasped the fingers and raised the back of my hand to his lips and kissed it vigorously. I was more than a bit flummoxed, maybe embarrassed by this gesture, and at once concluded that it was an idiosyncratic practice the old man harboured and done impulsively.

I had never even heard of anything like it before, let alone figure in such a ceremony. By that time I knew that the drink of whiskey on the threshold came from an old traditional custom; but not once did I suspect that there was anything ancient and ritualistic about the kissing of the back of the hand.

Séamas Ó Catháin, more knowledgeable than I about such Gaelic customs, asked softly did I know what the little ceremony meant. I did not. He explained:

" It's a very old Gaelic custom: you do that only to someone you think very highly about ".

The drink of whiskey on the threshold was of the ritual too; it signified the sincere depth and warmth of the welcome being extended.

I am still moved to recall those two so natural ceremonial scenes. Jemmy had heard me on the air and had read some of my newspaper pieces about The Fews and South Armagh, and he knew his Irish history. The ritual and welcome to me especially, genuine as it was personally, was, I like to believe, more of a gesture of recognition of what the history and tradition of The Fews symbolized to all Ireland, and at the same time he was acknowledging me as a fitting and appropriate representative and ambassador indeed because of the folk quest I was following.

Old Jemmy Flynn: an unforgettable Irishman of Glangevlin in County Cavan, with heart, soul and national spirit in the right place and proud of it; what a privilege to have met and known such people as I have all over Ulster.

Next time I heard of Jemmy Flynn he was dead and buried.

HUNTING GHOSTS ON CHRISTMAS EVE

IT was Christmas Eve; another traditional " set night " was ending. We were in Larkin's pub in Forkhill, South Armagh's gem of a village cradled atmospherically among hills that are mounds of legend and myth.

Our own expectations of ballad and good crack in Larkin's had been warmly fulfilled. They hadn't been loathe to wet their fingers either.

Donal's laconic geniality had reached to every corner of the house, and not even a dozen calls at once for his giving hand could restrain the familiar objurgation:

" Shocking quiet in this corner. I didn't hear a bar from here yet. Don't let down your art in the country ".

" Who can give us ' The Bogmen at McGuill's ' ? " someone wanted to know—quietly.

No one could—or would—but it started the talk of the ghosts; there were always more than one at McGuill's, as any South Armagh man will tell you. We had passed the ruin on our way from Dromintee without a thought.

Bullet-gouged

All day the clouds had sagged and dripped rain, and the bullet-gouged gables, as we went by, skulked under a damp stillness as black as its fire-scorched walls. Not a murmur came either from the few trees in front; maimed but vibrant effigies like stupefied sentries caught between life and death since that night of ambush and morning of blast and fire.

In Larkin's we talked of the ghosts. Someone whispered guardedly that " the Bogmen had caused the first one ".

Someone said not; hadn't a young man coming from abroad through Greenore and Moyra Castle been waylaid at McGuill's and drowned in the bog ?

No, we were told; the time McGuill's shifted the big corner stone the time it was a thatched house, that had started it. And everyone mentioned the famous ghost—the one they said which almost started a lawsuit till " Father Finnegan settled the playboy in a back room. Sure, the time after the ambush there was the room an' the door built up ".

" *The Playboy* "

So the " playboy " escaped, with other ghosts to keep it company.

Paddy, who had been in the ambush that night, said to old Mick: " It's a lot of nonsense. There's no ghosts—except with boots on. Drink that up ".

The way he said it was bound to draw old Mick. He got rid of much rebuke before he went on: " I heard a son-of-a-so-and-so one time on Glasgow Green say there was no heaven, no hell, no flamin' purgatory, no ghosts—no nothin'. Now you dare say to me—"

" If that pint's a ghost let it appear again. Donal! We're dry over here! "

" Bad luck from your long tongue ever day you rise. Don't you hear me shouting for ' Order ' for the song ".

That laid the ghost for the next few minutes. I remember Paddy settling that old argument in Genesis about Cain and Abel: " Who was Cain's wife? Any cod knows that. She was Mrs. Cain ".

He even threatened to sing himself when a song was " longsome " in coming " and because Mick was back on to the ghost at McGuill's. The night wore on; we had good songs and banter and " kept up our part of the world " against the boys of Mullabawn and elsewhere. And then we were leaving.

Open doorways of light burst upon the darkness like a cheer and streamers of talk held men in knots outside.

The sky was still clouded; but stars of candle-light were in the village windows, on the hills around, on Cloughinnea and Slieve Gullion beyond Monribba Bog.

Streeling Home

We streeled home. Mick, clearly disgruntled about Paddy's satire, was back on to McGuill's ghost. " It was the time them an' Farrelly that took over the shop was at loggerheads over the ghost; he wasn't told, you see. No one in the house at all, an' I seen every window alive with light ".

Paddy had overheard and came up with a vociferous paraphrasing: ' Come out you unmannerly ghost; why don't you ate your fill like another ghost an' leave the decent man from Dundalk alone. You're the unmanneriest ghost in all Ireland. Come out an' fight like a man '.

" That was Big Peter—scared half the country that night at McGuill's—an' scared himself the next day when he sobered up ".

" Strad-legs "

Paddy suddenly stopped everyone with his arms. McGuill's was there before us now. " Listen. There's no ghosts ". Mick asked him to prove it. " Fair enough, I'm goin' in now to McGuill's an' if I find one I'll lug him out an' leave him strad-legs across your shoulders the way the ghost rode Hero home. In uniform or out. I'll get you one if he's there ".

And he went ahead, past the maimed trees, over the mound of debris that had been the shop. I saw a torch flash among the ruins.

I don't know who challenged Joe to go in as well. Only when he was going in by the alleyway from the Newry road did I hear him: " Won't I? I never was afeared of nothin' alive or dead, a-foot or afloat ".

Paddy must have heard the footstep stumbling past a window. He says he waited and made a flying grab as he switched on the torch. What he cried we don't know, for Joe's yell must have put up crows in The Captain's Grove. I remember only the tattoo of his hobnails fading beyond the hill up the Newry road. Paddy had dropped his torch in the attempt and seemed to be more bothered about its loss than an escaping ghost. He wasn't praying for its recovery either.